The Forgotten
Spurgeon

The Forgotten Spurgeon

Iain H. Murray

The Banner of Truth Trust

THE BANNER OF TRUTH TRUST
78b Chiltern Street, London WIM IPS
P.O. Box 652, Carlisle, Pa 17013, U.S.A.

*

First published in this form 1966
Second edition published 1973
ISBN 0 85151 156 2

*

Printed in Great Britain by
Hazell Watson and Viney Ltd
Aylesbury, Bucks

*To the Office-Bearers and Congregation
of Grove Chapel, Camberwell,
with thankfulness for nine years
of fellowship and support in
the gospel of the Grace of God*

Preface to Second Edition

It is eleven years since the majority of these pages first appeared in *The Banner of Truth* magazine and in that period much has happened which is connected with Spurgeon though he died eighty years ago. There have been changes, for example, in regard to places associated with his memory. His first London home, in the New Kent Road, has been pulled down; the chapel in Artillery Street, off Hythe Hill, Colchester, where he was converted on that January Sunday in 1850, has been re-opened for evangelical services; and the Metropolitan Tabernacle, after some years of difficulties, has once more been extending its influence for the gospel in the heart of London. But over and above all has been the re-publication during the last four years of many of the volumes of his *Metropolitan Tabernacle Pulpit*. Until 1969, publishers on both sides of the Atlantic seem to have concluded that this great series of volumes – unquestionably the most influential of all that Spurgeon prepared for the press – would never again be re-issued *in toto*; consequently, they did no more than issue abridgements and selections of Spurgeon's writings. But since 1969 the publishers of this paperback have reprinted twelve of *The Metropolitan Tabernacle Pulpit* (that is volumes 26–37, the years 1880 to 1891), while Pilgrim Publications, Pasadena, Texas 77501, have to date re-issued sixteen volumes (8–23, the years 1862 to 1878), and hope to continue right through the whole series. A full textual index to the whole of Spurgeon's sermons is also available to purchasers of the British reprints. There could be no finer spiritual investment for young Christians and for all engaged in Christian work than to take the present opportunity to buy this set.

It will surely never be offered again at the current prices!

I have made a few changes in this second edition. In chapter 8 I have introduced several pages of evidence taken from newspaper cuttings contemporary with Spurgeon and collected by him in his scrapbooks which are now preserved in Spurgeon's College. Chapter 10 is an entirely new chapter. After the publication of the first edition of this book I had the opportunity to discuss some aspects of my subject with older Christians who remembered the Metropolitan Tabernacle in the earlier years of this century. One of them entrusted to me before his death the rare pamphlet by Charles Noble which I have added as an appendix to this edition. For me it was strong confirmation of the belief that lies behind this book, namely, that Spurgeon's successors and the modern evangelicalism which they helped to inaugurate has been in several respects weaker and less biblical than the school of faith to which he belonged. Today, however, there is a movement back to those living truths which Spurgeon believed that future generations would rediscover in God's time. Across the world young men and preachers are being gripped again by the very doctrines which were being generally cast aside towards the end of the last century. Certain it is that if the history of this present change of thought is ever written it must be said that, under the hand of God, Spurgeon's testimony exercised a powerful influence in the 1960's. That influence, we believe, will continue, and if it does so to the point of making the title of this book a complete *misnomer* no one will be better pleased than the author!

It only remains for me to thank Dr. G. R. Beasley-Murray for graciously giving me the facilities of the Heritage Room at Spurgeon's College and to record my debt to my friend S. M. Houghton of Charlbury whose ready help has once more made my work considerably easier.

Edinburgh   IAIN MURRAY
September 6, 1972

Contents

Illustrations appear between pages 126 and 127

Some Dates Concerning Spurgeon

1834	June 19	Born at Kelvedon, Essex
1850	January 6	Converted at Colchester
1851	October	Becomes pastor of Waterbeach Baptist Chapel, Cambridge
1854	April	Called to New Park Street Chapel, Southwark
1855	January	Publication of weekly sermon begins
	October	Baptist Confession of 1689 re-issued
1861	March 18	Metropolitan Tabernacle opened
1864	June 5	Sermon on 'Baptismal Regeneration'
1865	January	Publication of *The Sword and the Trowel* begins
1873–75		The first Moody-Sankey missions in Britain
1887		Commencement of Down-Grade controversy
	October 28	Resigns from Baptist Union
1888	April 20	By 2,000 votes to 7 the Baptist Union accepts a modified declaration of faith–unacceptable to Spurgeon
1891	June 7	Last sermon at Tabernacle
1892	January 31	Dies at Mentone
1897–1900		*The Autobiography* published
1898	April 20	The Tabernacle burnt down
1905	November	Spurgeon's library (containing probably the best private collection of Puritan literature in Britain) sold to William Jewell College, Missouri
1917	May	End of publication of weekly sermons

Why 'The Forgotten Spurgeon'?

My first acquaintance with Spurgeon arose out of a visit to a second-hand bookshop in Liverpool in 1950, though for some years after that the acquaintance was small. A few of his books were on my shelves, and being then a young Christian I could appreciate their evangelical warmth, but for the most part I viewed him from afar as a Victorian pulpit-wonder. The opinion of a recent writer who says that in 'an age of ponderous English sermons' Spurgeon 'mouthed rolling periods, piled metaphor upon metaphor' I would probably at that time have approved. Certainly I thought that there was nothing in his writings differing from the common run of more modern evangelical books unless it was their bulk. Not surprisingly, therefore, the purchases at the Liverpool bookshop were little used and my view of Spurgeon might have been the same to this day if my thinking had not been thoroughly disturbed and then set in another direction while I was studying at Durham. The new impetus to my spiritual life came from old books – dusty volumes of various shapes and sizes – which had a common feature in their adherence to the theology and experimental divinity associated with the Reformation and Puritan ages. The drawing power of these old writers was the way they opened up the Scripture and presented the doctrines of the grace of God with a richness which was new. Some of us will never forget the blessing of our first days in reading the Puritans and we turned to the Bible with greater appreciation than ever before.

It was while I was in this process of discovery that another of Spurgeon's books came into my hands in 1953; this was his *Commenting and Commentaries: Two Lectures together with A Catalogue of Biblical Commentaries and Expositions*. As those who know it are aware, the Catalogue traverses the whole field of expository works in the English tongue down to 1876, and while covering a wide variety of schools of thought from Anglo-Catholic to Plymouth Brethren, a main purpose was to draw attention to Puritan commentators and their successors. The slender work contains a mine of literary information on 17th century writings which might otherwise have been lost to modern times. Spurgeon was quite unashamed of his objective: he wanted more searching of the Scriptures and he believed Puritan writings were one of the finest inducements to obtain that result. 'Our Puritan forefathers were strong men, because they lived on the Scriptures. None stood against them in their day, for they fed on good meat, whereas their degenerate children are far too fond of unwholesome food. The chaff of fiction, and the bran of the Quarterlies, are poor substitutes for the old corn of Scripture.' It was not that Spurgeon ignored the latest commentaries of his day, but they fell short: 'Good as this volume is,' he wrote of F. Godet's *Studies on the New Testament* in 1877, 'it is nothing comparable in weight of thought and depth of instruction to the grand old Puritan writings, which to us at least are ever new and full of suggestiveness.' If I had not been already on the road to verifying statements like these I might have received *Commenting and Commentaries* with less interest; as it was the book became a *vade mecum* for me until I knew its salient names by heart. Yet though I was thus helped to read the Puritans I was not much further on in appreciating Spurgeon himself. No doubt I had now an exaggerated enthusiasm for what was generally to be found in old calf and folio; an enthusiasm which overlooked how the Holy Spirit has bestowed differing and distinct gifts upon men in various ages. To the Victorian age I was not drawn, and for the present my view of Spurgeon's chief value was that he acted as a kind of sign-post back to the 17th century. How Spurgeon related Puritan theology to his own ministry amongst the common people who had to work in the grind and fog of a commercial city, how he distilled old thoughts into plain English, how he used the solid doctrines of a bygone age to evangelize in a different historical context – these were all questions which I did not consider.

So far I had not seen the most valuable of all Spurgeon's publications, his sermons – to be distinguished from the selections and 'choice extracts' to be found in volumes of various sizes under his name. My first sight of the faded black binding of a set of *The Metropolitan Tabernacle Pulpit* and the even more worn *New Park Street Pulpit*, was in St John's Free Church, Oxford, where the minister, Sidney Norton, planted thoughts in my mind about Spurgeon which were later to develop.

There are various providences which control the bent of our reading. William Robertson Nicoll has described how as a 'probationer' minister in an Aberdeenshire village in 1874, where books were scarce, he had access to a set of Spurgeon's sermons and during six months 'went through all the volumes'![1] It was quite a different situation which at length drew me into a serious reading of the sermons. In 1961 I was called to the pulpit of Grove Chapel in Camberwell – an area very familiar to Spurgeon though greatly changed today. Humanly speaking, the prospects in our congregation were not encouraging and I was conscious that no mere repetition of old teaching could meet the problems of the 1960's. From a book in our church library fell a seat ticket for the Surrey Music Hall, signed by one of Spurgeon's deacons, and warning that reservations would only be kept until a certain hour on Sunday mornings. The age when such things happened in South London on the Lord's day seemed remote and of the practical contrast with the present day I did not need to be reminded. In

[1] *Princes of the Church*, 1922, 49.

4

this pastoral context I took up Spurgeon afresh and for a few years I had in my hand almost every week, one or other of the sixty-two volumes which make up the great series named above. The immediate object was help for my own congregation but out of the experience my whole conception of Spurgeon was radically and permanently changed. It seemed to me that the Spurgeon of the sermons was a forgotten man and the more I read the more the conviction deepened. By which I mean that despite the modern encomiums bestowed on him as 'the prince of preachers' and despite the anecdotes which still survive in the evangelical world about his abilities and his humour, some of the most important aspects of his ministry have been forgotten.

To provide proof for this assertion might at first sight seem hard. For Spurgeon's writings are so voluminous – extensive enough to fill the twenty-seven volumes of the ninth edition of the *Encyclopedia Britannica* – that perhaps anyone may extract enough passages on a pet subject to make him appear as the spokesman for causes which in fact did not have much importance in the context of his ministry considered in its entirety. Yet in Spurgeon's case this argument is not sound, though it could well be in the case of such 19th century pulpit figures as Henry Ward Beecher or Joseph Parker who had little or no system to their theology and who might say in one decade what they would disown in the next. What distinguished Spurgeon from so many of his contemporaries was that all his preaching was from within a definite framework of truth, a framework massive because Biblical and yet also simple enough to be stated within a narrow compass. Spurgeon could and did state his faith in definite confessional form, and his sermons, diversified though they are and ranging widely through Scripture, never lose touch with the system of gospel truth to which he held. 'It is perfectly extraordinary,' observed one critic, 'how able and powerful the great Baptist can be within his very narrow doctrinal limits'. Robertson Nicoll's prolonged reading of Spurgeon led him to assert that 'it cannot be doubted that his theology was a main element in his lasting attraction' and he asks the question, 'Why has Calvinism flourished so exceedingly in the damp, low-lying, thickly peopled, struggling regions of South London?' With this question I am not now concerned. The point of the quotations is that Spurgeon's theology is writ clear and large in his sermons – too plain to be misrepresented with any success. Furthermore the existence of a document like 'Spurgeon's Catechism'[2] – which gives the framework of all his preaching in a form which can be read through in ten minutes – is an effective safeguard against any distortion of his main emphases.

The only way to deal with Spurgeon's theology is to accept it or forget it: the latter is what I believe has largely happened in the 20th century. And Spurgeon without his theology is about as distorted as the cheap china figures of Spurgeon which were offered for sale by charlatans more than a century ago.

In the following pages the main subject is Spurgeon's thought and teaching. This is not a biography. Nevertheless, as the strong emphases in his preaching arose out of definite historical contexts, I have centred the chapters largely around the three major controversies of his ministry. The first concerns Spurgeon's early witness against a diluted evangelicalism and the controversy which ensued when, by reason of his Exeter Hall and Surrey Music Hall services, he began to draw the attention of ministers and newspapers who had long assumed that the kind of theology which Spurgeon was intent on restoring was a thing of the past. The second controversy arose out of a sermon on Baptismal Regeneration which he preached on June 5, 1864. This was the most widely circulated of all his sermons and it led to a debate considerably wider than the subject of baptism. The catalogue of the British Museum, under 'Spurgeon', gives nearly four columns to

[2] *Spurgeon's Catechism* is available from the Evangelical Press, 136 Rosendale Road, London S.E. 21.

6

books and pamphlets connected with this controversy. While not myself holding a position identical with Spurgeon's on the subject of baptism, I believe this was one of the most important unresolved controversies of the last century. The last great controversy, from 1887 to his death five years later at the age of fifty-seven, centres around his protest against the Down-Grade movement in the churches. This was certainly the most painful struggle in all his ministry and it was inevitable, for as E. K. Simpson has written, 'the cleavage between the critical libertines and the heralds of Christ crucified went down to the foundations'.

Of the first of these controversies a few words may be said here by way of introduction. According to modern standards it concerned a dispute which should never have arisen. The 'modern' approach is to shun words like Arminianism and Calvinism and to say that the Biblical evangelical is not a follower of any 'human' system. These old terms, it is said, would never have arisen if both sides had seen that each doctrinal scheme had a scriptural emphasis, human responsibility on the one hand and divine sovereignty on the other. The whole truth is larger than either side could see. But this solution to the controversy is not in fact new, it is exactly the same as that of the man whom Spurgeon criticizes for recommending in sermons 'three grains of Calvinism and two of Arminianism.'[3] Nor is it Biblical, for it really by-passes the issue of what the Scriptures mean by sovereignty and responsibility. The mere quoting of the term does not constitute a man a 'Biblical evangelical'.

In his early days Spurgeon tended to use 'Arminian' as a descriptive label to be applied to individuals; this practice which tends to impair the observation of the 'new commandment' of John 13:34, he later abandoned as far as possible and for a revival of the use in this sense there is nothing at all to be said. As long, however, as there is such a way of thinking

[3] *An All-Round Ministry*, 1960 reprint, 265.

about the gospel as is historically associated with Arminianism there is need of a theological term to denote that way of thinking. The hiding of the word is of no help to anyone; and if a man, as for example the eminent John Wesley, has thought through his Arminianism he is not ashamed of the title. To him it represents scriptural concepts. Similarly if there is a body of evangelical truth, rediscovered largely at the Reformation period, and if this differs in certain major respects from a more comprehensive and later evangelicalism, there is need of a term to mark the difference. It is almost an accidental fact of history that Reformation theology became known as 'Calvinism' but the name once established has served an important purpose: to the one who believes it, it is a scriptural system and its association with the name of the 16th century leader is merely incidental. This is the sense in which Spurgeon uses the term 'Calvinism'. For him it was a faith which belonged as much to Augustine and Paul as to the Genevan reformer. While we thus repudiate the use of these names as divisive labels, their occasional use in discussion is probably essential in the interests of clarity. It is pointless to claim to be merely Biblical when the whole question is, What do the Scriptures actually teach on certain issues?

There is one other preliminary matter connected with the above discussion. When Calvinism is spoken of as a 'system' – a theology which makes up a coherent whole – there is certain to be raised in some minds the idea that this is its weakness rather than its strength. Is it not the pitfall of this position that it drives logic and reason to extremes?

I raise this point now so that readers can be prepared to assess the justice of the charge in the subsequent chapters. If Spurgeon is taken as a fair spokesman for the system which upholds fully the doctrines of sovereign grace it may be found that the cap has been put on the wrong head. As we shall see, both Hyper-Calvinism and Arminianism took issue with Spurgeon, and strangely enough on the same ground. Spur-

8

geon held, because he believed Scripture teaches it, that man is responsible to believe the gospel, yet on account of sin wholly unable to do so. But how, asks reason, can a person be held responsible for an action of which he is not capable? Hyper-Calvinism, accepting reason's question, solves the problem by denying there is a universal obligation to trust in Christ, while Arminianism also follows reason and then solves the problem differently by affirming that ability must be universal. Again, Spurgeon, in line with the historic school to which he belonged, believed that none would be saved except through the special and effectual grace of God, to which reason responds that the rest of mankind must therefore be under a necessity to perish in sin. So Hyper-Calvinism (in its worst forms) resigns itself to inactivity, while Arminianism, also regarding this response as logically inevitable if the doctrine of special grace is accepted, abandons the whole doctrine as monstrous – and monstrous it would be if all that reason has to say on the subject were legitimate. The only reply which true Calvinism can make to the rational deductions of the Hyper-Calvinist and the Arminian is to assert, as Paul asserts in Romans 9, the inadmissibility of man's reasoning processes when they are applied to subjects which God has not chosen to explain. In so far as would-be exponents of Calvinistic theology have departed from this attitude they have given just grounds for other Christians to complain, but a survey of the position of those who have stood out as teachers of this system would bear record to the fact that the strength of these men has been their determination to resolve all by Scripture alone and where Scripture offers no resolution of difficulties to be silent and worship a great God.[4] 'Faith,' says Spurgeon, 'is reason at rest in God.'

[4] William Tyndale, for example, lays down the general position of the 16th century reformers on this subject when he says' 'Why doth God open one man's eyes and not another's? Paul (Rom. ix) forbiddeth to ask why; for it is too deep for man's capacity. God we see is honoured thereby, and His mercy set out and the more seen in the vessels of mercy. But the popish can suffer

Nevertheless this same school which has taught humility of mind before God has also been strongest in affirming the Church's duty of holding a system of theology and there is no inconsistency here because the science of systematic theology concerns the derivation of truths from Scripture and the formulation of them, as far as possible, in a connected body of doctrine. To reject this science as an intrusion of reason upon Scripture is to *pre-suppose* that Scripture provides no adequate material or guidance for the formulation of what may justly be called a Biblical system. This presupposition, which has not infrequently been regarded as preserving the Scripture from 'human systems', is itself unbiblical. Spurgeon writes: 'To affirm of any human production that it contained many great and instructive truths which it would be impossible to systematise without weakening each separate truth, and frustrating the design of the whole, would be a serious reflection upon the author's wisdom and skill. How much more to affirm this of the Word of God! Systematic theology is to the Bible what science is to nature. To suppose that all the other works of God are orderly and systematic, and the greater the work the more perfect the system; and that the greatest of all His works, in which all His perfections are transcendently displayed, should have no plan or system, is altogether absurd. If faith in the Scriptures is to be positive, if consistent with itself, if operative, if abiding, it must have a fixed and well-defined creed. No one can say that the Bible is his creed, unless he can express it in words of his own.'[5]

Turning from these reflections connected with the first

God to have no secret, hid to Himself. They have searched to come to the bottom of His bottomless wisdom: and because they cannot attain to that secret, and be too proud to let it alone, and to grant themselves ignorant, with the apostle, that knew no other than God's glory in the elect; they go and set up free-will with the heathen philosophers, and say that a man's free-will is the cause why God chooseth one and not another, contrary unto all the scripture.' *An Answer to Sir Thomas More's Dialogue*, Parker Soc. reprint, 1850, 191.

[5] *The Sword and the Trowel*, 1872, 141. This is part of a review of Charles Hodge's *Systematic Theology*.

controversy, I comment next on a general objection likely to be raised over the method I have followed in this book, namely, Is it right to high-light Spurgeon in terms of these three controversies? In so far as such an objection draws attention to the impossibility of dealing with a man so many-sided as Spurgeon in a book of this size I am in perfect agreement. This is not a substitute for a biography nor an alternative to reading his sermons at first-hand; a reason why I have documented my quotations from the latter is to encourage the follow-up of what are only extracts. One thing that the reader will find in the sermons is that Spurgeon was always preaching a great deal which belongs to the main stream of Catholic Christianity and this has made him valued by Christians in so many sections of the Church. I should not like to represent Spurgeon as doing the very thing which he exhorted his students not to do, namely, to 'rehearse five or six doctrines with unvarying monotony of repetition'.

The objection, however, goes further. Controversy and theological debate, it is said, were not Spurgeon's roles and in so far as he engaged in them he was out of his true calling. From this opinion I entirely dissent though one cannot but be aware how many advocates it has had. From Victorian times until now he has been applauded in almost every role except that of a man who had a vital witness to bear against errors in the Church. As a personality, preacher, author, Baptist, mystic and philanthropist, Spurgeon has been described and discussed, but meanwhile the great controversies in which he engaged so earnestly and the theology to which he held so tenaciously have, by and large, been allowed to fall into oblivion. And this has been justified on the ground that the controversial aspects of his ministry are the least important because theology was not his forte. Thus, when the Down-Grade controversy was at its height, John Clifford, the vice-president of the Baptist Union, declared, 'it pains me unspeakably to see this eminent "winner of souls" rousing the energies of thousands of Christians to engage in personal wrangling and strife, instead of inspiring them, as he might, to sustained and heroic effort to carry the good news of God's Gospel to our fellow-countrymen!'[6] Four years later, a religious journal, writing Spurgeon's obituary, echoed the prevailing mood: 'We turn away from his "Calvinistic theories" to his Christian life, and here we find solid kindness, his genuine loving character, in direct contrast with his narrow creed'.[7]

Just as the image of the Puritans after 1662 was formed largely by the smart sayings of those who had no relish for their religion, so the image of Spurgeon which has been projected into the 20th century is largely the work of men who had little or no sympathy with his doctrine and who discredited him as a theologian.[8] Apart from Robert Shindler, who wrote briefly before Spurgeon's death,[9] and Charles Ray, who seems to have done little more than write a good abridgement of the autobiography,[10] no biographer of Spurgeon readily comes to mind who could have honestly subscribed to the confession of faith affirmed by Spurgeon when he went to New Park Street Chapel. W. Y. Fullerton and J. C. Carlile, who in the third and fourth decades of the 20th century wrote what have sometimes been regarded as standard biographies of Spurgeon, could not have done so, and while these authors throw partial light on some of the controversies, they remind one too much of the 'men of willow and plaster of Paris' of whom Spurgeon speaks. An exposition of Spurgeon's doctrine cannot be found

[6] G. Holden Pike, *The Life and Work of Charles Haddon Spurgeon* (published for subscribers only in the 1890's), vol. 6, 297.
[7] Pike, 6, 352.
[8] William Robertson Nicoll, editor of *The British Weekly*, was one of the few literary critics of the age who saw the injustice of the judgment which ignored Spurgeon as a teacher. His opinion was that 'the church does not yet know what a great saint and doctor she possessed in Mr Spurgeon', and again, 'a great and trained theologian, master in every part of his own system, he preached nothing that he had not proved'. Introduction to *Sermons by Rev. C. H. Spurgeon*, undated, 8.
[9] *From the Usher's Desk to The Tabernacle Pulpit*, The Life and Labours of Pastor C. H. Spurgeon, 1892.
[10] *The Life of Charles Haddon Spurgeon*, 1903.

in their pages. When T. R. Glover wrote of Spurgeon in *The Times* in 1932 and A. Cunningham-Burley published his *Spurgeon and His Friendships* in 1933, the interpretation of the late pastor of the Metropolitan Tabernacle had reached rock bottom.[11] The latter book admirably suits a comment which Spurgeon once passed upon another work, 'valuable to housemaids for lighting fires'.

So by the 1930's the Victorian prediction that Spurgeon was 'the last of the Puritans' (a phrase coined by Nonconformist liberals) seemed to be amply demonstrated. 'The old-fashioned Gospel' for which he said his church and college had been 'set for a sign' was largely forgotten except by a few who spoiled the force of the denominational tributes being offered to Spurgeon's memory around the time of the centenary of his birth in 1934 by asking such questions as 'Who of these "best known Baptist ministers" proclaims the truth of Divine Election as Spurgeon did? Who of them glories in the precious blood of our Lord Jesus Christ as Spurgeon did?'[12] These things being so it is not surprising that the modern view of Spurgeon discounts his theological importance.

Wilbur Smith wrote in 1955: 'I have tried to read again most of the significant autobiographical and biographical volumes of Charles H. Spurgeon, and in so doing, I have come to the

[11] An exception to this was a fine article by Edmund K. Simpson, in reply to Glover, entitled 'Spurgeon's Intellectual Qualities', published in *The Evangelical Quarterly*, Oct., 1934.

[12] Quoted from *Our Outlook*, A Quarterly Message in connection with Highgate Road Chapel, London, N.W.5, edited by John Wilmot, Vol. for 1937-39, 179. In 1939 Spurgeon's College was re-affiliated with the Baptist Union and the same year the College Principal, Percy W. Evans, was elected Chairman of the Union. One periodical commented: 'This is an interesting appointment because in Spurgeon's time the College left the Union owing to theological differences, and Dr Evans has been largely instrumental in bringing the College back again. Dr Evans has maintained the orthodox and evangelical traditions of the College, but he is more broadminded than the famous founder.' At the same time a writer in the *Bible League Quarterly* regretted that he had failed in correspondence with the Principal of Spurgeon's College, 'to secure the assurance that today the historic doctrine of the verbal inspiration of Holy Scripture as originally given is taught as it was by the founder of the College'. ibid., 198-9.

strong conviction that the Christian church today has not yet seen a fully adequate, definitive life of this mighty preacher of the grace of God'.[13] This conclusion, I believe, was perfectly right.

My main defence of the method I have followed in this book does not, however, consist in a criticism of the biographers who have minimized or ignored these three controversies. I rest the case on Spurgeon's own conviction that the stand he took on the doctrines involved in these controversies was of great importance – a conviction abundantly witnessed to by his sermons, his *Autobiography* and his monthly magazine *The Sword and the Trowel* which he edited for twenty-seven years. Speaking to his students three years before his death he says: 'I shall be gone from you ere long. You will meet and say to one another, "The President has departed. What are we going to do?" I charge you, be faithful to the gospel of our Lord Jesus Christ, and the doctrine of His grace.' This was characteristic of Spurgeon's priorities and it was out of concern for the same priorities that he wrote, 'Controversy for the truth against the errors of the age is, we feel more than ever convinced, the peculiar duty of the preacher'. Mrs Spurgeon and J. W. Harrald were in full harmony with Spurgeon's viewpoint when, in his *Autobiography*, they commented on the Down-Grade controversy: 'Many people were foolish enough to suppose that he had adopted a new *role*, and some said that he would have done more good by simply preaching the gospel, and leaving the so-called "heretics" to go their own way! Such critics must have been strangely unfamiliar with his whole history, for, from the very beginning of his ministry, he had earnestly contended for the faith once for all delivered to the saints'.[14]

[13] In an Introduction to *The Treasury of Charles H. Spurgeon*, 1955, 19.
[14] *C. H. Spurgeon's Autobiography*, 2, 259. The Autobiography, compiled by his wife and private secretary, was first published in the years 1897–1900. The major part of volumes one and two, with a few additions, was reprinted in 1962 under the title *The Early Years*. When I am quoting from the first half of the

People may, of course, disagree with Spurgeon's own assessment of the controversies. By some it will be said that the controversies arose more out of personal factors than out of important doctrinal issues: in his early years of great success in London (when he was not without some tinge of egotism) he aroused the envy, and hence opposition, of other ministers; while in the final controversy of 1887–92, Spurgeon mistook an unwillingness to follow his leadership as a general defection of Baptists from Christianity, and this, coupled with his gout and rheumatism, produced his gloomy spirit![15] In the following pages I do not enter into any discussion of these views. To do so thoroughly would be more the proper work of a biographer and in any case I am personally convinced that the *main* factor in each controversy was scriptural and not personal. I mention these opinions in order to say that while writers are entitled to their own views they are not entitled to suppress Spurgeon's own convictions on the issues concerned. Yet suppression has occurred, for we have been living through a dreary age when, as Spurgeon anticipated, much has been done against the truth and the memory of its upholders: 'I am quite willing to be eaten of dogs for the next fifty years,' he said in 1889, 'but the more distant future shall vindicate me'.[16] My personal conviction is that there will be no re-appraisal of Spurgeon until these three controversies are re-examined. While such a study will not tell a man everything he can profit-

Autobiography I shall give the reference henceforth in *The Early Years* as it is more accessible to most readers. The *Autobiography* will always be the most important source of biographical information on Spurgeon and the next source (excepting *The Sword and the Trowel*) is G. Holden Pike's six-volume work already cited.

[15] The most wounding criticism along these lines was perhaps Joseph Parker's 'open letter' to Spurgeon in *The British Weekly*, April 25, 1890. But Parker was by no means alone in this kind of interpretation of the Down-Grade controversy. Cf. Pike, 6, 299. Robertson Nicoll would not have any part in criticism of Spurgeon's character: to one of Spurgeon's accusers, he wrote: 'I never knew a sign that his immense popularity turned his head. Rather the other way – it made him often very melancholy and depressed'. *William Robertson Nicoll*: Life and Letters, T. H. Darlow, 1925, 103.

[16] *An All-Round Ministry*, 360.

ably learn about Spurgeon, it will bring to the fore the things which Spurgeon firmly believed a future generation of Christians would be enabled by the grace of God to establish again in the earth. Examined in this context, Spurgeon is seen as no genial pulpiteer and humorist, but a man of granite, who thundered out to his generation the timeless truths of the Word of God. Like John Ploughman he drove a straight furrow and from his example we may gain fresh vision and determination.

One could write the history of Spurgeon as a great success story. As the settled pastor of a congregation he preached to more people on successive Sundays than the Christian church has yet witnessed in any other quarter.[17] When a general census of church attendance was taken on an ordinary Sunday in London in 1886 the total congregations at the Metropolitan Tabernacle, morning and evening, exceeded 10,000 people![18] Further, if the readers of the sermons were included, says G. H. Pike, 'Spurgeon's congregation was thought to be not less than a million persons'. So great was the popularity of the sermons that at one time there was even an attempt made, without Spurgeon's leave, to cable the Sunday morning sermon to America for publication in Monday's papers. By 1899 over a hundred millions of his sermons had been issued in twenty-three languages;[19] before his death 120,000 volumes of his largest expository work *The Treasury of David* were sold and to these figures must be added the influence of more than 125 other books which bore his name plus the issues of *The Sword and the Trowel*.[20]

[17] In 1874 the membership at the Tabernacle stood at 4,366 and 'now ranked as the largest in the world; the second largest was said to be the First African congregation at Richmond, Virginia'. Pike, 5, 124. The Tabernacle was built to hold 6,000 and was apparently generally full, with occasions when, it is said, 'half as many more turned away unable to gain admission'. ibid., 138. The great building was burnt down on April 20, 1898.
[18] *William Robertson Nicoll*: Life and Letters, 72.
[19] cf. *A Marvellous Ministry*, The Story of C. H. Spurgeon's Sermons, 1855 to 1905, Charles Ray, 1905.
[20] George J. Stevenson in his *Pastor C. H. Spurgeon*, His Life and Work to

It is tempting to turn these statistics to account in interpreting Spurgeon to the present day; to argue, for instance, that if ministers followed his example, or espoused his full theology, there would be like results in this age of small things. But the legitimacy of this line of argument cannot be accepted for it ignores primary Biblical considerations. God does not merely give opportunities to preachers and leave the rest to them. He gives the men and prepares the times in which they are to act. As Spurgeon says in reference to John Wycliffe, 'God fits the man for the place and the place for the man; there is an hour for the voice and a voice for the hour'. By upbringing, by the possession of superb natural gifts, by the enduement of the Holy Ghost, Spurgeon was fitted to work in a *reaping* time in English church history. 'My life,' he could say, 'has been one long harvest home'! Long before his death, however, the spiritual condition of the land was changing and Spurgeon saw the change; whereas he used to hold out the prospect of a full church to the man who preached the Gospel faithfully, he had to revise his opinion: 'Compared with what it used to be, it is hard to win attention to the Word of God. I used to think that we had only to preach the gospel, and the people would throng to hear it. I fear I must correct my belief under this head...We all feel that a hardening process is going on among the masses'.[21]

Robertson Nicoll's idea that there was a kind of natural affinity between the working-class masses of South London and a firm Calvinism, is one which no one born in the 20th century would care to own. Spurgeon himself would have disowned it. He foresaw an age coming for the church when success would not be the norm and when statistics and majorities would be a very misleading guide to the truth. He did not claim attention to his message because of its success but

his 43rd birthday, 1877, says that *The Sword and the Trowel* had at that date a monthly circulation of 15,000 'with a steady advancement.'
[21] *An All-Round Ministry*, 196.

because of its Divine authority. 'Long ago I ceased to count heads,' he said in 1887, 'truth is usually in the minority in this evil world'.

For these reasons I am not interested in a success-story view of Spurgeon and would disclaim any desire to impose beliefs upon readers in the following pages because 'Spurgeon said it'. For the revival of the kind of Spurgeon 'cult' which existed in some circles in former days I have no pleas to make. The cult was basically unhealthy; it doubtless led some to accept beliefs because Spurgeon taught them rather than because they saw them clearly in the Scripture, and in so far as it did this it was detrimental to the cause which was closest to Spurgeon's heart. For this kind of attitude negatives the great emphasis of his ministry. Spurgeon's legacy is neither his oratory nor his personality – these things have gone the way of all flesh – but his testimony to the whole counsel of God and his utterance of the great Reformation principle that the Lord alone must be before our eyes and His honour the ultimate motive in all our actions. In this connection it was no coincidence that, like John Calvin who desired no epitaph to mark his grave, Spurgeon wished for nothing more than the letters 'C.H.S.' to mark his tombstone.

One hundred years ago Charles Haddon Spurgeon wrote: 'It is, of course, the most easy to flesh and blood to deal in generalities, to denounce sectarianism, and claim to be of an ultra-Catholic spirit; but though rough and rugged, it is required of the loyal servant of King Jesus to maintain all His crown rights and stand up for every word of His laws. Friends chide us and foes abhor us when we are very jealous for the Lord God of Israel, but what do these things matter if the Master approves? The words of Rutherford, in his letter to William Fullarton, ring in our ears, "I earnestly entreat you to give your honour and authority to Christ, and for Christ; and be not dismayed for flesh and blood while you are for the Lord, and for His truth and cause. And howbeit we see truth

18

put to the worse for the time, yet Christ will be a friend to truth, and will act for those who dare hazard all that they have for Him and for His glory. Sir, our fair day is coming, and the court will change, and wicked men will weep after noon, and sorer than the sons of God who weep in the morning. Let us believe and hope for God's salvation.'[22]

[22] *The Metropolitan Tabernacle Pulpit*, 11, vi.

I feel that, if I could live a thousand lives, I would like to live them all for Christ, and I should even then feel that they were all too little a return for His great love to me.

C. H. S. SERMONS, 48, 274

Must I be carried to the skies
On flowery beds of ease,
While others fought to win the prize,
And sailed through bloody seas?

Sure I must fight if I would reign
Increase my courage, Lord,
I'd bear the toil, endure the pain,
Supported by thy Word.

Isaac Watts, lines often quoted by C.H.S.

1: The Preacher in Park Street

It is impossible to estimate the significance of the life of C. H. Spurgeon without knowing something of the religious condition of the land at the time when his ministry commenced in the middle of the last century. Protestant Christianity was more or less the national religion; Sunday was strictly observed; the Scriptures were respected; and, apart from the untouched thousands in some of the larger cities, church-going was the general custom. These things were all so commonly accepted and apparently entrenched that the spiritual changes that have since swept the nation were as remote to the mid-Victorians as motor-cars or aeroplanes. Yet one does not have to look long at the prevailing Christianity of the 1850's to observe some signs that are hardly akin to what we find in the New Testament – it was too fashionable, too respectable, too much at peace with the world. It was as though such texts as 'the whole world lieth in wickedness' were no longer correct.

The Church was not lacking in wealth, nor in men, nor in dignity, but it was sadly lacking in unction and power. There was a general tendency to forget the difference between human learning and the truth revealed by the Spirit of God. There was no scarcity of eloquence and culture in the pulpits, but there was a marked absence of the kind of preaching that broke men's hearts. Perhaps the worst sign of all was the fact that few were awake to these things. The Church was outwardly prosperous enough to be content to carry on the routine of past years. One contemporary writer, lamenting this dull formality, observed: 'The preacher speaks his usual time; the people sit patiently enough perhaps; the usual number of verses are sung and the business of the day is over; there is generally no more about it. No one can deny that this is neither more nor less than a simple statement of the real state of matters in the majority of our churches at the present day. Should the preacher let fall his handkerchief on the Psalm-book, or give one thump louder than usual with the fist ecclesiastic, that will be noted, remembered, and commented on, while there is all but total oblivion of the subject and the nature of the discussion.'

Spurgeon was soon to attack this lifeless traditionalism in more direct language: 'You think that because a thing is ancient, therefore it must be venerable. You are lovers of the antique. You would not have a road mended, because your grandfather drove his wagon along the rut that is there. "Let it always be there," you say; "let it always be knee-deep." Did not your grandfather go through it when it was knee-deep with mud, and why should not you do the same? It was good enough for him, and it is good enough for you. You always have taken an easy seat in the chapel. You never saw a revival; you do not want to see it.'[1]

The evangelical sections of the Church had not escaped from the prevailing tendencies of the times. The work of Whitefield and Wesley was admired, but it was little followed. The cutting edges of evangelical truth had been gradually softened down. Those rugged Methodist doctrines which had shaken the land a century before had not been abandoned – and by a few they were still fervently preached – but the gen-

[1] *New Park Street Pulpit*, 4, 167–8. All my quotations from Spurgeon's sermons, unless indicated otherwise, are from the original *New Park Street* and *Metropolitan Tabernacle Pulpit* volumes. In further references I will give only volume and page numbers. From 1855 onwards Spurgeon published a sermon every Thursday; these were re-published in volume form at the end of each successive year. So until the time of Spurgeon's death, 1892, the year in which the sermon was preached can generally be calculated, if the reader wishes, from the volume number. The title of the series was changed after the erection of the Tabernacle in 1861.

eral feeling was that a more refined presentation of the gospel
was needed in the Victorian era. With this kind of outlook
abroad it was inevitable that the strong and clear-cut Reformed
theology of 16th and 17th century England was quite out of
favour. The Reformation historian Merle d'Aubigné of
Geneva, who visited this country in 1845, says that he was
forced to ask himself whether Puritanism 'still exists in England? Whether it has not fallen under the influence of national
developments, and the sneer of novelists? Whether, in fine, it
would not be necessary to go back to the 17th century in order
to meet with it?'[2] It is nevertheless true that some of the
evangelical leaders of the land, particularly the older ones,
were deeply concerned about the spiritual condition of the
churches. John Angell James, for example, who had been
ministering at the famous Congregational church at Carr's
Lane, Birmingham, since 1805, wrote in 1851, 'The state of
religion in our country is low. I do not think I ever preached
with less saving results since I was a minister; and this is the
case with most others. It is a general complaint.'

If these things were true of the country in general they were
particularly true of London, and the Baptist Chapel at New
Park Street, situated in a 'dim and dirty' region close to the
south bank of the Thames in Southwark, was no exception.
The congregation had a great history stretching back into the
17th century, but now they were left like barges in the nearby
mud when the tide was out. For some years they had been in a
state of decline and the large and ornate building, built to seat
about a thousand, was three-quarters filled with empty pews.
This was the scene that confronted the nineteen-year-old
Essex youth when he first stood in the pulpit of New Park
Street Chapel on the cold and dull morning of December 18,
1853. It was the first time Spurgeon's voice had been heard in
London, but almost immediately he was called to commence

[2] *Germany, England and Scotland*, Recollections of a Swiss minister, J. H.
Merle d'Aubigné, London, 1848, 89.

24

a pastorate which was to continue for thirty-eight years until his death on January 31, 1892.

If one had to give an outline of Spurgeon's life it would more or less resemble one of his own sermons – an introduction and three divisions. Spurgeon a child and youth, being moulded and prepared in the countryside of Essex and Cambridgeshire – that would be the introduction. Then the first period, Spurgeon at New Park Street, a time of awakening and uproar, of ridicule and bitter opposition. The second division would be Spurgeon in the middle period of his life, after he had settled at the Metropolitan Tabernacle and the storm had gradually subsided into long years of quiet progress and blessing. His position was recognized and he became the admired and popular evangelical leader of London. The last 'head' would be the five or so years before his death at the age of fifty-seven. In these closing days the peace was suddenly broken. Once more Spurgeon found himself at variance with the evangelical majority around him and he became the centre of the Down-Grade controversy – a controversy which was to have far-reaching consequences in this land. Although he was still respected he was no longer so widely followed. It was almost as though the wheel of his ministry had gone round a full circle and he was back in the early years when he had felt the censure and suffering and loneliness of bearing a faithful testimony to truths that were not wanted by the professing Church. The words he had spoken at the beginning were true at the end: 'All the way to heaven, we shall only get there by the skin of our teeth. We shall not go to heaven sailing along with sails swelling to the breeze, like sea birds with their fair white wings, but we shall proceed full often with sails rent to ribbons, with masts creaking, and the ship's pumps at work both by night and day. We shall reach the city at the shutting of the gate, but not an hour before.'[3]

The Spurgeon who is best remembered today is the Spurgeon of the middle period, the popular preacher, the man whose sermons were printed in twenty-three languages and issued to the extent of a hundred million copies by the end of the 19th century. The Spurgeon of New Park Street, the man whose message was so unwelcome that the only place that would sell his books in Cambridge was a grocer's shop, and who could speak of himself as being 'reckoned the scum of creation, scarcely a minister looks on us or speaks favourably of us,' this Spurgeon has been largely forgotten. Likewise the Spurgeon of the Down-Grade controversy – the prophet who warned his fellow-evangelicals, 'We are going down hill at breakneck speed,' and who said, 'It is mere cant to cry, "We are evangelical; we are all evangelical" and yet decline to say what evangelical means' – this Spurgeon is little known today. Yet we believe the fact is that it is the burden of Spurgeon's early and closing years which is most relevant to ourselves at the present time, for the emphasis of his teaching at these periods throws much light on the condition of evangelicalism today. In this chapter we shall not attempt to elaborate the outline of his life, but rather concentrate mainly on one year of his ministry – the year 1856 when he was twenty-two. This year was to Spurgeon what the year 1739 was to George Whitefield, and just as one cannot understand Whitefield's life without knowing what happened when he was twenty-four, so a study of Spurgeon at the age of twenty-two provides us, as it were, with a key to the understanding of the future course of his life and it also gives us a close-up view of what one contemporary called 'the most romantic stage even in Mr Spurgeon's wonderful life.'

Great changes had swept New Park Street Chapel since the early days of 1854. By the autumn of that year five hundred people were in regular attendance at the weekly prayer meeting. The church was filled and even enlarged, but it was still inadequate for the number of hearers. It was soon evident that something was happening in London which had not happened since the days of Whitefield and Wesley. A minister from Scotland who visited New Park Street early in 1856 has given the following description of the numbers at the evening service. He arrived, he says, with two friends, about six, the service commencing at half-past:

'To our dismay we found crowds already at the door waiting for admission. Those only who had tickets were now permitted to enter; as we had none, we almost despaired of getting in. One of my friends, however, went up to a police officer, and told him I was a clergyman from Scotland, and was anxious to be admitted. The police officer, hearing this, said, very politely, he would allow us to enter the church, but would not promise us seats. This was all we wanted. One of us (a lady) was kindly favoured with a seat; my other friend and myself thought ourselves happy in being permitted to sit "in a window," with a dense crowd in the passage at our feet. I asked a man near me if he came regularly; he said he did. "Why then," I asked, "do you not take a seat?" "Seat!" he replied; "such a thing is not to be had for love or money. I got a ticket for leave to stand." The church, I was told, is seated for 1,500; but what with the schoolroom and the passages, which were choke-full, there could not have been fewer in it than 3,000.'[4]

There seemed to be no limit to the number of hearers who were anxious to hear Spurgeon's message. The Exeter Hall in the Strand, which held about 4,000, was frequently used on a Sunday evening instead of the chapel, until at length the managers of the Exeter Hall complained that they could not rent the hall indefinitely to members of one denomination. It was this that led in October 1856 to the use of the Surrey Gardens Music Hall, a vast building just erected for the concerts of a popular musician, M. Jullien, and capable of holding six to ten thousand people. That multitudes are prepared to listen to the gospel is not in itself a proof of a true revival, but there is good reason to believe that this time hundreds were actually entering

[4] Pike, 2, 225.

the kingdom of God. In 1857 Spurgeon said, 'In one year it was my happiness personally to see not less than a thousand who had been converted.'[5] It was Spurgeon's conviction that his church was in the midst of a great spiritual awakening; in fact this was a solemn argument he used with those who still slept, 'Unbelief makes you sit here in times of revival and of the outpouring of God's grace, unmoved, uncalled, unsaved.'[6] 'I do think,' he said on another occasion, 'that many an old Puritan would jump out of his grave if he knew what was doing now.'[7]

But it would be a serious misunderstanding to imagine that these were days of unmixed happiness for Spurgeon, for he was at this very time in the midst of one of the most bitter persecutions any minister of the gospel has ever singly endured in this country. In the bedroom of their home at 217 New Kent Road, Mrs Spurgeon hung the text, 'Blessed are ye, when men shall revile you, and persecute you, and shall say all manner of evil against you falsely, for my sake. Rejoice, and be exceeding glad: for great is your reward in heaven: for so persecuted they the prophets which were before you.' The words more or less describe Spurgeon's daily experience at the age of twenty-two. His name was lampooned in the press and 'kicked about the street as a football.' The newspapers could not ignore him, for his ministry was now a subject of conversation in all parts of England, but neither would they commend him, for he outraged the respectable religion which they patronized. *The Illustrated Times* wrote on October 11, 1856; 'Mr Spurgeon's popularity is unprecedented; at all events, there has been nothing like it since the days of Whitefield. Park Street Chapel cannot hold half the people who pant to hear him, and even Exeter Hall is too small. Indeed, it is re-

[5] *The Early Years*, 452. Light is thrown on the numbers under spiritual concern by an occasional, almost incidental, comment in his sermons. Preaching in December 1859, he mentions 'the thousands of letters that I continually receive from my congregation'. 6, 38.
[6] 1, 23.   [7] 3, 256.

ported on good authority that his friends mean to hire the
Concert Rooms at the Surrey Gardens, and firmly believe that
he will fill that. Nor is his popularity confined to London; lately
we ourselves saw, on a week-day, in a remote agricultural
district, long lines of people all converging to one point, and on
enquiring of one of the party where they were going, received
for answer, "We're a goin' to hear Maester Spudgin, Sir." '
The paper went on to predict that it was only a matter of time
before the current of popularity would 'turn and leave him.'[8]

In many parts of the country the local press joined in the
hue and cry. The following quotation from a Sheffield paper is
typical of the view that was generally expressed: 'Just now, the
great lion, star, meteor, or whatever else he may be called, of
the Baptists, is the Rev. Mr Spurgeon, minister of Park Street
Chapel, Southwark. He has created a perfect *furor* in the religious world. Every Sunday, crowds throng to Exeter Hall, as
to some great dramatic entertainment. The huge hall is crowded to overflowing with an excited auditory, whose good for-
tune in obtaining admission is often envied by the hundreds
outside who throng the closed doors . . . Mr Spurgeon preaches
himself. He is nothing unless he is an actor – unless exhibiting
that matchless impudence which is his great characteristic,
indulging in coarse familiarity with holy things, declaiming in
a ranting and colloquial style, strutting up and down the platform as though he were at the Surrey Theatre, and boasting of
his own intimacy with heaven with nauseating frequency . . .
It would seem that the poor young man's brain is turned by
the notoriety he has acquired and the incense offered at his
shrine. . . . To their credit be it spoken, Mr Spurgeon receives
no countenance or encouragement from the ornaments of his
denomination . . . He is a nine days' wonder – a comet that has
suddenly shot across the religious atmosphere. He has gone
up like a rocket, and ere long will come down like a stick.'[9]

The newspapers failed to silence Spurgeon, but the object

[8] *The Early Years*, 325–6.   [9] ibid., 321–2.

was nearly accomplished by other means on the night of Sunday, October 19, 1856. For the first time the New Park Street congregation was meeting at the Surrey Gardens Music Hall and the vast building with its three galleries was filled from floor to ceiling. When the service had begun and Spurgeon was engaged in prayer a shout of 'Fire!' commenced in more than one place. In the confusion and panic which immediately followed further shouts were raised, 'The galleries are giving way!' 'The place is falling!' A stampede ensued in which seven people were killed and twenty-eight taken to hospital seriously bruised and injured. The instigators of this false alarm – for such it was – were never discovered, but the terrible consequences remained vividly before Spurgeon's mind all his life, and such was the shock he suffered that for a time it was even in doubt whether he would ever preach again.[10]

Following the Surrey Music Hall disaster the press attacks on Spurgeon reached their height. *The Saturday Review* wrote on October 25:

'Mr Spurgeon's doings are, we believe, entirely discountenanced by his co-religionists. There is scarcely a Dissenting minister of any note who associates with him. We do not observe, in any of his schemes or building operations, the names, as trustees or the like, of any leaders in what is called the religious world ... It is generally felt that religion is not benefited by his abnormal proceedings. ... This hiring of places of public amusement for Sunday preaching is a novelty, and a painful one. It looks as if religion were at its last shift. ... After all, Mr Spurgeon only affects to be the Sunday Jullien. We are told of the profanity which must have been at the bottom of the clerical mind when the Church acted miracle plays, and tolerated the Feast of the Ass; but the old thing reappears when popular preachers hire concert-rooms, and preach Particular Redemption in saloons reeking with the perfume of

[10] Spurgeon described the Music Hall disaster as 'the great and terrible catastrophe invented by Satan to overturn us'. 6, 436.

tobacco, and yet echoing with the chaste melodies of *Bobbing Around* and the valse from the *Traviata*. . . .

'The Surrey Gardens affair was a great coup. The deplorable accident, in which seven people lost their lives, and scores were maimed, mutilated, or otherwise cruelly injured, Mr Spurgeon only considers as an additional intervention of Providence in his favour. "This event will, I trust, teach us the necessity of" – being sober, rational, and decent? – No; – "having a building of our own." Preach another crowd into a frenzy of terror, – kill and smash a dozen or two more, – and then the speculation will have succeeded.'[11]

Turning from what the world thought of Spurgeon in 1856, let us consider some of the factors that had made him the instrument of this great awakening. In the first place, Spurgeon possessed outstanding natural abilities which were all devoted to the cause of the proclamation of the Word. His powers of imagination and description enabled him to present familiar truths with arresting vividness. Take the following statement in which he is exhorting believers to awake to the urgency of making known the gospel: 'Christian man, while you are sleeping, remember time is running on. If you could stop the hands of time you might afford yourselves a little leisure; if you could, as we say, take him by the forelock, you might pause awhile; but you must not rest, for the tremendous wheels of the chariot of time are driven at such a fearful rate that the axles thereof are red-hot with speed, and there is no pause in that tremendous rush? On, on, on it goes, and a century has fled like a watch in the night.' Such language was a startling contrast to the dull pulpit style of mid-Victorianism. It was an impudent thing in the eyes of the religious world for a young upstart to popularize a new style of preaching. But that is, in fact, what Spurgeon did, and in doing so he proved he possessed a self-confidence and an originality of no common order. He scorned a dignified, impersonal presentation of the gospel and spoke to his hearers as though he was seizing them personally by the hand and talking to them in the street.

Spurgeon took 'commonplace' truths and subjects that had come to be regarded as somewhat dull and heavy, and presented them in such clear and forceful language that men could hardly prevent themselves from being gripped and stirred to their depths. What a wealth of language, doctrine and illustration there is, for example, in the following quotation on the perpetuity of the Church:

'Reflect first that a Church exists. What a wonder this! It is perhaps the greatest miracle of all ages that God has a Church in the world. . . . Always a Church! When the full force of the Pagan Emperors came like a thundering avalanche upon her, she shook off the stupendous load as a man shaketh the flakes of snow from his garment, and she lived on uninjured. When papal Rome vented its malice yet more furiously and ingenuously; when cruel murderers hunted the saints among the Alps, or worried them in the low country; when Albigenses and Waldenses poured out their blood in rivers, and dyed the snow with crimson, she lived still, and never was in a healthier state than when she was immersed in her own gore. When after a partial reformation in this country, the pretenders to religion determined that the truly spiritual should be harried out of the land, God's Church did not sleep or suspend her career of life or service. Let the covenant signed in blood witness to the vigour of the persecuted saints. Hearken to her psalm amidst the brown heath-clad hills of Scotland, and her prayer in the secret conventicles of England. Hear ye the voice of Cargil and Cameron thundering among the mountains against a false king and an apostate people; hear ye the testimony of Bunyan and his compeers who would sooner rot in dungeons than bow the knee to Baal. Ask me "Where is the Church?" and I can find her at any and every period from the day when first in the upper room the Holy Ghost came down even until now.

In one unbroken line our apostolic succession runs; not through the Church of Rome; not from the superstitious hands of priest-made popes, or king-created bishops (what a varnished lie is the apostolic succession of those who boast so proudly of it!), but through the blood of good men and true, who never forsook the testimony of Jesus; through the loins of true pastors, laborious evangelists, faithful martyrs, and honourable men of God, we trace our pedigree up to the fishermen of Galilee and glory that we perpetuate by God's grace that true and faithful Church of the living God, in whom Christ did abide and will abide until the world's crash.

'The chief wonder is that she abides perfect. Not one of God's elect has gone back; not one of the blood-bought has denied the faith. Not one single soul which ever was effectually called can be made to deny Christ, even though his flesh should be pulled from his bones by hot pincers, or his tormented body flung to the jaws of wild beasts. All that the enemy has done has been of no avail against the Church. The old rock has been washed, and washed, and washed again by stormy waves, and submerged a thousand times in the floods of tempest but even her angles and corners abide unaltered and unalterable. We may say of the Lord's tabernacle, not one of the stakes thereof has been removed, nor one of her cords been broken. The house of the Lord from foundation to pinnacle is perfect still: "The rain descended and the floods came, and the winds blew, and beat upon that house and it fell not"; nay, nor a single stone of it, "for it was founded upon a rock".'

There can be no doubt that one prominent reason for Spurgeon's influence was that he possessed abilities which enabled him to break through the long established conventions of his age, and then the confidence to withstand the storm which his actions aroused. 'Often,' he declared in a sermon on prayer, 'because I have not chosen to pray in any conventional form, people have said, "That man is not

reverent!" My dear sir, you are not a judge of my reverence.
... Brethren, I would like to burn the whole stock of old
prayers that we have been using this fifty years. That "oil that
goes from vessel to vessel" – that misquoted, mangled text,
"where two or three are met together, thou wilt be in the
midst of them, and that to bless them," – and all those other
quotations which we have been manufacturing, and dislocating,
and copying from man to man. I would we came to speak to
God, just out of our own hearts.'[12] He was equally as un-
wavering in replying to the critics of his preachings: 'I am not
very particular about how I preach. I have not courted any
man's love; I asked no man to attend my ministry; I preach
what I like, when I like, and as I like.'

There have probably been only two evangelists in English
Church history with whom Spurgeon can be adequately compared. In several of his natural gifts he resembles Hugh Lati-
mer and George Whitefield, but in one natural gift he went
well beyond either of these predecessors. He had a mental
power which enabled him to assimilate and digest and later
popularize practically everything he read.[13] Then we must add
to this the fact that Spurgeon's upbringing was such that by
the time he came to London he had read an enormous amount
for his age. He was steeped in what he called the golden era of

[12] 6, 338. 'I can at the prayer-meetings,' he says in another place, 'readily tell
when the brother is praying, and when he is only performing, or playing at
prayer. You know how it is with some prayers – they are like an invoice, "as
per usual", or a list of goods with "ditto, ditto" every here and there. Oh, for
a living groan! One sigh of the soul has more power in it than half an hour's
recitation of pretty pious words. Oh, for a sob from the soul, or a tear from
the heart!'

[13] 'His power of reading was perhaps never equalled. ... He took in the
contents almost at a glance and his memory never failed him as to what he read.
He made a point of reading half-a-dozen of the hardest books every week.
I several times had an opportunity of testing the thoroughness of his reading
and I never found him at fault.' (Dr Wright, quoted in Spurgeon's *Autobiography* 4, 273.) At the time of his death Spurgeon had a library of 12,000
books and it is said 'he could have fetched almost any one of them in the
dark.'
Similarly, we read that 'Mr Spurgeon at one time as he sat on his platform,
could name every one of his five thousand members'.

English theology – the Puritan period,[14] and above all he had been a fluent reader of the Bible since the age of six. What Spurgeon wrote of Bunyan is equally applicable to himself: 'Read anything of his, and you will see that it is almost like reading the Bible itself. He had studied our Authorized Version, which will never be bettered, as I judge, till Christ shall come; he had read it till his whole being was saturated with Scripture. . . . Prick him anywhere; and you will find that his blood is Bibline, the very essence of the Bible flows from him. He cannot speak without quoting a text, for his soul is full of the Word of God.'[15]

It would be wrong to ignore Spurgeon's natural gifts and his deep study, but it would be a much greater wrong to imagine that these things explain the character of his early ministry. To imply that they did would be a contradiction of all that he taught. Spurgeon came to London conscious that God had been hiding His face from His people. His knowledge of the Bible and of Church history convinced him that, compared with what the Church had a warrant to expect, the Spirit of God was in great measure withdrawn, and if God continued to withhold His face, he declared to his people, nothing could be done to extend His Kingdom. It is not your knowledge, nor your talent, nor your zeal, he would say, that can perform God's work. 'Yet, brethren, this can be done – *we will cry to the Lord until He reveals His face again.*' 'All we want is the Spirit of God. Dear Christian friends, go home and pray for it; give yourselves no rest till God reveals Him-

[14] Spurgeon's opinion of the Puritans, with whom he was first acquainted in his childhood, remained with him all his days. He said in 1872, 'We assert this day that, when we take down a volume of Puritanical theology we find in a solitary page more thinking and more learning, more Scripture, more real teaching, than in whole folios of the effusions of modern thought. The modern men would be rich if they possessed even the crumbs that fall from the table of the Puritans.' 18,322. Spurgeon had no patience with those who said, ' "We will not read anything except *the book* itself, neither will we accept any light, except that which comes in through a crack in our own roof. We will not see by another man's candle, we would sooner remain in the dark." Brethren, do not let us fall into such folly.' 25, 630.
[15] *Autobiography*, 4, 268.

self; do not tarry where you are, do not be content to go on in your everlasting jog-trot as you have done; do not be content with the mere round of formalities. Awake, O Zion; awake, awake, awake!'[16]

Before many months had passed it was manifest that the congregation at New Park Street was awakening, and as travail in prayer became the characteristic of the church one common burden spread from pastor to people. 'The Lord send a blessing. He must send it, our hearts will break if He does not.' What a change took place in the prayer meetings! Now instead of the old, dull prayers, 'Every man seemed like a crusader besieging the New Jerusalem, each one appeared determined to storm the Celestial City by the might of intercession; and soon the blessing came upon us in such abundance that we had not room to receive it.'[17]

To the end of his life Spurgeon pointed back to the revival at New Park Street as one sure evidence that God answers prayer, and he would often remind his congregation of those early days. 'What prayer meetings we have had! Shall we ever forget Park Street, those prayer meetings, when I felt compelled to let you go without a word from my lips, because the Spirit of God was so awfully present that we felt bowed to the dust.'[18] ... 'And what listening there was at Park Street, where we scarcely had air enough to breathe! The Holy Spirit came down like showers which saturate the soil till the clods are ready for the breaking; and then it was not long before we heard on the right and on the left the cry, "What must we do to be saved?" '

Some of the most solemn warnings Spurgeon ever gave his congregation were of the danger of their ceasing to be depend-

[16] The reason why the site of the chapel (built in 1833) is sometimes called 'New Park Street' and, more often in contemporary references, 'Park Street' is not clear. Newspapers quoted on pp. 35–6 above, speak of 'Park Street Chapel'. Apparently both names were in use. On a map in the records of Southwark Borough Council it is noted that the word 'New' was officially abolished in 1872.
[17] *The Early Years*, 263.   [18] II, 397.

ent upon God in prayer. 'May God help me, if you cease to pray for me! Let me know the day and I must cease to preach. Let me know when you intend to cease your prayers and I will cry, "O my God, give me this day my tomb, and let me slumber in the dust".'[19] These words were not the eloquence of a preacher; rather they expressed the deepest feelings of his heart.[20] He *believed* that without the Spirit of God nothing could be done. When his congregation should cease to feel their 'utter, entire, absolute dependence upon the presence of God,' then he was sure they 'would ere long become a scorn and a hissing, or else a mere log upon the water.'[21] Throughout Spurgeon's ministry this concern remained uppermost in his heart. 'If there were only one prayer which I might pray before I died, it should be this: "Lord, send thy Church men filled with the Holy Ghost and with fire." Give to any denomination such men, and its progress must be mighty: keep back such men, send them college gentlemen, of great refinement and profound learning, but of little fire and grace, dumb dogs which cannot bark, and straightway that denomination must decline.'[22]

The true explanation of Spurgeon's ministry, then, is to be found in the person and power of the Holy Spirit. He was himself deeply conscious of this. It was not man's admiration he wanted, but he was jealous that they should stand in awe of God. 'God has come unto us, not to exalt *us*, but to exalt *Himself*.' Moreover he saw nothing singular in his confidence in the Holy Spirit, for he regarded this as the mark of every true messenger of God. A preacher, he says, 'ought to know that he really possesses the Spirit of God, and that when he

[19] 3, 255–6.
[20] On one of his visits to the Continent Spurgeon met an American minister who said, 'I have long wished to see you, Mr Spurgeon, and to put one or two simple questions to you. In our country there are many opinions as to the secret of your great influence. Would you be good enough to give me your own point of view?' After a moment's pause, Spurgeon said, 'My people pray for me.'
[21] 13, 118–19.   [22] 10, 337–8.

speaks there is an influence upon him that enables him to speak as God would have him, otherwise out of the pulpit he should go directly; he has no right to be there. He has not been called to preach God's truth.'[23]

The presence of the Holy Spirit was manifested in Spurgeon's ministry in two prominent respects. Firstly, in *the spirit of his preaching*. Like the Apostle Paul he preached 'in weakness, and in fear, and in much trembling' (1 Cor. 2: 3). 'We tremble,' he says, 'lest we should misbelieve; and tremble more – if you are as I am – lest we should mistake and misinterpret the Word. I believe Martin Luther would have faced the infernal fiend himself without a fear; and yet we have his own confession that his knees often knocked together when he stood up to preach. He trembled lest he should not be faithful to God's Word. To preach the whole truth is an awful charge. You and I, who are ambassadors for God, must not trifle, but we must tremble at God's Word.'[24] When the Holy Spirit takes up a man He gives him something of that same care for the souls of men and women that was seen in the earthly ministry of Christ. 'Jesus never preached a careless sermon,' said Spurgeon, and he sought to be conformed to his Lord. Following this supreme example he was sometimes led into heights of joy – in preaching on John 17:24, he exclaimed, 'I had a thought, but I cannot express it. Easily could I step into heaven; so I feel at this moment' – but he was also taken into those Gethsemane-like depths of agony where one is conscious of the terrible reality of the judgment of God against human sin. 'Our heart is ready to break,' he said, 'when we think how the multitude reject the gospel,' and it was in that spirit that he always sought to speak: 'I can say at this moment,' he exclaimed in the course of a sermon, 'I do feel a

[23] 1, 203. See also his searching but too infrequently read address on *The Holy Spirit in Connection with our Ministry*, in which he shows that 'The lack of distinctly recognizing the power of the Holy Ghost lies at the root of many useless ministries.' *Lectures to my Students*, 2nd Series, 1–22.
[24] 35, 105.

38

longing for the conversion of my hearers, such as I cannot describe. I would count it a high privilege if I might sleep in death this morning, if that death could redeem your souls from hell.'[25]

The pulpit to Spurgeon was the most solemn spot in the world and nothing could be further from the truth than the suggestion that he made it a place of entertainment. Rather from his early days his work in the service of the Lord was marked by its seriousness. When he became a Sunday School teacher in the year of his conversion (1850) he had noted in his diary after a teachers' business meeting, 'Too much joking and levity to agree with my notions of what a Sunday School teacher should be'. Three years after Spurgeon's death, Robertson Nicoll, an acute judge of preachers, wrote while on a visit to New York: 'Evangelism of the humorous type may attract multitudes but it lays the soul in ashes and destroys the very germs of religion. Mr Spurgeon is thought by those who do not know his sermons to have been a humorous preacher. As a matter of fact there was no preacher whose tone was more uniformly earnest, reverent and solemn'.[26]

[25] 8, 64. In later years Spurgeon greatly feared the consequences of a growing disbelief in the reality of hell. In 1865 he said, 'There is a deep-seated unbelief among Christians just now, about the eternity of future punishment. It is not outspoken in many cases, but it is whispered; and it frequently assumes the shape of a spirit of benevolent desire that the doctrine may be disproved. I fear that at the bottom of all this there is a rebellion against the dread sovereignty of God. There is a suspicion that sin is not, after all, so bad a thing as we have dreamed. There is an apology, or a lurking wish to apologize for sinners, who are looked upon rather as objects of pity than as objects of indignation, and really deserving the condign punishment which they have wilfully brought upon themselves. I am afraid it is the old nature in us putting on the specious garb of charity, which thus leads us to discredit a fact which is as certain as the happiness of believers.' 10, 670-1. 'Some cannot bear the thought; but to me it seems inevitable that sin must be punished. . . . If sin becomes a trifle, virtue will be a toy.' 31, 498.
[26] Yet the old travesty persists in those who are ignorant of the real Spurgeon, e.g. Kenneth Slack, who speaks of him as 'a great entertainer, using every artifice of wit, humour, ingenuity and dramatic daring'. *The British Churches Today*, 1961, 73. Spurgeon would have agreed with Charles Simeon who, referring to preachers of a jocular manner, comments: 'St Paul said of sinners: "Of whom I tell you *weeping* that they are the enemies of the cross of Christ,

Spurgeon sought to treat his congregation as William Grimshaw had treated his many hearers at Haworth in the 18th century Awakening. On one occasion when Whitefield was preaching for Grimshaw the latter interrupted him with the words, 'Brother Whitefield, don't flatter them, I fear that half of them are going to hell with their eyes open'.

Every minister can understand what John Wesley meant when he said, 'Were I to preach one whole year in one place, I should preach both myself and most of my congregation to sleep,' and there were times when Spurgeon wished that the burden of preaching year after year to thousands might be lightened: 'There are times without number in which I have wished that I could become the pastor of some little country church, with two or three hundred hearers, over whose souls I could watch with incessant care.'[27] But he knew it was not to be, and he prayed that God would seal his mouth in eternal silence rather than let him grow careless or contented while souls were being damned: 'It were better for me that I had never been born than that I preach to these people carelessly, or keep back any part of my Master's truth. Better to have been a devil than a preacher playing fast and loose with God's Word, and by such means working the ruin of the souls of men. . . . It will be the height of my ambition to be clear of the blood of all men. If, like George Fox, I can say in dying, "I am clear, I am clear," that were almost all the heaven I could wish for.'[28]

whose end is destruction, who mind earthly things". Phil. 3: 18. But such preachers tell you these things laughing instead of weeping. They seem to want the awe and reverence with which we all, especially ministers, should approach God, and God's Word. The Christian should shudder at the idea of levity in such things'. On this subject cf. *An All-Round Ministry*, 335. I am not of course denying that true humour is a wholesome and refreshing gift; the above comments concern only the inappropriateness of its exercise when a man, in public worship, is speaking in the name of God. For charming examples of Spurgeon's humour, as well as other valuable material, see *Personal Reminiscences of C. H. Spurgeon*, W. Williams, 1895, and *Autobiography*, 3, 339–61.

[27] 19, 365.   [28] 19, 370; 27, 310.

40

To describe the spirit in which Spurgeon preached is not, however, to state the ultimate evidence for our belief that the Holy Spirit was abundantly present in his ministry. The *content of his message* was more important to him than the manner of his preaching, and it is this second point which we must now consider. The quotations given above are not only incomplete but, on their own, they could even be misleading. A solemn sense of responsibility was not the impelling motive of his preaching, he was constrained by something higher than the call of duty –

> *Yet if I might make some reserve,*
> *And duty did not call,*
> *I love my God with zeal so great*
> *That I would give Him all.*

These words take us to the heart of Spurgeon's preaching. He *loved* to proclaim 'the glory of God in the face of Jesus Christ.' Christ – He was the 'glorious, all-absorbing topic' of Spurgeon's ministry and that Name turned his pulpit labours into 'a bath in the waters of Paradise.'[29]

The story of how an unnoticed workman was awakened through a text which Spurgeon announced in the deserted Crystal Palace, when he was testing the acoustics in preparation for a service, is well known, but the verse which Spurgeon gave out is no incidental part of the picture. When, as he thought, he had no congregation and no hearers the words which came most simply and naturally to his lips were, 'Behold the Lamb of God, which taketh away the sin of the world.'

Is it then surprising that glancing over the titles of his sermons in 1856 and 1857 we find this constantly recurring Name – 'Christ about His Father's Business'; 'Christ – the Power and Wisdom of God'; 'Christ lifted up'; 'The Condescension of Christ'; 'Christ our Passover'; 'Christ Exalted'; 'The Exaltation of Christ'; 'Christ in the Covenant'? Let us glance

[29] *The Early Years*, 403.

for a moment at one such sermon, entitled 'The Eternal Name'
and preached early in 1855 when he was twenty years old. In
the course of this sermon he depicts what would become of
the world if the Name of Jesus could be removed from it, and
unable to restrain his own feelings he exclaimed, 'I would
have no wish to be here without my Lord; and if the gospel
be not true, I should bless God to annihilate me this instant,
for I would not care to live if ye could destroy the name of
Jesus Christ.'[30] Many years later Mrs Spurgeon had not
forgotten this same sermon and she describes its close, when
Spurgeon's voice was almost breaking in physical exhaustion,
in the following words:

'I remember, with strange vividness at this long distance of
time, the Sunday evening when he preached from the text,
"His Name shall endure for ever." It was a subject in which he
revelled, it was his chief delight to exalt his glorious Saviour,
and he seemed in that discourse to be pouring out his very soul
and life in homage and adoration before his gracious King.
But I really thought he would have died there, in face of all
those people! At the end of the sermon, he made a mighty
effort to recover his voice; but utterance well-nigh failed, and
only in broken accents could the pathetic peroration be heard,
– "Let my name perish, but let Christ's Name last for ever!
Jesus! *Jesus*! Jesus! Crown Him Lord of all! You will not hear
me say anything else. These are my last words in Exeter Hall
for this time. Jesus! *Jesus*! Jesus! Crown *Him* Lord of all!"
and then he fell back almost fainting in the chair behind him.'[31]

Is there any stronger evidence of the presence of the Holy
Spirit in a man's ministry than this? If there is, perhaps it is
that awareness, unknown to all save the preacher, of Christ's
own presence with him as he speaks – 'Scarcely is it possible
for a man, this side of the grave, to be nearer Heaven' than
when enjoying this, writes Spurgeon, and there were times
when he could testify, 'I have discerned the special presence of

42

my Lord with me by a consciousness as sure as that by which I know that I live. Jesus has been as real to me, at my side in this pulpit, as though I had beheld Him with my eyes.'

We cannot leave the subject of the theme of Spurgeon's ministry without giving one example of how he preached Christ to every class of hearer and Christ as the *only* need of every heart: 'Remember, sinner, it is not *thy hold* of Christ that saves thee – it is Christ; it is not *thy joy* in Christ that saves thee – it is Christ; it is not even faith in Christ, though that is the instrument – it is Christ's blood and merits; therefore, look not to thy hope, but to Christ, the source of thy hope; look not to thy faith, but to Christ, the author and finisher of thy faith; and if thou doest that, ten thousand devils cannot throw thee down. . . . There is one thing which we all of us too much becloud in our preaching, though I believe we do it very unintentionally – namely, the great truth that it is not prayer, it is not faith, it not our doings, it is not our feelings upon which we must rest, but upon Christ, and on Christ alone. We are apt to think that we are not in a right state, that we do not feel enough, instead of remembering that our business is not with self, but Christ. Let me beseech thee, look only to Christ; never expect deliverance from self, from ministers, or from any means of any kind apart from Christ; keep thine eye simply on Him; let His death, His agonies, His groans, His sufferings, His Merits, His glories, His intercession, be fresh upon thy mind; when thou wakest in the morning look for Him; when thou liest down at night look for Him.'[32]

Such was the spirit and message of C. H. Spurgeon at the age of twenty-two, and as we leave this side of his ministry who is there that does not feel we need to know again today the meaning of being constrained by the love of Christ? An oft-repeated verse expressed Spurgeon's prayer, let us make the words our own:

[32] 2, 375–6.

A very wretch, Lord! I should prove,
  Had I no love for Thee;
Rather than not my Saviour love,
  O may I cease to be!

Mr Spurgeon is a Calvinist, which few of the dissenting ministers in London now are. He preaches salvation, not of man's free will, but of the Lord's good will, which few in London, it is to be feared, now do.

John Anderson of Helensburgh
THE EARLY YEARS, 339

I do not hesitate to say, that next to the doctrine of the crucifixion and the resurrection of our blessed Lord – no doctrine had such prominence in the early Christian Church as the doctrine of the election of grace.

C.H.S. SERMONS, 6, 302

The doctrine of grace has been put by in the lumber chamber. It is acknowledged to be true, for it is confessed in most creeds; it is in the Church of England articles, it is in the confessions of all sorts of Protestant Christians, except those who are avowedly Arminian, but how little is it ever preached! It is put among the relics of the past. It is considered to be a respectable sort of retired officer, who is not expected to see any more active service.

C.H.S. SERMONS, 12, 429.

2 : The Lost Controversy

In the previous chapter we sought to recover the image of
Spurgeon as he was in the days of his New Park Street ministry. The picture which emerged was not that of a jovial pulpit
phenomenon upon whom men lavished their praise but rather
of a youth whose arrival amidst the soothing and sleepy
religious life of London was about as unwelcome as the
Russian cannons which were then thundering in the far-off
Crimea. The facts come as somewhat of a jolt to us, for we
have more or less become accustomed to look upon Spurgeon
as a benign grandfather of modern evangelicalism. When the
revival of 1855 and onwards shook Southwark out of its
spiritual slumber, the name of the pastor of New Park Street
was a symbol of reproach, and blows were rained on him
from every direction; the name has since been turned into a
symbol of evangelical respectability and we tend to comfort
ourselves amidst the prevailing defection from evangelical
principles with the thought that the religious world has still
some remembrance of a man holding our position whose
influence not so many years ago encircled the globe. Yet when
we recall the real character of his ministry our comfort may
evaporate, for we are faced with the question, not how much
do we admire Spurgeon, but what would a man like this think
of the Church today?

We have already spoken of the general characteristics of his
early life and they need to be borne in mind as we turn to more
detailed aspects of the doctrine he preached. It would be an
injustice to the man in any way to separate the truth which he

held from *the spirit* in which he lived. His doctrinal convictions were not formulated in the cool detachment of intellectual study, rather they were burned into him by the Holy Spirit, irradiated by his love for his Redeemer, and kept fresh in his ministry by communion with God. Spurgeon had little sympathy for men who held an orthodox system which was devoid of the living unction of the Spirit.

One of the first attacks which was made on Spurgeon's ministry after his settlement in London came from a section of the Baptist community which could at that time be described as 'Hyper-Calvinist'. The label is not one that Spurgeon liked to use, for he regarded the introduction of the great Reformer's name as a misnomer: 'Calvinists, such men may call themselves, but, unlike the Reformer, whose name they adopt, they bring a system of divinity to the Bible to interpret it, instead of making every system, be its merits what they may, yield, and give place to the pure and unadulterated Word of God.' In the January, 1855, issue of *The Earthen Vessel*, an anonymous writer of this school cast doubt on Spurgeon's whole position and call to the ministry. Spurgeon's untraditional phraseology, the crowds which followed him, his general invitations and exhortations to all hearers to repent and believe the Gospel, and the 'broadness' of his theology were all grounds for suspicion. He was neither narrow enough nor discriminating enough for his critic, who complained: 'Spurgeon preaches all doctrine and no doctrine; all experience, and therefore no experience.'

For a reason which will later be apparent, the youthful preacher was not concerned to meet this attack, nevertheless he did sometimes pause in the course of a sermon to deal with the views of the Hyper-Calvinists. Sometimes his reflections are semi-humorous, as the following:

'Is there not many a good "Hyper" brother, who has a full knowledge of the doctrines of grace; but when he is reading the Bible, one day, he finds a text that looks rather wide and general, and he says, "This cannot mean what it says; I must trim it down and make it fit into Dr Gill's commentary"?' More often he deals much more sharply with the principles which lead to this kind of practice, for Hyper-Calvinism not only causes personal lopsidedness, but what is more serious, it prevents a full preaching of the gospel:[1] 'I do not believe,' he declares in the course of a sermon on the Good Samaritan, 'in the way in which some people pretend to preach the gospel. They have no gospel for sinners as sinners, but only for those who are above the dead level of sinnership, and are technically styled *sensible* sinners.' We must break the quotation for a moment to clarify his terminology: Hyper-Calvinism in its attempt to square all gospel truth with God's purpose to save the elect, denies there is a universal command to repent and believe, and asserts that we have only warrant to invite to Christ those who are *conscious* of a sense of sin and need. In other words, it is those who have been spiritually quickened to seek a Saviour and not those who are in the death of unbelief and indifference, to whom the exhortations of the gospel must be addressed. In this way a scheme was devised for restricting the gospel to those who there is reason to suppose are elect. 'Like the priest in this parable,' Spurgeon continues, 'they see the poor sinner, and they say "He is not conscious of his need, we cannot invite him to Christ;" "He is dead," they say, "it is of no use preaching to dead souls;" so they pass by on the other side, keeping close to the elect and quickened, but having nothing whatever to say to the dead, lest they should make out Christ to be too gracious, and his mercy to be too

[1] 'They have been obliged to cover up such a passage as this, because they could not understand it: "O, Jerusalem, Jerusalem, how often would I have gathered thy children together as a hen gathereth her chickens under her wing, but ye would not." They durst not preach upon such a text as this: "As I live saith the Lord, I have no pleasure in the death of him that dieth, but had rather that he should turn unto me and live." They are ashamed to say to men, "Turn ye, turn ye, why will ye die." They dare not come out and preach as Peter did — "Repent ye, and be converted that your sins may be blotted out."' 6, 302.

free. . . . I have known ministers say, "Well, you know, we ought to describe the sinner's state, and warn him, but we must not invite him to Christ." Yes, gentlemen, you must pass by on the other side, after having looked at him, for on your own confession you have no *good* news for the poor wretch. I bless my Lord and Master he has given me a gospel which I can take to *dead* sinners, a gospel which is available for the vilest of the vile.'[2]

Spurgeon was urgent upon this issue because he saw that if the sinner's warrant for receiving the gospel lies in any internal qualifications or feelings, then the unconverted, as such, have no immediate duty to believe on Christ, and they may conclude that because they do not feel any penitence or need, the command to believe on the Son of God is not addressed to them. On the other hand, if the warrant rests not in anything in the sinner but solely in the command and invitations of God, then we have a message for every creature under heaven. Spurgeon did not believe that the fact of election should be concealed from the unconverted, but he held that Hyper-Calvinism, by directing men's attention away from the centrality of personal faith in Christ, had distorted[3] the New Testament emphasis and bolstered up complacency in unbelievers. It had alleged that because faith is wrought in man by the power of the Spirit of God, then we cannot command men to believe, but in so doing it by-passed the stark fact that unbelief is always presented to us in Scripture as sin for which we are responsible: 'If you had not fallen you would

[2] 8, 55.
[3] 'You have seen those mirrors,' he says (referring to fair-grounds) 'you walk up to them and you see your head ten times as large as your body, or you walk away and put yourself in another position, and then your feet are monstrous and the rest of your body is small; this is an ingenious toy, but I am sorry to say that many go to work with God's truth upon the model of this toy; they magnify one capital truth till it becomes monstrous; they minify and speak little of another truth till it becomes altogether forgotten." 8, 182. For a short summary of Spurgeon's views on 'Preaching to Sinners' see his book of addresses entitled *Only A Prayer-Meeting*, 301–5.

come to Christ the moment he was preached to you; but you do not because of your sinfulness.' Man's failure to comply with the gospel, instead of being excusable, is the highest expression of his depravity.

It should be clear from this that Hyper-Calvinism is more than a mere theoretical deviation from the gospel, and Spurgeon spoke strongly because he knew by experience that it reduces churches to inactivity or even complete paralysis. 'I have met with some brethren who have tried to read the Bible the wrong way upwards. They have said, "God has a purpose which is certain to be fulfilled, therefore we will not budge an inch. All power is in the hands of Christ, therefore we will sit still;" but that is not Christ's way of reading the passage. It is, "All power is given unto me, *therefore go ye*, and do something." '[4] 'The lazy-bones of our orthodox churches cry, "God will do His own work"; and then they look out the softest pillow they can find, and put it under their heads, and say, "The eternal purposes will be carried out: God will be glorified." That is all very fine talk, but it can be used with the most mischievous design. You can make opium out of it, which will lull you into a deep and dreadful slumber, and prevent your being of any kind of use at all.'[5]

At no point was Hyper-Calvinism more seriously at fault, in Spurgeon's eyes, than in its failure to be characterized by zeal for militant and world-wide evangelism. While he knew that not a few Christians of this persuasion were better than their creed, he saw clearly that both the theological and historical evidence indicated that the influence of this teaching never promoted earnest missionary work. If the gospel is only for *sensible* sinners, how then can the Church act under the compulsion of her commission to 'Go into all the world and preach the gospel to every creature'? If the warrant to believe only belongs to the penitent, then it does not belong to all men everywhere, for the multitudes of the earth are not in that

[4] 42, 234.   [5] 30, 630.

condition: 'I would like to carry one of those who only preach to sensible sinners, and set him down in the capital of the kingdom of Dahomey. There are no sensible sinners there! Look at them, with their mouths stained with human blood, with their bodies smeared all over with the gore of their immolated victims – how will the preacher find any qualification there? I know not what he could say, but I know what my message would be. My word would run thus – "Men and brethren, God, who made the heavens and the earth, hath sent His Son Jesus Christ into the world to suffer for our sins, and whosoever believeth in Him shall not perish, but have everlasting life.'[6]

'The day was,' he says in another sermon, 'when the very idea of sending the gospel to the heathen was regarded by our orthodox brethren as a piece of Don Quixotism, not to be attempted, and even now, if you say, "All the world for Jesus," they open their eyes and say, "Ah, we are afraid you are tainted with universal redemption, or are going off to the Arminian camp." God grant these dear brethren new hearts and right spirits; at present their hearts are too small to bring Him much glory. May they get larger hearts, hearts something like their

[6] 9, 538, a sermon on 'The Warrant of Faith.' 'The command to believe in Christ must be the sinner's warrant. . . . Unless the warrant be a something in which every creature can take a share, there is no such thing as consistently preaching to *every creature*.' cf. also another sermon on the warrant, *May I?* 30, 613. Perhaps no last-century Christian leader gave such clear teaching on the question of the warrant as the saintly Professor John Duncan of Edinburgh. With his customary habit of simplifying a problem in a few sentences, he says: 'If only convinced sinners are warranted to embrace Christ, then I must, ere I can be warranted to embrace Him, be convinced that I am a convinced sinner. But the Holy Spirit is the only source of infallible conviction, and the Holy Spirit is nowhere promised to convince of conviction; He is only promised to convince of sin. True, the convinced sinner is the only capable subject of saving faith, but it is not as a convinced sinner I am called upon to come to Christ. . . . None are so unwilling to consider themselves convinced as those who really are. . . . The convinced sinner would be the last to embrace an offer made to convinced sinners; but proclaim the gospel to a vile, guilty sinner, and he saith, "That is I". . . . God needs to do a great deal *to* sinners, in order to turn them; but God is requiring nothing *of* sinners but that they return.' *Recollections of the late John Duncan*, A. Moody Stuart, 1872, 96–7, 219.

Lord's, and may they have grace given them to estimate the precious blood at a higher rate, for our Lord did not die to buy a few hundred of souls, or to redeem to Himself a handful of people; He shed His blood for a number which no man can number, and His elect shall excel in multitude the sands which belt the sea.'[7]

The above quotations are vitally important for a variety of reasons. Firstly, they indicate that there is a real difference between Biblical Calvinism and Hyper-Calvinism. The latter term is sometimes used as though it were simply a stronger formulation of Scriptural doctrines – something beyond a 'moderate' position – but this is an incorrect usage, for the system deviates seriously from Scripture and falls short of Scripture. Another wrong usage of the term, which is even more common, is for the label 'hyper' or 'ultra' Calvinist to be attached to those who are in fact opposed to Hyper-Calvinism. Being ignorant of the distinct theological differences which separate Hyper-Calvinism from the faith of the Reformers and Puritans, and being unaware of its different historical origins, some critics use the phrase as though it were the most suitable to describe anyone who is earnest in opposing the tenets of Arminianism. But while this may be a convenient way to brand 'extremists', it reveals the spiritual muddle of those who thus use it. Spurgeon, however, had frequently to put up with this treatment and it is not unknown today.

If the reader turns to the twentieth-century biographies of Spurgeon he will have no difficulty in finding references to the preacher's opposition to the 'hyper' school. J. C. Carlile, for example, says, 'Naturally Mr Spurgeon's theology often brought him into controversy,' and he immediately proceeds to mention the controversy we have sketched above. We are left with the impression that Spurgeon was just like we are – opposed to extremes, and we are confirmed in this feeling when we are told by W. Y. Fullerton that 'he broke away

[7] 20, 239.

from the sterner school.'[8] Of course we are given a vague statement of Spurgeon's Calvinism, but Carlile adds that 'the stern truths of the Calvinist faith were held practically by all Protestants.'[9] So with such assurances we are unsuspectingly allowed to suppose that the *doctrinal* content of Spurgeon's preaching caused no great uproar in the religious world of his day. This is all thoroughly misleading. The twentieth-century biographers have in fact entirely passed over *the* greatest controversy of his early ministry; there is not even a whisper of the word which echoes through the six volumes of the New Park Street sermons; it cannot be found in the indexes to these biographies. Why should modern evangelicals be so much concerned to make the word 'Arminianism' vanish away?[10]

Whatever be the purpose, this method of dealing with Spurgeon has quite effectively created an impression of the man which has wide currency today; yet we believe this impression of the nature of Spurgeon's 'evangelicalism' is one which a study of his Autobiography and a study of his unabridged sermons thoroughly demolishes. When a small selection of his sermons, entitled *Revival Year Sermons*, was published in 1959, commemorating the revival of a century earlier, some British reviewers could not refrain from expressing their feeling that the sermons were 'hand-picked' in an attempt to put over a party position which was not really Spurgeonic at all, and when the same sermons were translated into Spanish by a minister of that country, Spanish Baptists questioned the

[8] *C. H. Spurgeon*, W. Y. Fullerton, 1920, 290. Fullerton appears to be im-plying that Spurgeon left Hyper-Calvinism, but it is quite clear from his Autobiography that he never was a Hyper-Calvinist! It was this fact which occasioned a difference with one of his deacons at Waterbeach – his first pastorate. cf. *The Early Years*, 221–2.
[9] *C. H. Spurgeon: An Interpretative Biography*, J. C. Carlile, 1933, 147.
[10] More seriously, 'Arminianism' has even been removed from the text of some of Spurgeon's Sermons reprinted in the Kelvedon edition, though no warning of abridgement is given to the reader. Compare, for example, the sermon preached on 18 October, 1857 which is No. 159 in *New Park Street Pulpit*, Volume 3 and which appears in volume 13 (Sermons of Comfort and Assurance), page 222 of the Kelvedon edition published by Marshall, Morgan & Scott.

veracity of the translation! We may smile at the story of the Victorian schoolboy who thought that Spurgeon was the Prime Minister of England but it seems there are similar wild ideas about what kind of man he really was, current at the present time.

In expanding these statements it is first necessary to show that the prevalent doctrinal outlook in the 1850's was not Calvinistic, as Carlile affirms, but rather Arminian, and it was chiefly because Spurgeon stood against this that his arrival in London was looked upon with such disfavour by the religious world. Spurgeon's exchanges with Hyper-Calvinism were only skirmishes compared to the battle which he had to fight on quite a different and much wider front; he judged that Hyper-Calvinism was held only by a group, with comparatively small and scattered influence, within the Baptist denomination, whereas he regarded Arminianism as an error which was influential throughout Nonconformity, as well as within the Church of England. He consequently devoted more time and energy to the exposing of the latter, and the correctness of his assessment of the position is borne out by the strength of the opposition he soon encountered.

The few religious periodicals which favoured Hyper-Calvinism could never have caused the storm which raged round Spurgeon's ministry in its early years. The newspapers generally, religious and secular, were indeed so far from Hyper-Calvinism that they were not even aware that Spurgeon was opposed by Hyper-Calvinists!

There is no shortage of literary evidence indicating that Spurgeon's doctrinal position was his chief offence in the eyes of his contemporaries. For example, Silas Henn introduced his book *Spurgeon's Calvinism Examined and Refuted*, published in 1858, with these words:

'By many, the Calvinistic controversy has been considered as long since settled, and comparatively few in these times, amid such enlightened views of Christianity, dare to proclaim, openly and without disguise, the peculiar tenets of John Calvin. Even in many professedly Calvinistic pulpits, the doctrines are greatly modified, and genuine Calvinism is kept back. But there are some who hold it forth in all its length and breadth, and among these, the Rev. C. H. Spurgeon, the notorious preacher at the Music Hall, Royal Surrey Gardens, is the most prominent.'

The same criticism is commonly to be found in many of the newspapers of that period. *The Bucks Chronicle* accused Spurgeon of making Hyper-Calvinism essential for entrance to heaven; *The Freeman* deplored that he denounced Arminians 'in almost every sermon'; *The Christian News* likewise decried his 'doctrines of the most rampant exclusiveness' and his opposition to Arminianism; and *The Saturday Review* was pained, as we have noted earlier, at the profanity of his preaching 'Particular Redemption in saloons reeking with the perfume of tobacco'.

Perhaps *The Patriot*, a Nonconformist journal, best summarized in the following broadside why they were all so much offended at the young preacher:

'All, in turn, come under the lash of the precocious tyro. He alone is a consistent Calvinist; all besides are either rank Arminians, licentious Antinomians, or unfaithful professors of the doctrines of grace. College training does but wean young men's sympathies from the people; and "really ploughmen would make a great deal better preachers." The doctrine of election is, "in our age, scorned and hated." "The time-serving religion of the present day" is "only exhibited in evangelical drawing rooms." "How many pious preachers are there on the Sabbath-day who are very impious preachers during the rest of the week!" He "never hears" his brother ministers "assert the positive satisfaction and substitution of our Lord Jesus Christ." These fishers of men "have been spending all their life fishing with most elegant silk lines and gold and silver hooks, but the fish will not bite for all that; whereas we of the rougher sort," adds the self-complacent censor, "have put the hook into the jaws of hundreds." Still "rougher", if possible, is Mr Spurgeon's treatment of theologians not of his own especial school. "Arminian perversions, in particular, are to sink back to their birthplace in the pit." Their notion of the possibility of a final fall from grace is "the wickedest falsehood on earth." '[11]

These quotations are coloured by the annoyance of the writers but they are all unanimous in two charges: namely that Spurgeon's doctrine was not that which was characteristic of contemporary Protestantism and secondly that he openly and repeatedly opposed Arminianism. Instead of clearing himself from the guilt of these charges Spurgeon readily accepted them.[12] 'We need not be ashamed of our pedigree,' he says, 'although Calvinists are now considered to be heterodox.' His estimate of the religious situation was that the Church was being tempted 'with Arminianism by the wholesale'[13] and that her primary need was not simply more evangelism nor even more holiness (in the first place) but a return to the full truth of the doctrines of grace – which, for convenience, he was prepared to name as Calvinism. It is clear that Spurgeon did not view himself simply as an evangelist but also as a reformer whose duty it was 'to give more prominence in the religious world to those old doctrines of the gospel'[14]....
'The old truth that Calvin preached, that Augustine preached, that Paul preached, is the truth that I must preach today, or else be false to my conscience and my God. I cannot shape the truth; I know of no such thing as paring off the rough edges of

[11] Pike, 2, 196.
[12] 4, 341. 'Scarcely a Baptist minister of standing will own me', Spurgeon wrote in a letter to a friend, and in another he commented that contemporary preachers 'are afraid of *real Gospel Calvinism*' (*The Early Years*, 342–3). The eminent Thomas Binney, after hearing a sermon on behalf of the London Association of Baptist Churches in 1855 in which the pastor of New Park Street spoke against Arminianism, declared 'I never heard such things in my life before'!
[13] 1, 208.   [14] *The Early Years*, 350.

a doctrine. John Knox's gospel is my gospel. That which thundered through Scotland must thunder through England again.'[15] These words take us back to the heart of his New Park Street ministry; there is a reforming zeal and prophetic fire about the man which, while it awakened some, aroused others to wrath and hostility. Spurgeon spoke as a man convinced that *he knew* the reason for the Church's ineffectiveness, and though he might have to say it alone, he would not be silent:

'There has sprung up in the Church of Christ an idea that there are many things taught in the Bible which are not essential; that we may alter them just a little to suit our convenience: that provided we are right in the fundamentals, the other things are of no concern ... But this know, that the slightest violation of the divine law will bring judgments upon the Church, and has brought judgments, and is even at this day withholding God's hand from blessing us ... The Bible, the whole Bible, and nothing but the Bible is the religion of Christ's Church. And until we come back to that the Church will have to suffer ...

'Ah, how many have there been who have said, "The old puritanic principles are too rough for these times; we'll alter them, we'll tone them down a little." What are you at, Sir? Who art thou that darest to touch a single letter of God's Book which God has hedged about with thunder, in that tremendous sentence, wherein He has written, "Whosoever shall add unto these things, God shall add unto him the plagues that are written in this book; and whosoever shall take away from the words of the book of this prophecy, God shall take away his part out of the book of life, and out of the holy city." It besomes an awful thing when we come to think about it, for men not to form a right and proper judgment about God's Word; for man to leave a single point in it uncanvassed, a single mandate unstudied, lest we shall lead others astray, while we ourselves are acting in disobedience to God ...

[15] ibid., 162.

'Our victories of the Church have not been like the victories of the olden times. Why is this? My theory to account for it is this. In the first place, the absence of the Holy Spirit in a great measure from us. But if you come to the root of it to know the reason, my fuller other answer is this: the Church has forsaken her original purity, and therefore, she has lost her power. If once we had done with everything erroneous, if by the unanimous will of the entire body of Christ, every evil ceremony, every ceremony not ordained of Scripture were lopped off and done with; if every doctrine were rejected which is not sustained by Holy Writ; if the Church were pure and clean, her path would be onward, triumphant, victorious . . .

'This may seem to you to be of little consequence, but it really is a matter of life and death. I would plead with every Christian – think it over, my dear brother. When some of us preach Calvinism, and some Arminianism, we cannot both be right; it is of no use trying to think we can be – "Yes", and "no", cannot both be true . . . Truth does not vacillate like the pendulum which shakes backwards and forwards. It is not like the comet, which is here, there, and everywhere. One must be right; the other wrong.'[16]

This reforming element in Spurgeon's early ministry can only be rightly interpreted if we understand his convictions on the theological drift of his age. He believed that God had called him to stand for a reviving of the old Calvinistic evangelicalism once predominant in England and it was because this conviction was so intertwined with the course of his ministry during his first years in London that he has a chapter in his Autobiography, at this point, entitled '*A Defence of Calvinism.*' An interesting letter of Spurgeon's which has only recently come to light bears out the same point. The letter is to Charles Spiller, a Baptist minister in Chipping Campden, and while Spurgeon mentions the attack he has suffered from

[16] 6, 166–70.

the Hyper-Calvinistic quarter in *The Earthen Vessel*, it is plain that his main attention is turned in quite a different direction. He rejoices that through the platform of Exeter Hall God has given him an opportunity to disturb the general religious malaise which he believed to be connected with an absence of the old orthodoxy.

> 75 Dover-road,
> Boro.
> 13th February, 1855.

My Dear Brother,

Amid the labour of an enormous correspondence I yet find a moment to acknowledge your note. I bless God that I have sounded an alarm in Zion for I find the sound has gone forth. You may conceive my position, a young man under 21 preaching on that occasion to all the ministers of London (nearly), but I thank God I never yet feared man and although last Sabbath more than 4,000 were assembled in Exeter Hall, though every inch was occupied and they clinging to pillars and everywhere, yet I feel unawed by it, for the God within makes even the Babe mighty. My position, as Pastor of one of the most influential churches, enables me to make myself heard and my daily labour is to revive the *old* doctrines of Gill, Owen, Calvin, Augustine and *Christ*.

My sermons are printed weekly, I enclose one – the sale is great – and you can procure them at your bookseller by order. They are also printed in the Penny Pulpits.

If you have ever seen 'The Earthen Vessel' you will see how I have been attacked, and set down as a deceiver – the consequence has been that more interest was excited, all 'The Earthen Vessels' were sold – hundreds of rejoinders were sent to the Editor – while I have quietly looked on, and rejoiced that all things work together for good. I think you will be amused if you read that magazine for December, January and February. I am not very easily put down, I go right on and care for no man on God's earth.

You may well pray that I may be kept near to God, for with knocks up, and kicks down – if I did not lean on His arm I were of all men most miserable. It is no easy matter to be belaboured, both by high and low, and stand still firm.

I bless God my church increases at a hopeful rate, 20 to hear tonight before the church, and more to come. All honour to God – for His name I can bear reproach – but the truth I must proclaim. Your note is like a flower in winter – it has the bloom of the summer on it, oh, to have Christ in the *Heart*, the *Holy Ghost in the soul* and glory in prospect – for this we might well barter worlds, and for this let us strive not only in words in the pulpit but in verity and truth in *our* closets alone with our Father.

> I am,
> Yours fraternally,
> C. H. Spurgeon.[17]

That it was his emphasis on reviving the old doctrine which aroused intense opposition to his ministry, Spurgeon had not the slightest doubt: 'We are cried down as *hypers*; we are reckoned the scum of creation; scarcely a minister looks on us or speaks favourably of us, because we hold strong views upon the divine sovereignty of God, and his divine electings and special love towards his own people'.[18] Preaching to his own congregation in 1860 he said: 'There has been no single church of God existing in England for these fifty years which

[17] This letter was first printed in *The Baptist Times*, 17th January, 1963.

At this period Spurgeon evidently had the same doctrinal emphasis in his many preaching visits to the provinces. A writer in 1879, for example, recalls how he first heard Spurgeon at Arley Chapel, Bristol, nearly a quarter of a century earlier. After describing his manner and appearance, he continues: 'I still see and hear Mr Spurgeon as he preached that morning at Arley Chapel. The point in the sermon which remains clearest in my mind was the very pronounced teaching of the doctrine of election, and the preacher's assertion of his being at one with Calvin and Augustine, of whom, as well as of the doctrine, my knowledge at that time was by no means extensive.' *Sword and Trowel*, 1879, 420.
[18] 2, 391.

has had to pass through more trial than we have done ...
scarce a day rolls over my head in which the most villainous
abuse, the most fearful slander is not uttered against me both
privately and by the public press; every engine is employed
to put down God's minister – every lie that man can invent is
hurled at me. . . . They have not checked our usefulness as a
church; they have not thinned our congregations; that which
was to be but a spasm – an enthusiasm which it was hoped
would only last an hour – God has daily increased; not because of me, but because of that gospel which I preach; not
because there was anything in me, but because I came out as
the exponent of plain, straight-forward, honest Calvinism,
and because I seek to speak the Word simply.'[19]

Spurgeon was not surprised at the enmity that was manifested towards his proclamation of the doctrines of grace:
'Brethren, in all our hearts there is this natural enmity to God
and to the sovereignty of His grace.'[20] 'I have known men bite
their lip and grind their teeth in rage when I have been preaching the sovereignty of God. . . . The doctrinaires of today will
allow a God, but he must not be a King: that is to say, they
choose a god who is no god, and rather the servant than the
ruler of men.'[21] 'The fact that conversion and salvation are of
God, is an humbling truth. It is because of its humbling
character that men do not like it. To be told that God must
save me if I am saved, and that I am in his hand, as clay is in
the hands of the potter, "I do not like it" saith one. Well, I
thought you would not; whoever dreamed you would?"[22]

On the other hand Spurgeon regarded Arminianism as
popular because it served to approximate the gospel more to
the thinking of the natural man; it brought the doctrine of the
Scripture nearer to the mind of the world. The common view
of Christianity was accepted by men simply because it was
not the teaching of Christ: 'had the religion of Christ taught

[19] 6, 435–6.   [20] 29, 85.   [21] 36, 416.
[22] 6, 258.

us that man was a noble being, only a little fallen – had the
religion of Christ taught that Christ had taken away by His
blood, sin from every man, and that every man by his own
free-will, without divine grace, might be saved – it were indeed a most acceptable religion to the mass of men.' [23] The
sting in Spurgeon's comment was occasioned by the fact that
this was precisely what a superficial Protestantism was preaching as the Christian Faith! So in attacking the worldly notions
of Christianity which were current, Spurgeon could not help
also undermining what so many within the Church were
actually preaching. No wonder there was a great uproar! But
Spurgeon did not flinch, for he believed the old truths were
powerful enough to turn his age upside down. In a sermon on
'The World Turned Upside Down,' he declared: 'Christ has
turned the world upside down, as to our *religious notions*. Why,
the mass of mankind believe, that if any man wills to be saved,
that is all which is necessary. Many of our preachers do in
effect preach this worldly maxim. They tell men that they
must make themselves willing. Now, just hear how the gospel
upsets that. "It is not of him that willeth, nor of him that run-
neth, but of God that showeth mercy." The world will have an
universal religion too; but how Christ overturns that: "I pray
for them; I pray not for the world." He hath ordained us *from
among* men: "Elect according to the foreknowledge of God,
through sanctification of the Spirit, and belief of the truth." ' [24]

Spurgeon obviously regarded the difference between Calvinism and Arminianism as something concrete and definable,
and not merely a matter of 'balance' or proportion of truth.
By Arminianism he did not mean an 'emphasis' on human
responsibility, for he preached man's responsibility as strongly
as anyone who ever lived.[25] Still less did he think that a consistent Scriptural position embraces both positions, indeed he

[23] 7, 475–6.   [24] 4, 230.
[25] The error of Arminianism is not that it holds the Biblical doctrine of
responsibility but that it *equates* this doctrine with an unbiblical doctrine of
'free-will' and preaches the two things as though they were synonymous. But

found it hard to be patient when he met such confusion: 'Do not think,' he says, 'you need have errors in your doctrine to make you useful. We have some who preach Calvinism all the first part of the sermon, and finish up with Arminianism, because they think that will make them useful. Useful nonsense! – That is all it is. A man, if he cannot be useful with the truth, cannot be useful with an error. There is enough in the pure doctrine of God, without introducing heresies to preach to sinners.[26] The fact is that there are definite doctrinal issues involved in the controversy between the two systems and when faced with these issues a man must hold either to the one or the other.

Some of these issues may be stated as follows:

Is there an eternal plan of redemption by which God has

man's will is always exercised in harmony with his nature and, as his nature is at enmity to God, so is his will. Man being fallen, his will *cannot* be neutral or 'free' to act contrary to his nature. 'Free-will has carried many souls to hell, but never a soul to heaven yet.' cf. 'Free-Will – A Slave,' 1, 395, and for a more mature treatment, 'God's Will and Man's Will,' 8, 181. Man's spiritual inability is due solely to his sin and therefore it in no way lessens his responsibility. That man must be *able* to believe and repent in order to be responsible for unbelief and impenitency is a philosophical conception nowhere found in Scripture; in fact it is directly contrary to Scripture because, if responsibility were to be measured by ability, then it would mean that the more sinful a man becomes the less he is responsible!

Spurgeon, and Reformed theologians, when speaking of man's free-agency – which is essential to moral responsibility – occasionally refer to man's will as being 'free', that is, from any external compulsion to sin; in this sense man has a free-will (which is obviously different from the Arminian usage of the term) and it makes our position one of terrible personal accountability for our actions. cf. Spurgeon on Acts 13: 46, 48, 'You choose sin; you choose to remain uncleansed from guilt; you choose to abide under the wrath of God. . . . This is a fearful thing. . . . It will be hell to a man to have his own voluntary choice confirmed, and made unchangeable. O sirs, I dread above all things that throughout eternity you will be left to your own free wills!' 34. 532–3. True Calvinism has never minimized this. Spurgeon would have agreed entirely with the words of John Duncan, 'The older I grow, the subject of the human will seems more awful to me – the power to forsake God.' *Colloquia Peripatetica*, 1907, 168.

[26] 1, 381. 'We have known men who believed Calvinistic doctrines, but who preached Calvinism in the morning and Arminianism in the evening, because they were afraid God's gospel would not convert sinners, so they would manufacture one of their own.' 2, 179.

determined to save, through Christ, certain persons whom He has chosen?

Does this plan provide for the free bestowal of all things necessary for its fulfilment or is its fulfilment conditioned by man's acceptance?

Did Christ in dying infallibly secure the redemption of all whom He represented as a substitute?

Does the Holy Spirit in regenerating sinners fully carry out the purpose of the Father and unfailingly apply the redemptive work of Christ?

Can the regenerating work of the Spirit be resisted?

Do we become regenerate, or re-born, because of our faith and repentance, or is faith the *effect* and result of regeneration?

There will probably be some who would object to the very formulation of questions like these. The brief doctrinal articles of modern evangelicalism – as distinct from the Reformed confessions of the 16th and 17th centuries – have nothing to say on these issues, presumably because it is no longer thought to be necessary. The prevalent attitude has been to frown on distinct and definite propositions of truth and to contend for obscurity and indefiniteness as though the latter were more spiritual and Biblical, and more preservative of unity. It is therefore not surprising that in such an atmosphere of low spiritual visibility the idea has become current that a man can be both an Arminian and a Calvinist. William Cunningham states the true position with his usual exactness when he says that a consideration of all the discussions and controversies on these points, 'decidedly confirms the impression that there is a clear line of demarcation between the fundamental principle of the Augustinian or Calvinistic, and the Pelagian or Arminian, systems of theology, – that the true *status quæstionis* in the controversy between these parties can be easily and exactly ascertained, – that it can, without difficul-

64

ty, be brought to a point where men may and should say either Aye or No, and, according as they say the one or the other, may be held to be, and may be warrantably called, Calvinists or Arminians.'[27]

We do not intend to formulate Spurgeon's answers to the questions above (they will in any case be obvious enough in quotations which are to follow) but rather to examine, in the next two chapters, why he believed the errors of Arminianism to be so detrimental to the Church. Whether he was right in his attitude and in warning contemporary Protestantism as he did, can only be determined from Scripture, but it should be obvious to all that this is a theme which is vitally important to us, as it will radically affect our view of evangelicalism at the present time. In exploring the reasons for Spurgeon's stand against Arminianism we are therefore not simply excavating some old battlefield of theological antiquities; the fact that the matter is still so controversial proves that it is very relevant to the current situation in the churches.

Before proceeding, however, it is necessary to state something on the negative side which may clear away a possible misunderstanding. Spurgeon did *not* attack Arminianism because he believed those errors meant that a person holding them could not be a Christian; he did not believe any such thing. Indeed he held that a man may be an evangelical Arminian, like John Wesley or John Fletcher of Madeley, and live 'far above the ordinary level of common Christians;'[28] he

[27] *The Reformers and the Theology of the Reformation*, 188.
[28] *The Early Years*, 173. At the same time, Spurgeon would have thoroughly agreed with the following words of William Cunningham: 'There is not a converted and believing man on earth, in whose conscience there does not exist at least the germ, or embryo, of a testimony in favour of the substance of the Calvinistic doctrine of election. This testimony may be misunderstood, or perverted, or suppressed; but it exists in the ineradicable sense which every converted man has, that if God had not chosen him, he never would have chosen God, and that if God, by His Spirit, had not exerted a decisive and determining influence in the matter, he never would have been turned from darkness to light, and been led to embrace Christ as his Saviour. This is really the sum and substance of Calvinism.' *The Reformers and the Theology of the Reformation*, 209.

knew that a man may be earnest for election and 'be as proud
as Lucifer', while other Christians may live humble and useful
lives who do not see these truths : 'Far be it from me even to
imagine that Zion contains none but Calvinistic Christians
within her walls, or that there are none saved who do not hold
our views.' In other words Spurgeon saw – what we need to
see – that a distinction must be drawn *between errors and persons*. All that are within the circle of Christ's love must be
within the circle of our love, and to contend for doctrine in a
manner which ignores this truth is a rending of the unity of
that Church which is His Body. Nevertheless it is equally
evident that no man's beliefs or preaching are above the need
of testing and it is the duty of ministers to oppose errors even
when they are held by sincere and saintly believers.[29] Spurgeon harmonized these two things when he wrote of John
Wesley, 'I can only say concerning him that, while I detest
many of the doctrines which he preached, yet for the man
himself I have a reverence second to no Wesleyan.' He summarizes his position thus: 'In attacking Arminianism we have
no hostility towards the men who bear the name and we are
opposed not to any body of men, but to the notions which they
have espoused.'[30] In our own charitable age it is at once pre-
sumed, even amongst evangelicals, that if any man's views are
opposed it is a reflection upon his whole person; but it ought

[29] 'I am quite sure that the best way to promote union is to promote truth. It
will not do for us to be all united together by yielding to one another's mis-
takes. We are to love each other in Christ; but we are not to be so united that
we are not able to see each other's faults, and especially not able to see our own.
No, purge the house of God, and then shall grand and blessed times dawn on
us.' 6, 171.
[30] 7,300. This quotation is from his introductory speech on April 11, 1861, a
day set aside for an 'Exposition of the Doctrines of Grace' by various ministers
at the Metropolitan Tabernacle. The Tabernacle had then been opened for
less than a month, and Spurgeon evidently intended to make clear by this
occasion the truths without which that building would never have come into
existence. At a later date he was to declare to his students: 'The buildings in
which you will preach were erected as monuments to the power of the doctrines
of grace. Mind you preach these doctrines in them. The doctrines some now
preach could not build a mousetrap.'

not to be so and we should all be ready to have our views judged by Scripture without taking personal affront. Too often the twentieth-century Church has succumbed to the temptation (which Spurgeon spoke of a century ago) to decry all controversy as 'party-spirit' and sectarianism. Speaking of the 'incalculable usefulness of controversy to arouse the natural lethargy of the Church', he declared:

'I glory in that which at the present day is so much spoken against – sectarianism. I find it applied to all sorts of Christians; no matter what views he may hold, if a man be but in earnest, he is a sectarian at once. Success to sectarianism; let it live and flourish. When that is done with, farewell to the power of godliness. When we cease, each of us, to maintain our own views of truth, and to maintain those views firmly and strenuously, then truth shall fly out of the land, and error alone shall reign.'[31]

[31] 8, 181.

I believe that very much of current Arminianism is simply ignorance of gospel doctrine.

C.H.S. SERMONS, 11, 29

When I was coming to Christ, I thought I was doing it all myself, and though I sought the Lord earnestly, I had no idea the Lord was seeking me. I do not think the young convert is at first aware of this. I can recall the very day and hour when first I received those truths in my own soul – when they were, as John Bunyan says, burnt into my heart as with a hot iron; and I can recollect how I felt that I had grown on a sudden from a babe into a man – that I had made progress in Scriptural knowledge, through having found, once for all, the clue to the truth of God.

C.H.S. THE EARLY YEARS, 164

3: Arminianism Against Scripture

It was obvious to Spurgeon, not only by Scripture but by his own experience, that a man – or child – may become a believer with very little knowledge besides the fact that the Son of God has borne his sins in His own body on the tree. What brought him to faith or what brought Christ to Calvary he may not then know – 'we did not know whether God had converted us, or we had converted ourselves.'[1] He gives us his own testimony on this point: 'I remember, when I was converted to God, I was an Arminian thoroughly. . . . I used sometimes to sit down and think, "Well, I sought the Lord four years before I found him".'[2] Again in another sermon, preached twenty-eight years after the one last quoted, he says, 'I have known some that, at first conversion, have not been very clear in the gospel, who have been made evangelical by their discoveries of their own need of mercy. They could not spell the word "grace." They began with a G, but they very soon went on with an F, till it spelt very like "freewill" before they had done with it. But after they have learned their weakness, after they have fallen into serious fault, and God has restored them, or after they have passed through deep depression of mind, they have sung a new song. In the school of repentance they have learned to spell. They began to write the word "free", but they went on from free, not to "will" but to "grace", and there it stood in capitals, "FREE GRACE". . . . They became

[1] 7, 85.   [2] 4, 339.

69

clearer in their divinity, and truer in their faith than ever they were before.'[3]

Recognizing then that wrong doctrine does not necessarily mean false experience, or the unchristianising of true believers, we return to the question, Why did Spurgeon oppose Arminianism so resolutely? If men can be brought to Christ under preaching which is not distinctly Calvinistic, and if they may be believers without apprehending clearly these doctrines, is this a subject which should ever disturb the peace of the Church? Is modern evangelicalism right after all in relegating the whole matter to limbo, and in regarding Arminianism as a kind of theological ghost, which may once have lived and may still drift about on occasions, but which no sensible Christian should waste time contending about? Or, to use the popular distinction, are we not in danger of confusing essentials with non-essentials if we give prominence to these issues? Let us then hear Spurgeon's justification of his position.

Firstly, Spurgeon held that Arminianism does not merely affect a few doctrines which can be separated from the gospel, rather it involves the whole unity of Biblical revelation and it affects our view of the whole plan of redemption at almost every point. He regarded ignorance of the full content of the gospel as a major cause of Arminianism, and the errors of that system then prevent men from grasping the whole divine unity of Scriptural truths and from perceiving them in their true relationships and in their right order. Arminianism truncates Scripture and it militates against that *wholeness* of view which is necessary for the glory of God, the exaltation of Christ and the stability of the believer. Anything which thus inclines Christians to rest short of this fulness of vision is therefore a serious matter which needs to be opposed : 'I would have you study much the Word of God till you get a clear view of the whole scheme, from election onward to final perseverance,

[3] 35, 226. In my documentation of Spurgeon's views on the doctrines of grace it will be seen that I am not confining myself to his early sermons.

and from final perseverance to the second advent, the resurrection, and the glories which shall follow, world without end.'⁴ Spurgeon never tired of introducing into his sermons summaries of the breadth and vastness of God's plan of salvation and yet the glorious unity of all its parts. The following is a typical example from a sermon on Galatians 1. 15, entitled 'It Pleased God.'

'You will perceive, I think, in these words, that the divine plan of salvation is very clearly laid down. It begins, you see, in the will and pleasure of God: "When it pleased God". The foundation of salvation is not laid in the will of man. It does not begin with man's obedience, and then proceed onward to the purpose of God; but here is its commencement, here the fountain-head from which the living waters flow: "It pleased God". Next to the sovereign will and good pleasure of God comes the act of separation, commonly known by the name of election. This act is said, in the text, to take place even in the mother's womb, by which we are taught that it took place before our birth when as yet we could have done nothing whatever to win it or to merit it. God separated us from the earliest part and time of our being; and indeed, long before that, when as yet the mountains and hills were not piled, and the oceans were not formed by his creative power, he had, in his eternal purpose, set us apart for himself. Then, after this act of separation came the effectual calling: "and called me by his grace". The calling does not cause the election; but the election, springing from the divine purpose, causes the calling. The calling comes as a consequence of the divine purpose and the divine separation, and you will note how the obedience follows the calling. So the whole process runs thus, – first the sacred, sovereign purpose of God, then the distinct and definite election or separation, then the effectual and irresistible calling, and then afterwards the obedience unto life, and the sweet fruits of the Spirit which spring therefrom. They do err, not knowing the Scriptures, who put any of these processes before the others, out of Scripture order. They who put man's will first know not what they say, nor whereof they affirm.'[5]

Arminianism is thus guilty of confusing doctrines and of acting as an obstruction to a clear and lucid grasp of the Scripture; because it mis-states or ignores the eternal purpose of God, it dislocates the meaning of the whole plan of redemption. Indeed confusion is inevitable apart from this foundational truth:

'Without it there is a lack of unity of thought, and generally speaking they have no idea whatever of a system of divinity. It is almost impossible to make a man a theologian unless you begin with this. You may if you please put a young believer to college for years, but unless you shew him this ground-plan of the everlasting covenant, he will make little progress, because his studies do not cohere, he does not see how one truth fits with another, and how all truths must harmonize together. Once let him get a clear idea that salvation is by grace, let him discover the difference between the covenant of works and the covenant of grace; let him clearly understand the meaning of election, as shewing the purpose of God, and its bearing upon other doctrines which shew the accomplishment of that purpose, and from that moment he is on the high road to become an instructive believer. He will always be ready to give a reason of the hope that is in him with meekness and with fear. The proof is palpable. Take any county throughout England, you will find poor men hedging and ditching that have a better knowledge of divinity than one half of those who come from our academies and colleges, for the reason simply and entirely that these men have first learned in their youth the system of which election is a centre, and have afterwards found their own experience exactly square with it. They have built upon that good foundation a temple of holy knowledge, which has made them fathers in the Church of God.

[5] 56, 230.

Every other scheme is as nothing to build with, they are but wood, hay, and stubble. Pile what you will upon them, and they will fall. They have no system of architecture; they belong to no order of reason or revelation. A disjointed system makes its topstone bigger than its foundation; it makes one part of the covenant to disagree with another; it makes Christ's mystical body to be of no shape whatever; it gives Christ a bride whom he does not know and does not choose, and it puts him up in the world to be married to any one who will have him; but he is to have no choice himself. It spoils every figure that is used with reference to Christ and his Church. The good old plan of the doctrine of grace is a system which when once received is seldom given up; when rightly learned, it moulds the thoughts of the heart, and it gives a sacred stamp to the characters of those who have once discovered its power.'[6]

It has frequently been said that Calvinism has no evangelistic message when it comes to the preaching of the Cross – because it cannot say that Christ died for the sins of all men everywhere. But the atonement lay at the centre of all Spurgeon's preaching and far from thinking that a universal atonement is necessary for evangelism, he held that if the Arminian position were true he would have no real redemption that he could preach, because it would throw the message of the gospel into confusion. He believed that once preachers cease to set the Cross in the context of the plan of salvation, and once the blood that was shed is not seen to be 'the blood of the everlasting covenant', then it is not only the extent of the atonement that is in question but its very nature. On the other hand, if we hold, with Scripture, that Calvary is the fulfilment of that great plan of grace in which the Son of God became the Representative and Head of those who were loved by the Father before the foundation of the world (Eph. 1:4), then at once both the nature and the extent of the atonement are settled. That His death was in its nature substitutionary (Christ bearing the penalty of the sins of others) and that it was suffered on behalf of those towards whom He stood related by an everlasting covenant, are two truths which are essentially connected.[7]

Against these persons, Scripture declares, no charge of sin can be laid, and the gift of Christ for them places beyond doubt the fact that God will also with Him freely give them *all things*. (Rom. 8:32-3).

This must be so, for the atonement means not only that salvation has been provided from sin as it affects human nature (the bondage and pollution of sin) but, more wonderful, from sin as it renders us guilty and condemned in the sight of God. Christ has borne the Divine condemnation, a condemnation which has no meaning unless we hold that it was the judgment due to the sins of persons,[8] and by His sacrifice He thus meets and removes the wrath due to His people. In His Person He has fully satisfied the demands of God's holiness and law, so that now, on the grounds of *justice*, the Divine favour has been *secured* for those in whose place the Saviour suffered and died. In other words, the Cross has a Godward reference; it was a propitiatory work through which the Father is pacified and it is on this ground, namely, Christ's obedience and blood, that

[7] As Hugh Martin shows in his work on *The Atonement, in its relations to the Covenant, the Priesthood, the Intercession of our Lord*, 1887, the surest way to meet an objection against the alleged injustice of a vicarious atonement (the Innocent dying instead of the guilty) is by setting forth the truth of 'Christ's covenant-headship and responsibility and of the covenant-oneness with Him of those whose sins He expiates by dying in their stead and room'. (p. 10). Covenant-oneness is the ground of His substitution and by this fact 'is the vicariousness of His sacrifice not merely brought to light but vindicated. It is not merely true that He suffers for us; it is also true that we suffer in Him. And the latter of these propositions justifies the truth and righteousness of the former. He is substituted *for us*, because He is one *with us* – identified with us, and we with Him'. (p. 43). Such is the great Biblical truth: Christ was by the decree and gift of the Father united to His people before His incarnation and it was because of this that He died for them.
[8] 'Just as sin belongs to persons, so the wrath rests upon the persons who are the agents of sin.' John Murray, monograph on *The Atonement*, 1962, cf. the same author on *The Epistle to the Romans*, vol. 1, 1960, 116–21.

all the blessings of salvation flow freely and surely to sinners. This is what is so clearly taught in Romans 3:25, 26. Writing on these verses, Robert Haldane says: 'God is shown not only to be merciful to forgive, but He is *faithful and just* to forgive the sinner his sins. Justice has received full payment, and guarantees his deliverance. Even the chief of sinners are shown in the propitiatory sacrifice of their Surety, to be perfectly worthy of Divine love, because they are not only perfectly innocent, but have *the righteousness of God*. 'He hath made him to be sin for us who knew no sin, that we might be made the righteousness of God in him.'[9] Spurgeon gloried in this truth: 'He has punished Christ, why should he punish twice for one offence? Christ has died for all his people's sins, and if thou art in the covenant, thou art one of Christ's people. Damned thou canst not be. Suffer for thy sins thou canst not. Until God can be unjust, and demand two payments for one debt, he cannot destroy the soul for whom Jesus died.'[10]

Evangelical Arminianism preaches a substitutionary atonement and it also clings to a universal redemption, but because it knows that this universality is one that does not secure universal salvation it must necessarily weaken the *reality* of the substitution, and represent it as a more indefinite and impersonal thing[11] – a substitution which does not actually *redeem* but which makes the redemption of all men possible. According to Arminianism, the atonement has no special relation to any individual person and it renders the salvation of

[9] *Exposition of the Epistle to the Romans*, 1958, 154.   [10] 5, 245.
[11] Thomas Goodwin in his commentary on Ephesians, chapters 1-2: 11, expounding 'the great love wherewith he loved us,' observes: '*That God in his love pitcheth upon persons*. God doth not pitch upon propositions only; as to say, I will love him who believeth, and save him, as those of the Arminian opinion hold; no, he pitcheth upon persons. And Christ died not for propositions only, but for persons. . . . He loved us nakedly; he loved *us*, *not ours*. It was not for our faith, nor for anything in us; "not of works", saith the Apostle; no, nor of faith neither. No, he pitcheth upon naked persons; he loves you, not yours. Therefore here is the reason that his love never fails, because it is pitched upon the person, simply as such. . . . The covenant of grace is a covenant of persons, and God gives the person of Christ to us, and the person of the Holy Ghost to us. . . .' *Works of Thomas Goodwin*, 1861, vol. 2, 151.

no one certain. For this same reason this teaching has also an inevitable tendency to underrate the meaning of propitiation and to obscure the fact that justification comes to sinners solely on account of Christ's work.[12] It is not faith which makes the atonement efficacious for us, rather the atonement has secured the justification and righteousness of sinners, and even the faith by which we apprehend these blessings is a gift of which Christ is the author and purchaser. So while Arminianism does not deny the nature of the atonement as vicarious, there is always the danger that it may do so, and this is one reason why, in more than one period of history, Arminianism has led to a Modernism which denies substitution and propitiation altogether. Once a blurred and indistinct view of the atonement is accepted in the Church it is more than likely that the next generation will come to the ultimate obscurity of a man like F. W. Robertson of Brighton, of whom it was said, 'Robertson believed that Christ did something or other, which, somehow or other, had some connection or other with salvation.'

Those who desire to study further the relationship between the doctrines of grace and the atonement will find an extensive examination of the relevant scriptures in John Owen's work, *The Death of Death in the Death of Christ*, and Spurgeon's

[12] As Charles Hodge says, commenting on the teaching of Romans 3:21–31, 'The ground of justification is not our own merit, nor faith, nor evangelical obedience; not the work of Christ in us, but His work for us, that is, His obedience unto death, v. 25.' Historically, Arminianism has repeatedly jeopardized the doctrine of justification, and this was exactly the danger which Calvin and other Reformers foresaw when they declared that agreement on justification is impossible unless we understand the doctrine in the context of God's gracious purpose to save the elect: 'Unless these points are put beyond controversy, though we may ever and anon repeat like parrots that we are justified by faith, we shall never hold the true doctrine of justification. It is not a whit better to be secretly seduced from the alone foundation of salvation than to be openly driven from it.' John Calvin, *Tracts*, vol. 3, 254. It is only when justification is not given its full content that Calvinism and Arminianism can be amalgamated. 'Most certain it is,' says Jerome Zanchius, 'that the doctrine of gratuitous justification through Christ can only be supported on that of our gratuitous predestination in Christ, since the latter is the cause and foundation of the former.'

position was the same as the great Puritan's.[13] Our purpose in raising this particular doctrine in the present context is only to show that Spurgeon regarded it as involving more than a dispute about the extent of redemption. Preaching on 'Particular Redemption' in 1858 he said: 'The doctrine of Redemption is one of the most important doctrines of the system of faith. A mistake on this point will inevitably lead to a mistake through the entire system of our belief.'[14] More than twenty years later this was still his conviction: 'The grace of God cannot be frustrated, and Jesus Christ died not in vain. These two principles I think lie at the bottom of all sound doctrine. *The grace of God cannot be frustrated after all.* Its eternal purpose will be fulfilled, its sacrifice and seal shall be effectual; the chosen ones of grace shall be brought to glory.'[15] 'The Arminian holds that Christ, when he died, did not die with an intent to save any particular person; and they teach that Christ's death does not in itself secure, beyond doubt, the salvation of any one man living . . . they are obliged to hold that if man's will would not give way, and voluntarily surrender to grace, then Christ's atonement would be unavailing. . . . We say Christ so died that he infallibly secured the salvation of a multitude that no man can number, who through Christ's death not only may be saved, but are saved, must be saved, and cannot by any possibility run the hazard of being anything but saved.'[16]

For Spurgeon the error of believing that Christ died equally for all men led to a further remove from the Bible in misleading Gospel hearers on the nature of saving faith:

'I have sometimes thought when I have heard addresses from some revival brethren who had kept on saying time after time,

[13] For Owen's opinion on the impossibility of a compromise with Arminianism, see his *Display of Arminianism*, Works of John Owen, vol. 10, 5–7. Spurgeon had well studied the texts which have been claimed as teaching a universal redemption and he was not afraid to expound them. See, for example, his solemn warning concerning those who 'destroy with their meat those for whom Christ died,' 12, 542.

[14] 4, 130.   [15] 26, 252.   [16] 4, 130, 135.

"Believe, believe, believe," that I should like to have known for myself what it was we were to believe in order to our salvation. There is, I fear a great deal of vagueness and crudeness about this matter. I have heard it often asserted that if you believe that Jesus Christ died for you, you will be saved. My dear hearer, do not be deluded by such an idea. You may believe that Jesus Christ died for you, and may believe what is not true; you may believe that which will bring you no sort of good whatever. That is not saving faith. The man who has saving faith afterwards attains to the conviction that Christ died for him, but it is not of the essence of saving faith. Do not get that into your head, or it will ruin you. Do not say, "I believe that Jesus Christ died for me," and because of that feel that you are saved. I pray you to remember that the genuine faith that saves the soul has for its main element – trust – absolute rest of the whole soul – on the Lord Jesus Christ to save me, whether he died in particular or in special to save me or not, and relying, as I am, wholly and alone on him, I am saved. Afterwards I come to perceive that I have a special interest in the Saviour's blood; but if I think I have perceived that, before I have believed in Christ, then I have inverted the Scriptural order of things, and I have taken as a fruit of my faith that which is only to be obtained by rights, by the man who absolutely trusts in Christ, and Christ alone, to save.'[17]

In more succinct language Charles Hodge has also indicated how Arminianism undermines the coherence of the whole Biblical revelation. After stating that the radical divergence between the Arminian and Augustinian systems concerns the doctrine of God's election of some of the fallen family of men to everlasting life (with the consequent provision of His Son for their redemption and of His Spirit to secure their repentance, faith and holy living unto the end) he continues: 'Although this may be said to be the turning point between these great systems, which have divided the Church in all ages, yet that point of necessity involves all the other matters of difference; namely, the nature of original sin; the motive of God in providing redemption; the nature and design of the work of Christ; and the nature of divine grace, or the work of the Holy Spirit. Thus, in a great measure, the whole system of theology, and of necessity, the character of our religion, depend upon the view taken of this particular question. It is, therefore, a question of the highest practical importance, and not a matter of idle speculation.'[18]

A second reason why Spurgeon opposed Arminianism so strongly was that he saw that the *spirit* of that system leads directly to legality,[19] for while evangelical Arminians deny salvation by works, the tendency of the errors they hold is to elevate the importance of the sinner's activity and to direct emphasis primarily to the human will and endeavour. This is the logical outcome of a system which regards the human decision as the crucial factor in determining who is saved, and which represents faith as something which every man may call into exercise if he so chooses. A modern evangelist, for example, has written, 'We do not know Christ through the five physical senses, but we know Him through the sixth sense that God has given to every man – which is the ability to believe.' If God has given this ability to all men then the turning point must depend on the human response, as clearly not all are saved. This consequence is accepted by Arminianism. In the words of a contemporary preacher of this view: 'This love of God, that is immeasurable, unmistakable and unending, this

[18] *Systematic Theology*, 2, 330-1. The theology which the Hodge family taught at Princeton for a century was the same as the system which Spurgeon sought to have implanted in the minds of his students at his Pastor's College. A. A. Hodge's *Outlines of Theology* was in fact their text book for systematic theology. On a visit to England in 1877, Dr Hodge was present at the annual picnic of the College when Spurgeon said, 'The longer I live the clearer does it appear that John Calvin's system is the nearest to perfection.' Pike, 6, 197. [19] 'The tendency of Arminianism is towards legality; it is nothing but legality which lays at the root of Arminianism.' 6, 304.

love of God that reaches to whatever a man is, can be entirely rejected. God will not force Himself upon any man against his will. . . . But if you really want it, you must believe – you must receive the love of God, you must take it.' The emphasis is intended to be upon 'you', and the impression is unavoidably given that it is only our faith which can save us – as though faith were the *cause* of salvation. This is the very reverse of Spurgeon's conception of the spirit of gospel preaching. 'I could not preach like an Arminian,' he says, and in the following passage he tells us precisely why: 'What the Arminian wants to do is to arouse man's activity; what we want to do is to kill it once and for all, to show him that he is lost and ruined, and that his activities are not now at all equal to the work of conversion; that he must look upward. *They* seek to make the man stand up; *we* seek to bring him down, and make him feel that there he lies in the hand of God, and that his business is to submit himself to God, and cry aloud, "Lord, save, or we perish." We hold that man is never so near grace as when he begins to feel he can do nothing at all. When he says, "I can pray, I can believe, I can do this, and I can do the other," marks of self-sufficiency and arrogance are on his brow.'[20]

Arminianism, by making the love and salvation of God to turn upon the fulfilment of conditions on the part of the sinner instead of entirely upon grace, encourages an error which cannot be too strongly opposed: 'Do you not see at once that this is legality,' says Spurgeon, ' – that this is hanging our salvation upon our work – that this is making our eternal life to depend on something we do? Nay, the doctrine of *justification* itself, as preached by an Arminian, is nothing but the doctrine of salvation by works, after all; for he always thinks faith is a work of the creature, and a condition of his acceptance. It is as false to say that man is saved by faith as a work, as that he is saved by the deeds of the Law. We are saved by faith as the gift of God, and as the first token of his eternal favour to us;

but it is not faith as our work that saves, otherwise we are saved by works, and not by grace at all.'[21] 'We did not ask him to make the covenant of grace,' he declares in another sermon, 'We did not ask him to elect us. We did not ask him to redeem us. These things were done before we were born. We did not ask him to call us by his grace, for alas! we did not know the value of that call, and we were dead in trespasses and sins, but he gave to us freely of his unsought, but boundless love. Prevenient grace came to us, outrunning all our desires, and all our wills, and all our prayers.'[22] 'Does God love me because I love him? Does God love me because my faith is strong? Why, then, he must have loved me because of something good in me, and that is not according to the gospel. The gospel represents the Lord as loving the unworthy and justifying the ungodly, and therefore I must cast out of my mind the idea that divine love depends on human conditions.'[23]

Arminianism, because it obscures the glory which belongs solely to the grace of God, comes under apostolic condemnation[24] and is therefore an error sufficiently serious for there to be no room for compromising. We may have fellowship with brethren who are under the influence of these errors but in the preaching and teaching of the Church there can be no wavering or indistinctness on such an issue.

On a personal level, it is the full proclamation of the doc-

[21] 6, 304. 'Our faith does not cause Salvation, nor our hope, nor our love, nor our good works; they are things which attend it as its guard of honour. The origin of Salvation lies alone in the sovereign will of God the Father; in the infinite efficacy of the blood of Jesus – God the Son; and in the divine influence of God the Holy Spirit.' 3, 357. 'I only know of one answer to this question, "Why did some believe?" and the answer is this, *because God willed it*. 9, 355.
[22] 14, 573.   [23] 24, 440.
[24] See Thomas Goodwin's profound handling of this in his exposition of Eph. 2:5. 'Our whole salvation by grace,' he says, 'is the greatest thing of all others, of the greatest moment for believers to know and to be acquainted with. "By grace ye are saved." This is the great axiom, the great principle he would beget in all their hearts. And it is to advance the design of God, the glory of his grace, so you have it, ver. 7. This is the sum and substance of the gospel, and it is the sum of the great design of God. . . . Therefore you shall find, that when a man doth step out of the way and road of free grace unto anything

trines of grace which gives the believer the peace so beautifully
expressed in Horatius Bonar's verses:

> *My love is oft-times low,*
> *My joy still ebbs and flows;*
> *But peace with Him remains the same –*
> *No change Jehovah knows.*
>
> *I change, He changes not,*
> *The Christ can never die;*
> *His love, not mine, the resting place,*
> *His truth, not mine, the tie.*

It was this faith which supported Spurgeon in the periods of
sickness and darkness through which he sometimes passed,
and he was expressing the feelings of his heart when he said, 'I
can never understand what an Arminian does, when he gets
into sickness, sorrow, and affliction'.[25] Nevertheless, C. T.
Cook expunges the words in the *Kelvedon Edition* reprint of
the sermon in which the remark occurs.[26] It hardly fits modern
notions to regard Arminianism as undermining peace of
heart, but where else can the believer rest in times of trouble
except in the assurance that he is saved, kept and destined for
glory solely by the eternal and unchanging grace of God!

On the same subject he gives this testimony in another place:
'I would cheerfully give up many doctrines if I believed that
they were only party watchwords, and were merely employed
for the maintenance of a sect; but those doctrines of grace,
those precious doctrines of grace, against which so many
contend, I could not renounce or bate a jot of them, because

else, he is said to turn from God. Gal. 1:6, "I marvel that you are so soon
removed from him that called you" – it was because they did not hold the
doctrine of free grace – "into the grace of Christ, unto another gospel". It was
God's great design to advance grace, and therefore he calls their stepping aside
from the doctrine thereof, a frustrating of the grace of God, Gal. 2. 21, which
men do by mingling anything with it.' *Works*, vol. 2, 230–1.
[25] 4, 463.
[26] See *Sermons of Comfort and Assurance*, C. H. Spurgeon, 1961, 36.

they are the joy and rejoicing of my heart. When one is full of health and vigour, and has everything going well, you might, perhaps, live on the elementary truths of Christianity very comfortably; but in times of stern pressure of spirit, when the soul is much cast down, you want the marrow and the fatness. In times of inward conflict, salvation must be all of grace from first to last.'[27]

Thirdly, Spurgeon stood against the teaching which was already current in the 1850's because he held that it contained errors which lessen the gravity of the position of the unconverted. Arminianism does not fully disclose the Biblical testimony concerning the condition of sinners and it does not do justice to the terrible extent of their needs. The Scripture represents us, by nature, as not only in need of salvation from the guilt of sin, but in need of an omnipotent power to quicken us from being 'dead in trespasses and in sins'. We are not only under condemnation through our offences, but we are under the dominion of a *fallen nature* which is at enmity against God. It is not only that we have committed sins for which we need mercy, but we have a sinful nature which needs to be made anew. Arminianism preaches the new-birth but it preaches it as a consequence of or an accompaniment to the human decision; it represents man as being born again by repenting and believing, as though these spiritual acts are within the ability of the unconverted. This teaching is only possible because of an under-estimation of the total ruin and impotence of the sinner. The Scripture says that the natural man *cannot* receive spiritual things and it is because of this that the Divine quickening *must* precede the human response.

The call of God which effects the new birth causally precedes faith and justification as the New Testament evidence shows.[28] In the statement of *The Baptist Confession*, reprinted by Spurgeon in 1855: 'This effectual call is of God's free and special grace alone, not from anything at all foreseen in man,

[27] 18, 621.   [28] See note at the end of this chapter.

84

nor from any power or agency in the creature, being wholly passive therein, being dead in sins and trespasses, until being quickened and renewed by the Holy Spirit, he is thereby enabled to answer this call, and to embrace the grace offered and conveyed in it.'

In other words, calling is the act of God which summons a sinner out of the kingdom of darkness. It is efficacious because it carries with it operative saving grace, which inwardly renews those who are thus called and enables them to respond in conversion – that is to say, in repentance and faith. Conversion is caused by regeneration which in turn is related to God's call and eternal purpose. It was Spurgeon's grasp of this sequence which made him affirm: 'If any man is saved, it is not because he willed to be saved. If any man be brought to Christ, it is not of any effort of his, but the root, the cause, the motive of the salvation of any one human being, and of all the chosen in heaven, is to be found in the predestinating purpose and sovereign distinguishing will of the Lord our God.'[29]

Let it be noted that the point in dispute between the Biblical teaching and Arminianism is not whether man's will is active in *conversion*; on this there can be no question; the issue concerns how that activity originated. In a sermon, 'All of Grace,' published a few years before his death, Spurgeon says:

'The man believes, but that belief is only one result among many of the implantations of divine life within the man's soul by God Himself.

'*Even the very will thus to be saved by grace is not of ourselves*, but is the gift of God. There lies the stress of the question. A man ought to believe in Jesus: it is his duty to receive Him whom God hath sent forth to be a propitiation for sins. But man will not believe in Jesus, he prefers anything to faith in his Redeemer. Unless the Spirit of God convinces the judgment, and constrains the will, man has no heart to believe in Jesus unto eternal life. I ask any saved man to look back upon his own conversion, and explain how it came about. You turned to Christ, and believed on His name: these were your own acts and deeds. But what caused you thus to turn? What sacred force was that which turned you from sin to righteousness? Do you attribute this singular renewal to the existence of a something better in you than has been yet discovered in your unconverted neighbour? No, you confess that you might have been what he now is if it had not been that there was a potent something which touched the spring of your will, enlightened your understanding, and guided you to the foot of the cross. Gratefully we confess the fact; it must be so.'[30] The consciousness of such a truth lifts us high above the realm of debate, and Spurgeon never tired of quoting in wonder and praise:

> *Why was I made to hear thy voice,*
> *And enter while there's room;*
> *When thousands make a wretched choice,*
> *And rather starve than come?*
>
> *'Twas the same love that spread the feast*
> *That sweetly forced me in;*
> *Else I had still refused to taste,*
> *And perished in my sin.*

The Arminian teaching reverses the Scriptural order and puts the human decision before the Divine act. Thus we find an evangelistic book written from this standpoint asserting the following: 'God's holy eye discerns the sinfulness of every heart and calls upon all to take sides with God against themselves. Until this is done, faith is absolutely impossible. This does not limit the grace of God, but repentance makes way for the grace of God.' The 'call' in this context is clearly not the inward special call of Christ but the outward general call

[30] *Sword and Trowel*, 1887, 8.

of the preacher which summons us to decision.[31] According to this view, until the decision is made, nothing further is possible. Repentance must precede the rebirth and the appeal which is the characteristic of such evangelism is consistent with this theology: 'You open your heart, and let Him come in. You renounce all sin and sins. You give up and surrender, by faith, to Him. At that precise moment the miracle of the new birth takes place. You actually become a new moral creature. There comes the implantation of the Divine nature.'

This is clearly not simply a difference in terminology, but a different assessment of the position of the unregenerate. These quotations reveal a belief that through a general influence of the grace of God the natural man may act in a way which will result in salvation. Grace in this context is clearly not saving grace because it is extended equally to those who perish; in fact it is not grace at all in the Scriptural usage of the term. The Calvinist has a different estimate both of the sinner and of grace. Concerning the sinner he believes that he has fallen into a condition far more terrible and that he has a need which is much more colossal. And concerning grace he glories that it is *efficacious* to reach men even in such a position: 'You look at the spiritual thermometer and you say, "How low will the grace of God go? Will it descend to summer heat? Will it touch the freezing point? Will it go to zero?" Yes, it will go below the lowest conceivable point, – lower than any instrument can indicate: it will go below the zero of death.'[32]

It is at that point of spiritual *death* that the Holy Spirit first meets men in saving power and raises them from sin's sepulchre. Not until life is implanted can repentance and faith be exercised and therefore these spiritual acts are 'the first apparent result of regeneration'.[33] 'Evangelical repentance never can

[31] In a review of W. B. Pope's *Compendium of Christian Theology*, Spurgeon names the failure to distinguish 'between the special and personal call and the general call of the gospel' as characteristic of the Arminian scheme. *Sword and Trowel*, 1877, 484.
[32] 30, 502.   [33] 35, 494.

exist in an unrenewed soul.' We are as helpless to co-operate in our regeneration as we are to co-operate in the work of Calvary, and as it is the Cross alone that meets the guilt of sin, so it is regeneration alone which meets its power. It is this doctrine which at once does justice both to the real nature of the sinner's condition and to the greatness of the Spirit's work:

> *Can aught beneath a power divine*
> *The stubborn will subdue?*
> *'Tis thine, Eternal Spirit, thine*
> *To form the heart anew.*
>
> *'Tis thine the passions to recall*
> *And upwards bid them rise;*
> *And make the scales of error fall*
> *From reason's darken'd eyes.*
>
> *To chase the shades of death away,*
> *And bid the sinner live;*
> *A beam of heaven, a vital ray,*
> *'Tis thine alone to give.*

Spurgeon held that the reality of the sinner's position cannot be fully recognized until this truth of the necessity of the special work of the Spirit of God is made unmistakably clear: 'Sinner, unconverted sinner, I warn thee thou canst never cause thyself to be born again, and though the new birth is absolutely necessary, it is absolutely impossible to thee, unless God the Spirit shall do it. . . .'[34] 'Do what you will, and still at your very best there is a division wide as eternity between you and the regenerate man. . . . The Spirit of God must new make you, ye must be born again. The same power which raised Christ Jesus from the dead must be exerted in raising us from the dead; the very same omnipotence, without which angels or worms could not have had a being, must again step forth

[34] 3, 340.

out of his privy chamber, and do as great a work as it did at the first creation in making us anew in Christ Jesus our Lord. Constantly the Christian Church itself tries to forget it, but as often as ever this old doctrine of regeneration is brought forward pointedly, God is pleased to favour His Church with a revival. . . .'[35] 'Unless God the Holy Spirit, who "worketh in us to will and to do", should operate upon the will and the conscience, regeneration is an absolute impossibility, and therefore so is salvation. "What!", says one, "do you mean to say that God absolutely interposes in the salvation of every man to make him regenerate?" I do indeed; in the salvation of every person there is an actual putting forth of divine power, whereby the dead sinner is quickened, the unwilling sinner is made willing, the desperately hard sinner has his conscience made tender; and he who rejected God and despised Christ, is brought to cast himself down at the feet of Jesus. There must be a divine interposition, a divine working, a divine influence, or else do what you may, without that you perish and are undone – "For except a man be born again he cannot see the kingdom of God" . . .'[36] 'Be it never forgotten by us that the salvation of a soul is a *creation*. Now, no man has ever been able to create a fly. . . . Jehovah alone creates. . . . No human or angelic power can intrude upon this glorious province of divine power. Creation is God's own domain. Now, in every Christian there is an absolute creation – "Created anew in Christ Jesus." "The new man, after God, is created in right-eousness." Regeneration is not the reforming of principles which were there before, but the implantation of a something which had no existence; it is the putting into a man of a new thing called the Spirit, the new man – the creation not of a soul, but of a principle higher still – as much higher than the soul, as the soul is higher than the body. . . . In the bringing of any man to believe in Christ, there is as true and proper a manifestation of creating power, as when God made the

[35] 7, 479.   [36] 3, 188.

heavens and the earth. . . .'[37] 'He only who fashioned the heavens and the earth could create a new nature. It is a work that is not to be paralleled, it is unique and unrivalled, seeing the Father, Son and Spirit must all co-operate in it; for to implant the new nature in the Christian, there must be the decree of the Eternal Father, the death of the ever-blessed Son, and the fulness of the operation of the adorable Spirit. It is a work indeed. The labours of Hercules were but trifles compared with this; to slay lions and hydras, and cleanse Augean stables – all this is child's play compared with renewing a right spirit in the fallen nature of man. Observe that the apostle affirms (Phil. 1:6) that this good work was *begun by God*. He was evidently no believer in those remarkable powers which some theologians ascribe to free will; he was no worshipper of that modern Diana of the Ephesians.'[38]

These words, it needs to be remembered, are the words not of a lecturer but of an evangelist and a soul-winner who longed to see men brought to Christ. To Spurgeon this was not just a question of theological orthodoxy; he knew that there is a profound practical impact upon the consciences of hearers made by these truths. They batter down self-sufficiency until men stand helpless in the sight of God and the desperate nature of their condition is inescapable: 'There is a something in these doctrines that drives right into the soul of man. Other forms of doctrine run off like oil down a slab of marble, but this chisels them, cuts into the very quick. They cannot help feeling there is something here, which if they kick against it has nevertheless force, and they must ask themselves, "Is the thing true or not?" They cannot be content with huffing it, and making themselves easy.'[39]

The glorious truth is that it is the very hopelessness of the sinner that shows him where real hope lies. To minimize that hopelessness – as Arminianism does – is therefore not the way to reveal the brightness of the hope which shines in the gospel.

[37] 9, 566.   [38] 15, 291.   [39] 6, 258.

Listen again to some of Spurgeon's closing words to a vast congregation in the Exeter Hall, 'You, who have not been converted, and have no part or lot in present salvation, to you I say this much: Man, man, you are in the hand of God. Whether you shall live to reach home today or not, depends absolutely upon His will.'[40] Is this sending men away to despair? No, it is shutting them up to God! It is the very truths which reveal our helplessness which turn us to our true hope and reveal that there is omnipotent grace in the Father of mercies to do for us what we cannot do for ourselves. 'Calvinism gives you ten thousand times more reason for hope than the Arminian preacher, who stands up and says, "There is room for everybody, but I do not think there is any special grace to make them come; if they won't come, they won't come, and there is an end of it; it is their own fault, and God will not make them come." The Word of God says they cannot come, yet the Arminian says they can; the poor sinner feels that he cannot, yet the Arminian declared positively that he could if he liked.'[41] When a man who has reached this point is told that *God has determined* to save sinners, that, just as He has appointed the means in the blood of Calvary, so He has given the Spirit to apply the merits of that sacrifice and to quicken the dead in sin – the purpose is His, the gift is His, the means are His, the power is His – this is exactly the good news that such a fainting soul needs.[42] To a person who is no longer dependent upon himself and who feels the desperate evil of his heart there could be no more needed message than one that teaches him to look and trust in the free grace of God: 'The great system known as "The Doctrines of Grace" brings before the mind of the man who truly receives it, God and not man. The whole scheme of that doctrine looks God-ward,'[43] and that is exactly the direction in which a convicted soul needs

[40] 6, 324.   [41] 53, 268.
[42] See 7, 565, on how the doctrines of grace are bread for hungry sinners.
[43] 34, 364.

to look. His flimsy notions of religion have been stripped from him – 'You formerly boasted, "I can believe in the Lord Jesus Christ whenever I like, and it will be all right." You once thought it such an easy thing to believe; but you do not find it so now. "Why", now you cry, "I cannot feel. What is worse, I cannot believe. I cannot remember. I cannot restrain myself. I seem possessed by the devil. God help me, for I cannot help myself." '44 . . . 'When a man knows and feels that he is in very deed a sinner before God, it is a miracle for him to believe in the forgiveness of sins; nothing but the omnipotence of the Holy Ghost can work this faith in him.'45

Spurgeon had enough knowledge of the real nature of conviction of sin to know that the preaching of irresistible grace is a sweet cordial to those whose hopes are in God alone. He gloried in setting forth the truth that human helplessness is no barrier to Divine omnipotence: 'The Lord, when he means to save sinners, does not stop to ask them whether they mean to be saved, but like a rushing mighty wind the divine influence sweeps away every obstacle; the unwilling heart bends before the potent gale of grace, and sinners that would not yield are made to yield by God. I know this, if the Lord willed it, there is no man so desperately wicked here this morning that he would not be made now to seek for mercy, however infidel he might be; however rooted in his prejudices against the gospel, Jehovah hath but to will it, and it is done. Into thy dark heart, O thou who hast never seen the light, would the light stream; if he did but say, "Let there be light", there would be light. Thou mayest bend thy fist and lift up thy mouth against Jehovah; but he is thy master yet – thy master to destroy thee, if thou goest on in thy wickedness; but thy master to save thee now, to change thy heart and turn thy will, as he turneth the rivers of water.'46

The title of the sermon from which the last quotation comes, 'A Revival Sermon', preached in January 1860, reminds us

[44] 36, 690.   [45] 29, 551.   [46] 6, 86.

that the source of this tremendous certainty lay in Spurgeon's conscious knowledge not only of the doctrine given by the Spirit but of the presence of that same mighty Spirit accompanying the preaching of the Word. Never did he more glory in the power of God than in these years of revival.

Among the memorable experiences of that time was the evening of September 4, 1855 when some 12,000 people stood in a field off King Edward's Road, Hackney, to hear the pastor of New Park Street. 'I think I shall never forget,' he later wrote in his Autobiography, 'the impression I received when, before we separated, that vast multitude joined in singing "Praise God from whom all blessings flow." That night, I could understand better than ever before why the apostle John, in the Revelation, compared the "new song" in heaven to "the voice of many waters". In that glorious hallelujah, the mighty waves of praise seemed to roll up towards the sky, in majestic grandeur, even as the billows of old ocean break upon the beach.'

A reading of the words that were preached that night makes it easy to understand why the service ended with hearts being raised heavenwards in wonder and praise. Preaching on the words, 'Many shall come from the east and west, and shall sit down with Abraham, and Isaac, and Jacob, in the Kingdom of heaven,' Spurgeon gloried in the triumph of grace:

'Oh! I love God's "shalls" and "wills". There is nothing comparable to them. Let a man say "shall", what is it good for? "I will", says man, and he never performs; "I shall", says he, and he breaks his promise. But it is never so with God's "shalls". If He says "shall", it shall be; when He says, "will" it will be. Now He has said here, "many *shall* come." The devil says, "they shall not come"; but "they shall come". You yourselves, say, "we won't come"; God says, "You shall come". Yes! there are some here who are laughing at salvation, who can scoff at Christ, and mock at the gospel; but I tell you some of you shall come yet. "What!" you say, "can God make me become a Christian?" I tell you yes, for herein rests the power of the gospel. It does not ask your consent; but it gets it. It does not say, will you have it? but it makes you willing in the day of God's power. . . . The gospel wants not your consent, it gets it. It knocks the enmity out of your heart. You say "I do not want to be saved"; Christ says you shall be. He makes your will turn round, and then you cry, "Lord save, or I perish!" Ah, might heaven exclaim, "I knew I would make you say that"; and then He rejoices over you because He has changed your will and made you willing in the day of His power. If Jesus Christ were to stand on this platform tonight, what would many people do with Him? If He were to come and say, "Here I am, I love you, will you be saved by me?" not one of you would consent if you were left to your will. He Himself said, "No man can come to me except the Father who hath sent me draw him." Ah! we want that; and here we have it. They shall come! They shall come! Ye may laugh, ye may despise us; but Jesus Christ shall not die for nothing. If some of you reject Him there are some that will not. If there are some that are not saved, others *shall* be. Christ *shall* see His seed, He *shall* prolong His days, and the pleasure of the Lord *shall* prosper in His hands. They shall come! And nought in heaven, nor on earth, nor in hell, can stop them from coming.'[47]

[47] I, 304–5.

NOTE ON REGENERATION AND FAITH

That the exercise of faith in conversion is the result of God's purpose and of His effectual call, renewing the nature of sinners, is clearly taught in a number of references: Acts 13:48, 'As many as were ordained to eternal life believed'; Rom. 8:30, 'Whom he did predestinate, them he also called: and whom he called, them he also justified'; John 6:65, John 10:26, 27, Eph. 2:1-8, etc. It has sometimes been argued that two texts, James 1:18 and 1 Peter 1:23, seem to teach that regeneration is 'by the word of God', and as the Scripture read or preached is not effective without faith, therefore the new birth must be determined in some way by the response of the hearer. But the exegesis of these two texts demands no such conclusion, rather the analogy of Scripture precludes it. The act of God which gives birth or life to the spiritually dead is distinct from the truth, just as the faculty of seeing is distinct from light; and because *quickening* is an immediate and creative act, no instrumental and secondary causes are conjoined to it. The Scripture is only effective in those who are renewed (1 Cor. 2:12-14), it cannot produce life. It is because a man is born of the Spirit that he *sees* (John 3:3), and once he possesses the faculty of sight the Word is indispensable to guide him in faith and repentance, so that regeneration only occurs, by the determination of God, where the Gospel message is present. Theologically, regeneration can be considered as a distinct part of salvation and a part which is not accomplished by the outward Word of truth, but in the experience of adults rebirth is immediately linked to conversion and in the process of conversion – namely, the activity of faith and repentance – the Word is indispensable (Rom. 10:17). 'It is by the Word,' says Charles Hodge, 'that the person and work of Christ are revealed, and all the objects on which the activity of the regenerated soul terminates, are presented to the mind. It is by the Word that all the graces of the Spirit are called into exercise, and without it holiness, in all its conscious manifestations, would be as impossible as vision without light.'

If the term regeneration is used in the wide and comprehensive sense as including conversion, then the Word of truth must be given an important instrumental place. James 1:18 and 1 Peter 1:23 point to this wider sense, but elsewhere in the New Testament the terms used to describe the new birth convey the narrower sense and refer to the instantaneous act of God in imparting new life. The wider sense is not the normal one and it is therefore erroneous to attribute, on the basis of these two texts, an instrumentality to the

Word in the act of quickening, for these two texts do not refer to the *act* but to the whole comprehensive change which occurs in those who are brought to Christ – a change in which regeneration and conversion are distinct though inseparable parts. cf. Charles Hodge, *Systematic Theology*, 1960, vol. 2, 702–3, and W. G. T. Shedd, *Dogmatic Theology*, 1960, vol. 2, 509.

In terms of the presentation of the Gospel the preacher's awareness of the necessity of regeneration to effect the conversion of his hearers does not hinder him in summoning all men to immediate faith in Christ. For as already mentioned in dealing with Hyper-Calvinism, the inability of sinners, arising out of their depraved natures, does not excuse them from responding to the command to believe, and because the priority of regeneration to conversion is one of order and nature only, not of time, there is no warrant for preachers to expect a time-lag between the effective work of the Spirit (which in any case is unseen by man) and the exercise of faith. As regeneration is not the act of man it is never presented as a duty (though John 3:7 is expounded frequently as if Christ taught this). The demands of the Gospel upon sinners are exclusively in terms of repentance and faith (Acts 20:21), and it is not unimportant to notice that while modern Arminianism has coined new phrases to describe the duties of the unconverted ('open your heart', 'decide for Christ', etc.), the old Reformed evangelism, which had a true doctrine of regeneration, also gave to faith the centrality which it has in the New Testament presentation of salvation. In this connection Spurgeon noted with concern in 1890 the new style of exhortations which was being used by preachers and teachers seeking a response from their hearers: 'The gospel is, "Believe on the Lord Jesus Christ, and thou shalt be saved". If we think we shall do more good by substituting another exhortation for the gospel command, we shall find ourselves landed in serious difficulties. If, for a moment, our improvements seem to produce a larger result than the old gospel, it will be the growth of mushrooms, it may even be the growth of toadstools; but it is not the growth of trees of the Lord.' *An All-Round Ministry*, 376. Terminology which Spurgeon mentions, like 'Give your heart to Christ', cannot be used without violating the New Testament gospel; whereas the doctrine of regeneration, as outlined above, safeguards the purity of evangelism and in no way displaces the apostolic emphasis upon faith. Commenting on Romans 1:16–17, John Murray underlines the scriptural teaching 'that salvation is not accomplished irrespective of faith' and he adds this note: 'The priority of effectual calling and of regeneration in the *ordo salutis* [order of salvation] should not be allowed to prejudice this truth either in our thinking or in the preaching of the gospel. It is true that regeneration is causally prior to faith. But it is only *causally* prior and the adult person who is regenerated always exercises faith. Hence the salvation which is of the gospel is never ours apart from faith. . . .There is order in the application of redemption, but it is order in that which constitutes an indissoluble unity comprising a variety of elements. It is salvation in its integral unity of which the apostle speaks and this is never ours without faith – we are saved by grace through faith (Eph. 2:8). The person who is *merely* regenerate is not saved, the simple reason being that there is no such person. The saved person is *also* called, justified, and adopted.' *Commentary on Romans*, 27. See also the same author's *Redemption: Accomplished and Applied*, chapters on 'Effectual Calling' and 'Regeneration'.

A. A. Hodge writing on the question, 'What is the difference between regeneration and conversion?' summarizes the Scriptural teaching thus:

'The term conversion is often used in a wide sense as including both the change of nature and the exercise of that nature as changed. When distinguished from regeneration, however, conversion signifies the first exercise of the new disposition implanted in regeneration, i.e. in freely turning unto God.

'Regeneration is God's act; conversion is ours. Regeneration is the implantation of a gracious principle; conversion is the exercise of that principle. Regeneration is never a matter of direct consciousness to the subject of it; conversion always is such to the agent of it. Regeneration is a single act, complete in itself, and never repeated; conversion, as the beginning of holy living, is the commencement of a series, constant, endless, and progressive.' *Outlines of Theology*, 1949, 460.

This was precisely Spurgeon's belief: 'Regeneration is an instantaneous work. Conversion to God, the fruit of regeneration, occupies all our life, but regeneration itself is effected in an instant.' 4, 293.

We believe, that the work of regeneration, conversion, sanctific-
ation and faith, is not an act of man's free will and power, but of
the mighty, efficacious and irresistible grace of God.

from the 'Declaration of Faith and Practice' held by the
New Park Street congregation. THE EARLY YEARS, 552

No more soul-destroying doctrine could well be devised than the
doctrine that sinners can regenerate themselves, and repent and
believe just when they please. . . . As it is a truth both of Scripture
and of experience that the unrenewed man can do nothing of
himself to secure his salvation, it is essential that he should be
brought to a practical conviction of that truth. When thus
convinced, and not before, he seeks help from the only source
whence it can be obtained.

Charles Hodge, SYSTEMATIC THEOLOGY, 2, 277

4: Arminianism and Evangelism

The extracts from sermons in our last chapter make it quite plain that Spurgeon did not believe that there is a gospel message which can somehow be detached from the whole structure of Biblical theology. He regarded all truth as having a place in evangelism. But what is likely to be questioned in view of the above statements which are so far removed from our modern conceptions of evangelism, is whether the gospel can be preached at all on a doctrinal basis such as this? It must at once be admitted that if by the gospel we mean that Christ has died for everybody, that God 'respects His gift of free-will to man', and that 'a decision for Christ' is the crux of salvation, then such a gospel is not at all recognizable in Spurgeon's sermons. But he did unceasingly set forth the greatness of Christ's love to sinners, the freeness of His pardon and the fulness of His atonement; and he persuaded and exhorted all to repent and trust in such a Saviour. The point at which he diverged from both Hyper-Calvinism and Arminianism is that he refused to rationalize *how* men can be commanded to do what is not in their power.[1] Arminians say that sinners are commanded, therefore they must be able; Hyper-Calvin-

[1] The same difficulty is raised when it is asked, How can men be responsible when they perish in sin if grace alone can prevent such an end? 'Someone says, "But I do not understand this doctrine." Perhaps not, but remember that, while we are bound to tell you the truth, we are not bound to give you the power to understand it; and besides, this is not a subject for understanding, it is a matter for believing because it is revealed in the Word of God. It is one of the axioms of theology that, if man be lost, God must not be blamed for it; and it is also an axiom of theology that, if man is saved, God must have all the glory of it.' 56, 294.

ists say they are not able, therefore they cannot be commanded. But Scripture and Calvinism sets forth *both* man's inability and his duty, and both truths are a necessary part of evangelism – the former reveals the sinner's need of a help which only God can give, and the latter, which is expressed in the exhortations, promises and invitations of Scripture, shows him the place in which his peace and safety lies, namely, the person of the Son of God.

The fact that regeneration is the work of God certainly forbids us to tell men they can be born again at a moment which they or the preacher may choose, but it does not hinder the evangelist from doing his true work, which is to show men that they must be saved by grace through faith, and that trust in Christ is the way to peace with God. However much it is beyond the power of reason to reconcile the command to sinners to believe on the Son of God for salvation with the truth that only grace can enable them to do so, there is no conflict between the two things in Scripture. Spurgeon took these two truths, man's *duty* to believe and his sinful *inability* to do so, and used them like the two jaws of a vice to grip the sinner's conscience. Take the following example:

'God asks you to believe that through the blood of Jesus Christ, He can still be just, and yet the justifier of the ungodly. He asks you to trust in Christ to save you. Can you expect that He will save you if you will not trust Him? Man, it is the most reasonable thing in the world that He should demand of thee that thou shouldst believe in Christ. And this He does demand of thee this morning. "Repent and believe the gospel". O friends, O friends, how sad, how sad is the state of man's soul when he will not do this! We may preach to you, but you never will repent and believe the gospel. We may lay God's commands, like an axe, to the root of the tree, but, reasonable as these commands are, you will still refuse to give God His due; you will go on in your sins; you will not come unto Him that you may have life; and it is here the Spirit of God must come in to work in the souls of the elect to make them willing in the day of His power. But oh! in God's name I warn you that, if, after hearing this command, you do, as I know you will do, without His Spirit, continue to refuse obedience to so reasonable a gospel, you shall find at the last it shall be more tolerable for Sodom and Gomorrah, than for you; for had the things which are preached in London been proclaimed in Sodom and Gomorrah, they would have repented long ago in sackcloth and in ashes. Woe unto you, inhabitants of London!'[2]

But he did not leave sinners at this point. Listen to the way in which he closes the sermon from which we have just quoted. With a great crescendo of truth he has been attacking the consciences of the unconverted from every direction and now, in an agony of earnestness, he reaches this tremendous conclusion: 'I charge you by the living God, I charge you by the world's Redeemer, I charge you by the cross of Calvary, and by the blood which stained the dust at Golgotha, obey this divine message and you shall have eternal life; but refuse it, and on your own heads be your blood for ever and ever!'[3]

Moreover, he not only exhorted sinners, he frequently directed them. In language which seems so far off from the present formula for closing an evangelistic message, he would counsel men how to seek Christ: 'Before you leave this place,' he says on one such occasion, 'breathe an earnest prayer to God, saying, "God be merciful to me a sinner. Lord, I need to be saved. Save me. I call upon thy name." Join with me in prayer at this moment, I entreat you. Join with me while I put words into your mouths, and speak them on your behalf – "Lord, I am guilty, I deserve thy wrath. Lord, I cannot save myself. Lord, I would have a new heart and a right spirit, but what can I do? Lord, I can do nothing, come and work in me to will and to do of thy good pleasure.

[2] 8, 405.   [3] 8, 408.

> *Thou alone hast power, I know,*
> *To save a wretch like me;*
> *To whom, or whither should I go*
> *If I should run from thee?*

But I now do from my very soul call upon thy name. Trembling, yet believing, I cast myself wholly upon thee, O Lord. I trust the blood and righteousness of thy dear Son. . . . Lord, save me tonight, for Jesus' sake." '

Another verse which he used in directing sinners was Charles Wesley's stanza:

> *O God, my inmost soul convert,*
> *And deeply on my thoughtful heart*
> *Eternal things impress;*
> *Give me to feel their solemn weight,*
> *And trembling on the brink of fate,*
> *Wake me to righteousness!*

In this way seeking souls were directed to God alone, and while the members of the Tabernacle were expected to be always looking out for those needing spiritual help, there was no outward or physical sign required of those who were under concern. It was just at that point, Spurgeon knew, that Arminianism works havoc by calling attention to the human action instead of the Divine. 'Go home alone', he would say, 'trusting in Jesus. "I should like to go into the enquiry-room." I dare say you would, but we are not willing to pander to popular superstition. We fear that in those rooms men are warmed into a fictitious confidence. Very few of the supposed converts of enquiry-rooms turn out well. Go to your God at once, even where you now are. Cast yourself on Christ, now, at once, ere you stir an inch!' These words were spoken before the enquiry-room had fully developed into the modern system of appeals and decisions; how sadly Spurgeon would have viewed such a development it is not hard to imagine. He recognized that once such things became a part of evangelism, men would soon begin to imagine that they could be saved by *doing* certain things or that these things would at least help to save them – 'God has not appointed salvation by enquiry-rooms' becomes a recurring warning in his later sermons.

Man has made a connection between coming forward after an appeal and 'coming to Christ', but Spurgeon would have strongly repudiated any such connection. Not only does such an evangelistic method not exist in Scripture, it vitiates what Scripture does teach on coming to Christ: 'It is a motion of the heart towards Him, not a motion of the feet, for many came to Him in body, and yet never came to Him in truth, . . . the coming here meant is performed by desire, prayer, assent, consent, trust, obedience.'[4] Furthermore, Spurgeon had enough experience of the powerful working of the Spirit to know that these human additions to preaching the gospel were not justified by their supposed helpfulness: the man genuinely convicted by the truth may be the last to desire to comply with the public actions which an 'appeal' would force on him: 'For the most part, a wounded conscience, like a wounded stag, delights to be alone that it may bleed in secret. It is very hard to get at a man under conviction of sin; he retires so far into himself that it is impossible to follow him.'[5] The practice at the Tabernacle was entirely in harmony with these convictions. At the close of services the congregation of 5,000 would be bowed in solemn stillness with no organ or other music to break the silence, and then members of the church would be ready to speak to any strangers who might be sitting near them and desiring help.

These considerations on the way Arminianism affects the presentation of the Gospel lead us to a final reason why the teaching must necessarily be regarded in a serious light. It is because this type of evangelism, wherever it prevails, has an

[4] 19, 280.   [5] 23, 428.

inevitable tendency to produce a dangerous religious superficiality. Arminianism in by-passing, as we have seen, the
offensive truth that all saving experience must *begin* with
regeneration, and because it implies that men come to faith and
repentance without the direct and prior work of the Holy
Spirit, sets up a pattern for conversion which is *below* the
Biblical one. The sinner is instructed, under Arminian preaching, that he must begin the work by becoming willing and God
will complete it; he must do what he can and God will do the
rest. So if a firm 'decision for Christ' is made, he is at once
counselled to trust that the Divine work has also been done,
and to regard such texts as John 1:12 as describing his own
case. But the truth is that Arminianism has erected a pattern of
conversion which is sub-scriptural and which unregenerate
men *can* attain to. By representing repentance and faith as
something possible to unrenewed men it opens the way to an
experience in which the self-will of the sinner and not the
power of God may be the main feature. The Scripture everywhere represents the will and power of God as first, not
second, in salvation, and a teaching which promises that God's
will must follow our will may have the effect of causing men
to trust in a delusion – an experience which is not salvation at
all. It is against such a delusion that Scripture frequently
warns us. And the urgency of the warning arises in part from
the fact that there is a 'faith' which can be exercised by unregenerate men, and the exercise of it may even lead to joy and
peace. But Arminianism, instead of cautioning men against this
danger, inevitably encourages it, for it throws men, not upon
God, but upon their own acts. The impression is distinctly
given to the gospel hearer that the choice is not God's but his
and that he is able there and then to decide the time of his rebirth. For example, a booklet, which is much circulated in
student evangelism at the present time, lays down 'Three
simple steps' to becoming a Christian: first, personal acknow-
ledgement of sin, and second, personal belief in Christ's sub-

stitutionary work. These two are described as preliminary, but 'the third so final that to take it will make me a Christian. ... *I must come to Christ and claim my personal share in what He did for everybody*.' This all-decisive third step rests with me, Christ 'waits patiently until I open the door. Then He will come in. ...' Once I have done this I may immediately regard myself as a Christian. The advice follows: 'Tell somebody *today* what you have done.'

On this basis a man may make a profession without ever having his confidence in his own ability shattered; he has been told absolutely nothing of his need of a change of nature which is not within his own power, and consequently, if he does not experience such a radical change, he is not dismayed. He was never told it was essential, so he sees no reason to doubt whether he is a Christian. Indeed the teaching he has come under consistently militates against such doubts arising. It is frequently said that a man who has made a decision with little evidence of a change of life may be a 'carnal' Christian who needs instruction in holiness, or if the same individual should gradually lose his new-found interests, the fault is frequently attributed to lack of 'follow-up', or prayer, or some other deficiency on the part of the Church. The possibility that these marks of worldliness and falling away are due to the absence of a saving experience at the outset is rarely considered; if this point were faced, then the whole system of appeals, decisions and counselling would collapse, because it would bring to the fore the fact that change of nature is not in man's power, and that it takes much longer than a few hours or days to establish whether a professed response to the gospel is genuine. But instead of facing this, it is protested that to doubt whether a man who has 'accepted Christ' is a Christian is tantamount to doubting the Word of God, and that to abandon 'appeals' and their adjuncts is to give up evangelism altogether. That such things can be said is tragic proof of the extent to which the Arminian pattern of conversion has come to be regarded as the

Biblical one. So much is this the case that if anyone raises an objection to the use of such unscriptural expressions as 'accepting Christ', 'opening your heart to Christ', 'letting the Holy Spirit save you', it would generally be regarded as merely cavilling about words.

Spurgeon saw Arminianism to be a departure from the purity of New Testament evangelism and, in asserting religious superficiality to be one of its attendant consequences, he recognized what has become so characteristic of modern Evangelicalism. It was not so much the advent of musical accompaniments and enquiry rooms that alarmed him, though he was troubled by these things and had no time for them, but rather the disappearing emphasis on the necessity of the Spirit's work and the stream-lining of conversion into a speedy business: 'Do you know,' he asked in a sermon entitled 'Sown Among Thorns' preached not long before his death, 'why so many professing Christians are like the thorny ground? It is because processes have been omitted which would have gone far to alter the condition of things. It was the husbandman's business to uproot the thorns, or burn them on the spot. Years ago, when people were converted, there used to be such a thing as conviction of sin. The great subsoil plough of soul-anguish was used to tear deep into the soul. Fire also burned in the mind with exceeding heat: as men saw sin, and felt its dreadful results, the love of it was burned out of them. But now we are dinned with braggings about rapid salvations. As for myself, I believe in instantaneous conversions, and I am glad to see them; but I am still more glad when I see a thorough work of grace, a deep sense of sin, and an effectual wounding by the law. We shall never get rid of thorns with ploughs that scratch the surface. . . .'[6]

With a lowered standard of conversion came a lowered con-

[6] 34, 473–4. Many similar quotations could be given. 'I must confess,' he says, 'my preference for these old-fashioned forms of conviction: it is my judgment that they produce better and more stable believers than the modern superficial methods.' 30, 446–7.

ception of the real nature of true Christian experience, and Spurgeon viewed with dismay the failure to apply searching Scriptural tests to those who professed conversion. 'I have heard young people say, "I know I am saved, because I am so happy." Be not sure of that. Many people think themselves very happy, and yet are not saved.'[7] A sense of peace he likewise regarded as no sure sign of true conversion. Commenting on the verse, 'The Lord killeth, and maketh alive: he woundeth, and his hands make whole', he asks: 'But how can He make those alive who were never killed? You that were never wounded, you who tonight have been sitting here and smiling at your own ease, what can mercy do for you? Do not congratulate yourselves on your peace.'[8] There is a peace of the Devil as well as the peace of God. Throughout his ministry Spurgeon warned men of this danger but in some of his later sermons this note of alarm is increasingly urgent. In one such sermon entitled 'Healed or Deluded? Which?' preached in 1882, Spurgeon speaks of the large numbers who are deceived by a false healing. This may even be the case, he shows, with those who have gone through a period of spiritual anxiety: 'Convinced that they want healing, and made in a measure anxious to find it, the danger with the awakened is lest they should rest content with an apparent cure, and miss the real work of grace. We are perilously likely to rest satisfied with a slight healing, and by this means to miss the great and complete salvation which comes from God alone. I wish to speak in deep earnestness to everyone here present upon this subject, for I have felt the power of it in my own soul. To deliver this message I have made a desperate effort, quitting my sick bed without due permit, moved by a restless pining to warn you against the counterfeits of the day.'[9]

Wherever Arminianism becomes the predominant theology, true religion is bound to degenerate and false security to be promoted. By separating the sinner's need to believe from his

[7] 23, 647.   [8] 36, 691.   [9] 28, 255.

need of regeneration, Arminianism places in the background
the fact that 'change of heart is the very core and essence of
salvation.'[10] It is inevitable that it should not give prominence
to the latter truth because no man can cause his nature to be
forever divorced from the love and rule of sin, and regeneration means nothing short of this. Instead Arminianism depicts
regeneration as something within the scope of man's choosing,
or something which will accompany his decision, and in so
doing its tendency is to make men imagine that the new birth
is something less than it actually is. 'Your regeneration,'
Spurgeon would say, 'was not of the will of man, nor of blood,
nor of birth; if it were so, let me tell you, the sooner you are
rid of it the better. The only true regeneration is of the will
of God and by the operation of the Holy Ghost.'[11]

Arminianism gives men no such warning and its silence is
dangerous because it fails to make clear the truth which safeguards men from false security – namely, that God never for-
gives sin without at the same time changing the nature of the
sinner. 'I speak advisedly,' Spurgeon declared, 'when I say
that the doctrine of "believe and live" would be a very dangerous one if it were not accompanied by the doctrine of
regeneration.'[12] By emphasizing that 'faith saves' without also
insisting that wherever true faith exists there is a new life,
created in likeness to the character of God and manifesting itself in a hatred of all sin, Arminianism opens the way for a
'believism' which debases the meaning of conversion and does
not give to that word its full content.

While the new life imparted in regeneration is *never* the
ground of our justification, nevertheless the Scripture knows
nothing of the possibility of a justified man who has not ex-
perienced 'the washing of regeneration' (Titus 3:5). Arminianism has frequently separated conversion and sanctification
because it has lost the truth that regeneration is the cause of
conversion; but once the Biblical doctrine of regeneration is

[10] 24, 526.   [11] ibid.   [12] 52, 163.

grasped it means that no man can be a *true* believer who does not possess a new life 'created in righteousness and true holiness' (Eph. 4.24). According to Scripture it is quite impossible to be justified by faith and not to experience the commencement of true sanctification, because the spiritual life communicated by the Spirit in the act of regeneration (which introduces the new power to believe) is morally akin to the character of God and contains within it the germ of all holiness. Thus saving faith is never found in isolation. As the Westminster Confession teaches, faith 'is the alone instrument of justification; yet it is not alone in the person justified, but is ever accompanied with all other saving graces.'

Because they teach this, the doctrines of grace are a barrier against carelessness and superficiality. The very system which has been accused of lessening man's responsibility has where-ever it has prevailed, produced generations of serious, God-fearing and saintly people, for Calvinism has always emphasized that it is by obedience and holiness that we fulfil the apostolic command to make our calling and election sure: 'If the divine calling has produced in us the fruit of obedience, then we may assuredly believe that we were separated unto God ere time began, and that this separation was according to the eternal purpose and will of God.'13 On the other hand, Arminianism, which claims to be the protector of the doctrine of human responsibility, has within its teaching an inevitable tendency to lower the Biblical standard of true Christian experience. In this connection it is significant that modern Evangelicalism has popularized the phrase 'the eternal security of believers', whereas historic Calvinism has maintained the final perseverance of *the saints:* 'We believe in the perseverance of the saints, but many are not saints, and therefore do not persevere.'14

It is true that Arminianism has been productive of many

[13] 56, 290.   [14] 35, 222.

'holiness' meetings and conventions, but this fact, instead of rebutting the charge made above, rather confirms it, because there was no need of special teaching on sanctification until Arminianism began to prevail in evangelism. Calvinism held that the *same* message which saves men makes them holy, and that a faith which is not bound up with holiness is not saving faith at all. It was because he knew this that Spurgeon took no part in holiness conventions, but had he been called upon to address worldly 'believers' who needed to be sanctified there is no question what he would have had to say: 'Those people who have a faith which allows them to think lightly of past sin, have the faith of devils, and not the faith of God's elect. ... Such who think sin a trifle and have never sorrowed on account of it, may know that their faith is not genuine. Such men as have a faith which allows them to live carelessly in the present, who say, "Well, I am saved by a simple faith", ... and enjoy the carnal pleasures and the lusts of the flesh, such men are liars; they have not the faith which will save the soul. ... Oh! if any of you have such faith as this, I pray God to turn it out bag and baggage.'[15]

As we shall see in a subsequent chapter, the Arminian view of conversion received a more concrete form in England in the 1870's when it came to logical fruition in Moody's method of giving an 'invitation' at the end of an evangelistic address. As it was not emphasized that a change of nature is necessary to effect a true response to the gospel, the idea was soon popularized that a man may be converted and then receive 'sanctification' at some later stage in his Christian life. The 'holiness teaching', as it came to be called, was largely based on a concept of sanctification as something separate and distinct from conversion, and it is significant that it came into vogue along with an evangelism which promoted a defective theology of the new-birth. As B. B. Warfield has pointed out the teaching owed not a little of its immense influence to the fact that it was 'embroidered on the surface' of the popular Moody and Sankey missions.[16] In a preface to his book *Holiness* J. C. Ryle, a critical Victorian contemporary of the 'holiness' movement, noted the fundamental flaw in the holiness teaching when he wrote: 'Many talk now-a-days about "*Consecration*" who seem to be ignorant of the "first principles of the oracles of God" about "*Conversion*".'[17]

The superficiality which is attendant upon Arminianism may be traced to the very centre of its system. 'If you believe that everything turns upon the free-will of man' says Spurgeon 'you will naturally have man as its principal figure in your landscape.'[18] This being the case there is inevitably the tendency to regard Divine truth only as a means to gain men, and whatever truth does not appear to us to be effective towards that end, or whatever truth seems an obstacle to the widest possible evangelism, it is consequently liable to be laid aside. The end must be greater than the means. But what is here forgotten is that the ultimate *end* of the gospel is not the conversion of men but the glory of God.

It is not man's need of salvation which is the supreme thing, and once this is realized, the attitude which thinks 'we must get men converted' and fails to ask whether the means are according to Scripture, is seen in its true light. 'In the church of the present age there is a desire to be doing something for God, but few enquire what He wills them to do. Many things are done for the evangelizing of the people which were never commanded by the great Head of the Church, and cannot be approved of by him.'[19] We know His will only by His Word and, unless truth comes before results, conversions will soon be regarded as more important than the Divine glory. Spurgeon denounced the kind of evangelism in which there is 'a wretched lowering of the truth upon many points in

[16] *Perfectionism*, 1931, I, 315.
[17] *Holiness*, 5th ed., 1900, viii. This preface is omitted from the modern reprint.
[18] 34, 364.   [19] 30, 245.

order to afford encouragement to men';[20] he saw that it would end 'in utter failure' and bring neither glory to God nor lasting blessing to the Church. He deplored the fact that men were being allowed 'to jump into their religion as men do into their morning bath, and then jump out again just as quickly, converted by the dozen, and unconverted one by one till the dozen has melted away.'[21] In contrast to this sort of thing, he declared solemnly on one occasion, 'I do not wish for success in the ministry, if God does not give it me; and I pray that you who are workers for God, may not wish to have any success except that which comes from God himself in God's own way; for if you could heap up, like the sand of the sea, converts that you have made by odd, unchristian ways, they would be gone like the sand of the sea as soon as another tide comes up.'[22]

Spurgeon's marks of a true conversion are as follows:

'When the Word of God converts a man, *it takes away from him his despair but it does not take from him his repentance.*

True conversion *gives a man pardon, but does not make him presumptuous.*

True conversion *gives a man perfect rest, but it does not stop his progress.*

True conversion *gives a man security, but it does not allow him to leave off being watchful.*

True conversion *gives a man strength and holiness, but it never lets him boast.*

[20] 30, 447. In his book, *Truth and Error*, Horatius Bonar summarized the cause of this growing habit: 'Our whole anxiety is, not how shall we secure the glory of Jehovah, but how shall we multiply conversions? The whole current of our thoughts and anxieties takes this direction. We cease to look at both things together; we think it enough to keep the one of them alone in our eye; and the issue is that we soon find ourselves pursuing ways of our own. We thus come to measure the correctness of our plans, simply by their seeming to contribute to our favourite aim. We estimate the soundness of our doctrine, not from its tendency to exalt and glorify Jehovah, but entirely by the apparent facility with which it enables us to get sinners to turn from their ways. The question is not asked concerning any doctrine, Is it in *itself* a God-honouring truth, but will it afford us facilities for converting souls?' 1861 edition, 16.
[21] 38, 434.   [22] 36, 688.

True conversion *gives a harmony to all the duties of Christian life;* . . . it balances all duties, emotions, hopes and enjoyments.

True conversion *brings a man to live for God.* He does everything for the glory of God, – whether he eats, or drinks, or whatsoever he does. True conversion *makes a man live before God.* . . . He desires to live as in God's sight at all times, and he is glad to be there. . . . And such a man now comes to *live with God.* He has blessed communion with him; he talks with him as a man talks with his friend.'[23]

Before we leave the subject of the relation between the doctrines of grace and evangelism we must hear a characteristic reply from Spurgeon to the objection that 'Calvinistic' belief must prove an obstacle to practical endeavour in Gospel witness. The objection has not infrequently been regarded as so valid that theological criticisms of Arminian evangelism have been impatiently set aside, the presumption being that if it were not for *such* evangelism there would be no evangelical endeavour at all. Spurgeon met this prejudice by turning from theories about the supposed effects of faith in God's electing love to the historical evidence of evangelistic zeal found in those whose theology was contrary to Arminianism. Upon this evidence he loved to expatiate:

'The greatest missionaries that have ever lived have believed in God's choice of them; and instead of this doctrine leading to inaction, it has ever been an irresistible motive power, and it will be so again. It was the secret energy of the Reformation. It is because free grace has been put into the background that we have seen so little done in many places. It is in God's hand the great force which can stir the church of God to its utmost depth. It may not work superficial revivals, but for deep work it is invaluable. Side by side with the blood of Christ it is the world's hope. How can men say that the doctrine of distinguishing grace makes men careless about souls? Did they never hear of the evangelical band

[23] 50, 79–80.

which was called the Clapham sect? Was Whitefield a man who cared nothing for the salvation of the people? He who flew like a seraph throughout England and America unceasingly proclaiming the grace of God, was he selfish? Yet he was distinctly a free-grace preacher. Did Jonathan Edwards have no concern for the souls of others? Oh, how he wept, and cried, and warned them of the wrath to come! Time would fail me to tell of the lovers of men who have been lovers of this truth.'[24]

[24] 34, 372.

I have been in my inmost soul bowed before the Lord with awful dread lest these days of the Son of Man which we have enjoyed in great measure so long should be taken away from us. I tremble lest we should go to sleep, and do nothing: I am alarmed lest there should be no conversions, and nobody caring that there should be any ... You Protestants who are today flinging away your liberties as dirt-cheap will one day rue the day in which you allowed the old chains to be fitted upon your wrists. Popery fettered and slew our sires, and yet we are making it the national religion!

C.H.S., November 12th, 1876, SERMONS, 22, 633–4

5: Church Issues Revived

One consequence of the Evangelical Revival of the 18th century was that the division between evangelicals in the Established Church and evangelical Nonconformists was, in the realm of spiritual activity at least, partially healed. Methodism, with its itinerant leaders, Whitefield and Wesley, did much to blur the old differences. The impact of ministries like William Grimshaw's in Yorkshire and John Newton's in Buckinghamshire worked likewise towards a new measure of harmony between Church and Dissent, while in London, as a result of joint endeavour, such evangelical and inter-denominational organizations as The London Missionary Society (1795) and The British and Foreign Bible Society (1804) showed the practical results of the new spirit. It is true that underlying tensions still remained, as was witnessed, for example, in Thomas M'Crie's clash with Charles Simeon in 1813 over the latter's sermons on 'The Excellency of the Liturgy'; nevertheless as the 19th century advanced all the probabilities appeared to be against a repetition of the controversies on church issues which had gone so deep two centuries earlier. Evangelicals in 'Church' or 'Chapel' were prepared for a greater measure of benevolent neutrality on issues not directly relevant to the progress of the Gospel, and we find the Congregational leader John Angell James, in 1844, counselling in regard to the formation of the Evangelical Alliance, that Prelacy should not be an object of antagonism: 'If we take up the latter,' he writes to a friend, 'we cannot carry Episcopalians with us.'[1]

[1] *Life and Letters of J. A. James*, R. W. Dale, 1861, 421.

In rural Essex the new spirit found genuine expression in the village of Stambourne where Spurgeon spent much of his childhood. Since 1662, when the rector of the parish was ejected from the Church of England, a Nonconformist meeting-house had borne witness to the Gospel. But in the 1830's when James Spurgeon, Spurgeon's grandfather, was the pastor of the Stambourne dissenters, the rector of the parish was again an evangelical, and the two men worked harmoniously together; it was one of the 'choice pleasures' of Stambourne, according to Spurgeon, when he, as a boy, ate sugared bread and butter, along with his grandfather and the rector at the Squire's house on a Monday afternoon! Spurgeon was thus taught to appreciate evangelical churchmen from his youth, and *The Evangelical Magazine*, edited by such men, was staple reading in the old manse at Stambourne. It was another sign of the religious tolerance of his dissenting background, when at the age of fourteen he became a boarder for a year at a Church of England school in Maidstone.

Despite all this, however, Spurgeon became involved in later years in one of the most violent ecclesiastical controversies of the last century. The controversy arose and blew over like a sudden storm in 1864, but although comparatively brief in its actual duration it is significant as marking a stage in a new religious trend – a trend which was against harmony and which worked powerfully for the reviving of issues which had long been allowed to rest.

For this trend Spurgeon was in no way responsible. It had begun in 1833 – the year before his birth – when the first of the 'Tracts for the Times' had been issued at Oxford, and though the first excitement and alarm occasioned by the spate of tracts died down after 1841, and though Nonconformity was slow to realize the long-term significance of what was happening in the Establishment, a movement had been set in motion which was to colour church issues for a long time to come. The theme of the Oxford tracts was 'the Church'. They called for reform; for a recognition that the Church is in no sense subordinate to state control or dependent on Parliament's legislation; and for a renewed realization that her officers receive their authority, and the Church her privileges, from Jesus Christ alone. If this was all that 'Tractarians' had said, such claims might have received considerable support from evangelicals; instead, the latter regarded the new movement as a direct threat to the purity and preservation of the gospel.

The Tractarian position, which was formulated by John Henry Newman (1801–1890), the learned vicar of St Mary's, Oxford, along with other Oxford men, was based on the same definition of the church as the defenders of the Papacy urged against the Reformers in the 16th century. 'The Lord Jesus Christ,' said Newman in Tract 1, 'gave His Spirit to His Apostles; they in turn laid their hands on those who should succeed them, and these again on others, and so the sacred gift has been handed down to our present bishops who have appointed us as their assistants, and in some sense representatives.' In other words apostolic authority continues in the 'episcopate', and it is upon the episcopate that the validity of the orders of other clergy and their right to administer the sacraments depends. So where there are no bishops there can be no ministry appointed by Christ and if there is no ministry there can be neither church nor salvation. This teaching of 'apostolic succession' was thus not only a matter of church government, it involved the whole question of salvation. It claimed that grace is conveyed by a series of clerical acts – baptism, confirmation and 'holy communion' – and the assurance that these acts have the blessing of Christ is that they are performed by the lawful successors of His apostles. So the Tractarians not only accepted the bishop-priest structure of the Church of England, they revived the 'suppressed truth' that this structure was to be revered not merely for its antiquity and because experience had shown it to be the best kind of church order, but rather because the very existence of the Church depended upon it.

Tractarianism, described by the then Bishop of Oxford as 'The most remarkable movement, which, for three centuries at least, has taken place among us,' was destined to change the whole outlook in the Church of England. Hitherto the Church, even when it had persecuted evangelicals, had generally been firmly Protestant in its attitude to the Papacy. Yet although the Tracts did not at first say so, it soon appeared that, if this teaching were true, the separation from Rome should not be permanently maintained. How could the standing of the English Church be justified apart from the descent of her bishops in historical succession from the great 'Catholic' Church of Medieval times? And as the same succession continued at Rome, were they not both still essentially one body? William Ewart Gladstone need not have been so greatly amazed in 1842 when he was confidentially told by a sympathiser with the Oxford Movement that reunion with Rome was the ultimate hope.

There were various reasons for the swift progress of Anglo-Catholicism – the name by which the movement ultimately became known. The Evangelical Awakening of the 18th century had never reached more than a minority of the clergy, and the nominal Protestantism of the majority did no more than leave them like a house 'swept and garnished'. For the most part, the parishes of England were ill prepared to meet an influence which only a full-orbed Gospel ministry could withstand. The same is true of the Bench of Bishops where evangelicals could never hope to be anything more than numerically weak.

But a different reason has sometimes been given to explain the progress of the Tractarians: it has been attributed to their readiness to indulge in a measure of intellectual dishonesty. Newman certainly laid himself open to such a charge when in February, 1841, he sought in Tract 90 to reconcile the 39

Articles with the Roman dogmas of the Council of Trent. Four years later he joined the Roman Church, but many other clergy who had come under the influence of the Oxford teaching continued in the Church, and while nominally upholding articles which teach that 'the sacrifices of Masses' are 'blasphemous fables' (Art. 31), they laboured to promote doctrine which was irreconcilable with their own profession.[2] Subscription to the Articles was in process of becoming worthless.

Yet it is not sufficient to represent the Tractarians as acting in a manner which was entirely inconsistent with the constitution of a Protestant Establishment. It also needs to be said that possibly the most important factor contributing to the ultimate success of their influence was the existence of points in the structure and formularies of the Church of England which could be appealed to as bearing witness to their teaching. Did not the Prayer Book assert that the orders of Bishops and Priests existed 'from the Apostles' time'?, that Episcopal consecration or ordination was necessary for a lawful ministry? that the Bishop should say while laying hands on priests in ordination, 'Receive the Holy Ghost'?, that only a Bishop may administer confirmation, laying his hands on candidates and claiming as he does so the warrant of 'the example of thy holy Apostles'? More than this, does not the Prayer Book teach that the person to whom baptism is administered is regenerate, 'made a member of Christ, the child of God,' and consequently at death (provided he is not excommunicate or a suicide) the priest is required to state that his burial is in 'true and certain hope of the resurrection to eternal life, through our Lord Jesus Christ'? Again, why is sanction given to the use of such terms as 'priest', and of such expressions as, 'I absolve thee from all thy sins,' if these words are not to be taken in their most natural sense?

[2] Foremost among this group was E. B. Pusey (1800–82) whose prominence in the Anglo-Catholic movement led to the coining of the derogatory term 'Puseyite'.

The Tractarians were quick to appeal to statements like these and the difficulty which their opponents had in making any simple reply made their appeals the more effective. Evangelicals in the Church could demonstrate that no Anglican leader in the early Elizabethan period interpreted these terms in a Roman sense. Yet this did not prove that the Roman sense was not the more ancient meaning. But it was asked by upholders of the Protestantism of the Establishment, how the Roman sense could be admissible, seeing that the same Reformers had authorized both Prayer Book and Articles? Would they have composed or accepted formularies which allowed both a Protestant and a Roman interpretation? Along such lines as these, evangelical churchmen laboured to show that everything in the Prayer Book could be reconciled with a pure gospel and an evangelical faith.

Significantly, the debate over Tractarianism demonstrated that the wheel had come almost full circle since Puritan times. In the 17th century the prelates and authorities in the Church had complained that the Puritan scruples over full conformity to the Book of Common Prayer were groundless, seeing there was nothing in the Book which supported the errors of Rome. To this the Puritans replied by pointing out the very things which – for an altogether different purpose – the Tractarians pointed out in the mid-nineteenth century. The Puritans claimed that the Prayer Book revealed the insufficiently Reformed character of the Church of England; it allowed nests of Popery to remain, and to these, they prophesied, 'the rooks' would one day return. But the strange thing was that it was now evangelicals who asserted that there were no 'nests' in the Prayer Book, whereas dignitaries and bishops began to talk about the 'Catholic' character of the Book. Either the Puritans or the 19th century evangelical churchmen were wrong.

Tractarianism thus revived the old issue, how far had the national church been reformed in accordance with Scripture at the time of the Reformation? If Newman in Tract 90 was erroneous in his interpretation of the Articles, were later Anglo-Catholics equally astray in finding a 'Catholic' meaning in the passages of the Prayer Book to which they appealed? And if, in fact, expressions in the Liturgy and rubrics suggest or leave room for false teaching not warranted by the Articles, how could such a discrepancy be explained? How much strength was there in the argument that the Reformers would not have drawn up formularies which did not fully harmonize with each other?

Questions like these inevitably called renewed attention to the character and nature of the reformation in England, and led to an upsurge of reprints and to fresh historical research into the history of the 16th century. On the evangelical side the Parker Society published its monumental edition of the works of the English Reformers and John Foxe's old *Acts and Monuments of the Martyrs* went through several new editions, but as far as the production of new and comprehensive histories of the reformation in England was concerned, the Anglo-Catholic side went far to carrying the day with writers like R. W. Dixon in his *History of the Church of England from the Abolition of the Roman Jurisdiction* (6 vols.) and James Gairdner in his *Lollardy and the Reformation in England* (4 vols.). These men worked with unflagging industry on the Reformation period and, while their dislike of evangelical Christianity coloured their whole outlook, they became well equipped through prolonged study to challenge a number of traditional Protestant assumptions in the field of history. By drawing attention to the mixed and worldly influences at work in the English Reformation they gave force to the plea that the legislation of that period should not be regarded as an all-time norm for the Establishment; by showing the oppressive nature of the secular power in altering the constitution of the Church of England they sought to underline the wrong of subordinating ecclesiastical to civil authority. On points such as these there was sufficient factual truth to give the

Anglo-Catholic re-interpretation of the Reformation a strong influence.

This new historical examination of the Reformation was a by-product of Tractarianism and it would be irrelevant to our purpose to comment further upon it except to note how, in this case also, Anglo-Catholics were pointing to matters which the Puritans had discussed and debated two centuries before. Puritanism had always seen a distinction between the Reformation as a spiritual movement and the official legislation reconstituting the English Church; in the Prayer Book that was drawn up and enforced upon all clergy the Puritans saw much that was scriptural, but also several things which, through the mixed character of the official reformation carried through by the government, were without any scriptural sanction. They argued that the Prayer Book reflected the character of the age in which it was drawn up, an era when clay was mixed with the gold. To shut one's eyes to the defects of the Reformation settlement in England, the 17th century Puritans had urged, was to shut one's eyes to Scripture, and Dixon, Gairdner and others unwittingly confirmed the Puritan findings when they said that it also meant shutting one's eyes to the facts of history.

The rapid progress made by Tractarianism was naturally viewed with grief by all who loved the Gospel in England. A number of clergy left the Establishment,[3] while others under the leadership of men like J. C. Ryle (1816–1900) sought to repel Romanizing influences by remaining within its pale. Ryle argued that the presence of evil in the Church was not sufficient reason for separation. That the Anglican system was now working badly was no proof in his eyes that the system *itself* was bad, or 'that the whole machinery of the Church of

[3] According to J. C. Philpot, between forty and fifty ordained clergymen in various parts of England left the Established Church in the years 1830–35. At one point Philpot seems to have anticipated a major secession of evangelicals but this did not occur. cf. *The Seceders*, The Story of J. C. Philpot and William Tiptaft, 1964, 85.

England is rotten and corrupt.' At the same time Ryle was realistic and he was not afraid to state that, in his own judgment, the situation might deteriorate to such an extent that to remain within it would become sin. If, for example, the Articles were altered or jettisoned, if a sacrificial dress were formally legalized for use at the communion table,[4] if re-union came with false Churches like the Eastern Orthodox,[5] above all, if the tenets of sacerdotalism were accepted in place of the Gospel of grace, then, he believed, the Establishment 'will not be worth preserving. She will be an offence to God, and not a resting place for any true Christian.'

In a sermon on 'Apostolic Fears', Ryle wrote:

'At the rate we are going, I think it quite within the verge of possibility that in a few years the Church of England may be re-united to the Church of Rome. The Crown of England may be once more on the head of a Papist. Protestantism may be formally repudiated. A Romish Archbishop may once more preside at Lambeth Palace – Mass may once more be said at Westminster Abbey and St Paul's. And one result will be that all Bible-reading Christians must either leave the Church of England or also sanction idol-worship and become idolaters! God grant we may never come to this state of things! But at the rate we are going, it seems to me quite possible.'[6]

[4] 'If any persons want a sacrificial dress to be formally legalized at the communion table of the Church of England, let us resolve firmly that we will never consent.' Quoted in an article on Ryle in *The Sunday at Home* (1876), 104.

[5] I infer this from a statement like the following where Ryle is speaking of the Armenian, Greek and Roman Churches: 'A wise man should beware of ever being tempted to belong to such Churches himself, or of ever thinking lightly of the conduct of those who join such Churches, as if they had only committed a little sin.' *Knots Untied*, 1896, 274.

[6] *Knots Untied*, 506. Contrast with this the words of M. A. P. Wood in his Presidential Address to the evangelical clergy meeting at the Islington Clerical Conference in 1960, when his only reference to Roman Catholicism was to chide 'the gloomy prophets who fear that the Roman Catholic Church wants to make a take-over bid for the Church of England'!

Yet, since Ryle wrote, full inter-communion between the Church of England and the Old Catholic Churches (Popish in all except adherence to Papal Infallibility) has been established; masses have been said at Westminster Abbey

126

On other occasions he declared:

'Let our common watchword throughout England and Wales be this – "A Protestant Established Church, or else no Established Church at all . . . I maintain that the Established Church of England had better be disestablished, disendowed, and broken to pieces, than re-united with the Church of Rome . . . Rather than be re-united with the idolatrous Church of Rome, I would willingly see my own beloved Church perish and go to pieces. Rather than become Popish once more, she had better die!'[7]

Against this background of a resurgent 'Catholicism' in the Establishment we return to Spurgeon and the once famous Baptismal Regeneration controversy of 1864. By the latter date Spurgeon had completed ten years in London and when, from time to time, he had made references to the Establishment, they were of a moderate character. Unsparing in dealing with ritualism and sacramentalism, he made no attack on the Anglican system as such: 'half reformed, in a transition state, somewhere between truth and error . . . too good to be rejected, too evil to be wholly received',[8] this was as far as he would go in his judgment. In 1864, however, Spurgeon's preaching on church issues entered upon a new phase and shortly evangelical churchmen were complaining that they would never have given any support to the building of the Metropolitan Tabernacle three years earlier if they had an-

and Southwark Cathedral, prayers for the dead have been declared legal in the Establishment; vestments having a traditional sacrificial significance have been legally reintroduced, with a unanimous episcopal vote, though at the same time it was affirmed that the Church of England attaches no doctrinal significance to what a minister wears; and the Bishop of Ripon (leader of Anglican observers at the Vatican Council) was not controverted by any of his episcopal colleagues when he declared his belief that the Anglican communion as a 'whole would be prepared to accept the fact of the Papacy' (cf. *The Times*, October 22, 1963). The archbishop of Canterbury's views on the latter subject are well-known. Not surprisingly, the Pope told the Bishops of Southwark and Salisbury at the Vatican in April 1964, 'You have always been awaited and expected'.
[7] *The Sunday at Home* op. cit. Charge to the Diocese of Liverpool, 1887, reprinted in *Charges and Addresses*, J. C. Ryle (1903). and *Knots Untied*, 505.
[8] 8, 112.

A portrait of Spurgeon in middle life.

The Metropolitan Tabernacle as it was in Spurgeon's day.

Spurgeon's birthplace at Kelvedon, Essex.

to defend him. Nevertheless, we recognise in his ministry a powerful agency for good, and we cannot bear to hear so eminent a preacher as Dr. Parker minimising this good, and especially when the doctor is anxious that charity shall have a wider and more satisfactory exemplification than it now has. That Mr. Spurgeon is doing a great work at his orphanage goes without saying, but that he is doing even a greater work in his public ministry is, in our judgment, still more self-evident. We are glad to believe that Dr. Parker is doing a great deal also, and that his sermons, which are printed in this journal, are read and appreciated by thousands. Nevertheless, we do not believe that Dr. Parker, even in his sermons, is accomplishing any more for Christ and humanity than Mr. Spurgeon is in his. As a matter of fact Mr. Spurgeon's Calvinism has very little to do with his preaching, for even when he introduces it at the beginning of his sermon he is sure to contradict it before he closes. We have often noticed this peculiar method of Mr. Spurgeon, and he himself would no doubt admit that what we say is true. He holds that both God's sovereignty and man's responsibility are taught in the book, and that it is his duty to insist upon both, and not his duty to re-concile them. This we believe does Mr.

A column from the Christian Commonwealth *commenting on Joseph Parker's attack on Spurgeon's Calvinism in the* British Weekly, *April 1890. This cutting is reproduced from Spurgeon's own scrapbook and the cross in thick blue pencil—probably from Spurgeon's own hand—registers his entire denial of the writer's statement. Such marks in the scrapbook are very unusual but a statement like this was altogether intolerable to Spurgeon.*

THE FUNERAL OF THE LATE MR. C. H. SPURGEON
ARRIVAL OF THE BODY AT THE GATES OF THE NORWOOD CEMETERY

A newspaper drawing of the vast crowds at the entrance gates of Norwood Cemetery, London, as the hearse entered on 4 February 1892.

ticipated it. He appeared to be adopting a new attitude. To some extent this was probably the case, and in the sermon which began the whole controversy, he was quite open in pointing out one subject upon which his convictions had changed:

'It is a most fearful fact, that *in no age since the Reformation has Popery made such fearful strides in England as during the last few years.* I had comfortably believed that Popery was only feeding itself upon foreign subscriptions, upon a few titled perverts, and imported monks and nuns. I dreamed that its progress was not real. In fact, I have often smiled at the alarm of many of my brethren at the progress of Popery. But, my dear friends, we have been mistaken, grievously mistaken . . .

'Popery is making advances such as you would never believe, though a spectator should tell it to you . . . And to what is it to be ascribed? I say, with every ground of probability, that there is no marvel that Popery should increase when you have two things to make it grow: first of all, the falsehood of those who profess a faith which they do not believe, which is quite contrary to the honesty of the Romanist, who does through evil report and good report hold his faith; and then you have, secondly, this form of error known as baptismal regeneration, and commonly called Puseyism, which is not only Puseyism, but Church-of-Englandism, because it is in the Prayer Book, as plainly as words can express it – you have this baptismal regeneration preparing stepping stones to make it easy for men to go to Rome. I have but to open my eyes a little to foresee Romanism rampant everywhere in the future, since its germs are spreading everywhere in the present. In one of our courts of legislature but last Tuesday, the Lord Chief Justice showed his superstition, by speaking of "the risk of the calamity of children dying unbaptized!" Among Dissenters you see a veneration for structures, a modified belief in the sacredness of places, which is

all idolatry; for to believe in the sacredness of anything but of
God and of His own Word, is to idolize, whether it is to
believe in the sacredness of the men, the priests, or in the
sacredness of the bricks and mortar, or of the fine linen, or
what not, which you may use in the worship of God. I see
this coming up everywhere – a belief in ceremony, a resting in
ceremony, a veneration for altars, fonts, and Churches – a
veneration so profound that we must not venture upon a
remark, or straightway of sinners we are chief. Here is the
essence and soul of Popery, peeping up under the garb of a
decent respect for sacred things. It is impossible but that the
Church of Rome must spread, when we who are the watch-
dogs of the fold are silent, and others are gently and smoothly
turfing the road, and making it as soft and smooth as possible,
that converts may travel down to the nethermost hell of
Popery. We want John Knox back again. Do not talk to me of
mild and gentle men, of soft manners and squeamish words, we
want the fiery Knox, and even though his vehemence should
"ding our pulpits into blads," it were well if he did but rouse
our hearts to action.'[9]

The above words were preached to some 5,000 hearers on
June 5th, 1864, in a sermon on Mark 16: 15–16, and its title
'Baptismal Regeneration' gave its name to the controversy
which immediately ensued. Soon, 180,000 copies of the sermon were in print (the figure increasing to 350,000) until there
was probably hardly a minister in the country who was unaware of the debate occasioned by its publication. 'Never',
wrote Dr John Campbell, the influential editor of *The British
Standard*, 'has the error been exhibited to the public eye with
colouring so vivid, and never was it pressed home on the
clerical conscience with a force so thrilling, resistless, and
terrible!'

A multitude of articles, pamphlets and sermons in reply to

Spurgeon was soon also in print.[10] Many of these were not written by defenders of baptismal regeneration but by evangelicals in the Establishment who were exasperated by Spurgeon's refusal to distinguish between Tractarianism and the Prayer Book, and in particular they repudiated as a dishonourable imputation Spurgeon's charge that they were guilty of equivocation and dishonesty in swearing their assent to a Book which teaches what they did not believe. Spurgeon had made this charge in his sermon when considering the case of clergymen in the Church who did not believe in baptismal regeneration. He made the same charge again three weeks later in another sermon, 'Let us Go Forth':

'I see before me now a Church which tolerates evangelical truth in her communion, but at the same time lovingly embraces Puseyism, and finds room for infidels and for men who deny the authenticity of Scripture. This is no time for us to talk about friendship with so corrupt a corporation. The godly in her midst are deceived if they think to mould her to a more gracious form . . .'[11]

The duty of believers, in such a situation, was the duty to 'come out of her, and bear your witness for the truth'. What held men back in an apostate church, he proceeded to say, was unwillingness to pay the cost of being 'without the camp'. In some cases, perhaps many, the charge was true, but what was startling and offensive was that Spurgeon made it in universal terms. He claimed that for any evangelical to exercise a ministry of baptizing all infants and burying all the dead according to the terms of the Book of Common Prayer was dishonesty because such practice could only be reconciled with gospel principles by evading the natural sense of words, and evasion argues an unwillingness to confess the whole truth.

This charge, as we have already said, was resented by

[10] Spurgeon collected enough pamphlets on the subject to be bound into five large volumes!
[11] 10, 370.

Protestant churchmen who argued that whatever the plausible or apparent sense of the words in the baptismal service, they were persuaded that the compilers of the Book never intended to imply that every administration of the sacrament was accompanied by the saving influences of the Holy Spirit (a dogma denied in article 25 of the 39 Articles); the meaning was only that the ordinance becomes a means of grace (not necessarily at the time it is administered) to those who rightly receive it. The warrant to baptize infants was through the covenant-standing of a *believing* parent and it was concerning such children, according to evangelicals in the Church, that the charitable supposition was made that they would be receivers of the grace of regeneration.

This is an interpretation of infant baptism which, when backed by Scripture, cannot be easily dismissed, and because some men were not conscious of any insincerity in believing that *this* was the viewpoint of the Prayer Book, Spurgeon was unwise in seeming to attribute an unworthy motive to all who, though evangelicals, accepted the Prayer Book service.

Upon the above argument, however, a few observations can be made: (1) There is evidence to indicate that a number of those associated with the formulation of the 1552 Prayer Book *did* believe that an efficacy accompanied infant baptism at the time of its administration[12] and it is very hard to deny that this belief is taught in the Catechism. (2) The warrant for the administration of baptism to children is not qualified in the Prayer Book in terms of the covenant promises of God to *believing* parents. It may be replied that the Christian standing of those who used the Prayer Book was assumed by its compilers, but such an assumption would be extraordinary when we bear in mind that the Prayer Book was meant to be en-

[12] cf. a letter of Peter Martyr to Bullinger, at the very time when the Book of Common Prayer was being drawn up: 'many will have it, and those otherwise not unlearned nor evil, that grace is conferred, as they say, by the sacraments'. Printed in *Letters, Treatises of John Bradford*, Parker Society, 1853, 403–6.

forced throughout the country at a time when the majority of people in English parishes were far from being Christians.[13] Furthermore the Canons of the Church, in response to the Puritan attempt to introduce discipline into the administration of baptism, explicitly require that, 'No Minister shall refuse or delay to christen any child, according to the form of the Book of Common Prayer, that is brought to the Church to him upon Sundays or Holy-days to be christened.' (Canon 68) When the weight of these two points is considered it bears heavily against the attempt to defend the practice of infant baptism as authorized in the formularies of the Church of England and it gives justification for asking whether evangelicals who submit to an ordination oath containing the declaration 'that the Book of Common Prayer containeth in it nothing contrary to the Word of God,' have not compromised their position.[14]

In his last sermon relating to this controversy, Spurgeon widened the area of debate by alleging that the issues involved extended beyond the wording of one or two particular services. On September 25th, 1864, he took up the whole subject of the authority of Scripture in a sermon on Ezekiel 11: 5: '*Thus saith the Lord*: or, *The Book of Common Prayer Weighed in the Balances of The Sanctuary*.' From his text he argued that 'Thus saith the Lord' is (1) the minister's message; (2) the

[13] I base this statement on the verdict of many of the reformers who in their letters and other writings give an assessment of the spiritual state of the people in King Edward's reign (1547–53).

[14] John Newton (1725–1807) is quite candid in dealing with the above difficulties and it is hard to see how his admissions did not lead him to question the rightness of the oaths required of the clergy. He writes: 'Some persons who had a share in Church councils in Edward the Sixth's time, though they could not wholly prevent the Reformation, had influence sufficient to impede and embarrass it. They would not accept the Scriptures alone, as the sufficient rule of faith and practice, but prevailed to superadd the fathers of the first six centuries . . . their authority gave sanction to several expressions and sentiments which the Scripture does not warrant, particularly with regard to baptism. . . ' The Fathers, or some of them, did indeed speak of baptism and regeneration or the new birth as synonymous; but while Scripture, experience, and observation contradict them, I pay little regard to their judgment.' *John Newton, An Autobiography and Narrative*, Josiah Bull, 1868, 316–7.

only authority in God's Church; (3) the most fitting word of rebuke for erring saints; (4) the only solid ground of comfort to God's people; (5) that with which we must confront the Lord's enemies; (6) an authority that is not to be despised without entailing upon the offender the severest penalty.'

After these general observations he proceeded to seven major counts upon which he held the Prayer Book or Constitution of the Established Church to be without Biblical authority. There is nothing original in his material; it had all been gone over many a time before the final rejection of the Puritans' petitions for reform in 1662.[15] The new element in the situation, which pointed a contrast with the 17th century, was that a substantial number of evangelicals could not see anything unscriptural in the Church's system, and therein Spurgeon grieved that they were failing to apply to themselves the authority of Scripture which they pleaded against Rome. He specifies, for example, the manner of the 'Ordering of Priests', the bishop laying his hands in apostolic manner on the head of the candidate and saying, 'Receive the Holy Ghost': 'Is the way of ordering priests in the Church of Rome much worse than this? That the apostles did confer the Holy Ghost we never thought of denying, but that Oxford, Exeter, or any other occupants of the bench can give the Holy Spirit, needs some proof other than their silk aprons or lawn sleeves can afford us.' Later in this same sermon he examines the words of absolution to be used by the priest in 'The Order for the Visitation of the Sick' and proceeds to this question:

'After this, how can the priests of the Church of England denounce the Roman Catholics? It is so very easy to fume and bluster against Puseyites and Papists, but the moment our charity begins at home and we give our Evangelical brethren

[15] Spurgeon, of course, realized this: 'The struggles of the Covenanters of old need to be renewed at this moment. The strife of the Puritanic age needs to return once more to the Church.' 10, 372.

the same benefit which they confer upon the open Romanists, they are incensed beyond measure. Yet will we tell them to their faces, that they, despite their fair speeches, are as guilty as those whom they denounce, for there is as much popery in this priest-making as in any passage in the mass-book. . . . I am clear of this matter before the Most High, or hope to be, ere I sleep in the grave; and having once sounded the trumpet, it shall ring till my lips are dumb.'[16]

In the remaining twenty-eight years of his life Spurgeon did not swerve from what he had taught concerning the State Church in 1864. A union of Church and State which denies the spirituality of the kingdom of Christ,[17] a liturgy 'which ignores the distinction between the regenerate and the unregenerate,'[18] clerical subscriptions which compelled men to swear to errors, the payment of men with 'the mark of the beast in their foreheads' to teach the people, the widespread practice of idolatry under episcopal connivance,[19] these were all things he continued to urge as marks of the spirit of Antichrist. The Roman and Anglican Antichrist he linked together: the latter being 'a stepping stone to Popery,'[20] and a system that one day would be judged: "Let all who love the Lord, and hate evil, come out of this more and more apostatising church, lest they be partakers of the plague which will come upon her in the day of her visitation.'[21] But he recognized that that day might not yet be at hand. Preaching from John 10:16 on March 25, 1883, he says:

'We hear a great deal about the unity of the Church, and

[16] 10, 544. On the claim that apostolic *charismata* are still conferred by episcopal hands see the fine article by R. L. Dabney, 'Prelacy A Blunder', in his *Discussions: Evangelical and Theological*, vol. 2, reprinted 1967.
[17] 24, 368; 19, 50; 17, 354.
[18] 29, 362.
[19] 'The idolatry which worships the image of the devil is less blasphemous than that which worships the image of Christ. It is an awful sacrilege to make the holy Jesus appear to be an accomplice in the violation of the divine command: yea, and to turn that blessed memorial of death into an idolatrous rite in which divine honours are given to a piece of bread.' 23, 378.
[20] 11, 392; 11, 605; 14, 333. etc.   [21] 15, 294.

notions upon this subject are rather wild. We are to have the
Roman and the Greek and the Anglican church all joined
together in one: if they were so, much evil would come of it.
God has, I doubt not, a chosen people amongst all these great
corporations, but the union of such questionable organizations
would be a dire omen of mischief to the world: the dark ages,
and a worse Popedom than ever, would soon be upon us.'[22]

Probably the most significant thing about the great controversy of 1864 was its three-cornered nature. It showed that the
Anglo-Catholic movement set in motion by the Tractarians
would not have to reckon on Protestant solidarity in its path;
for the growing harmony between evangelicals which, as we
have observed, marked the beginning of the century, had left
certain denominational differences unresolved. Tractarian
claims forced these underlying differences into prominence,
thus dividing once again evangelical churchmen from evangelical nonconformists. In the eyes of evangelicals in the
Establishment, Spurgeon's charges in 1864 were a service to
the cause of Popery because they weakened faith in the formularies of the national church at a time when these same
formularies – particularly the doctrine of the 39 Articles –
were already under attack from the ritualists. Spurgeon, on
the other hand, argued that it was only from outside the
Establishment that an effective stand could be made against
Rome, for evangelical churchmen were already compromised
in the struggle by ordination oaths which compelled acquies-
cence in unscriptural practices.

As noted earlier, John Angell James had argued in 1844
that silence on church issues in the Evangelical Alliance basis
would preserve evangelical unity; and that might have been
the case had circumstances not arisen which compelled men
who belonged to the Alliance to speak plainly on principles
which were purposely left unstated at the Alliance's formation.
Spurgeon's stand in 1864 rocked the Alliance and peace was

only restored by his resignation. This was the cause of his public 'Letter to the Evangelical Alliance'.[23]

The controversy, although long forgotten, points important lessons. The division between evangelicals in 1864 suggested where real danger lay for Protestantism in future years – the danger of major crises developing which would involve issues concerning which evangelicals were disunited. The Baptismal Regeneration controversy was a foretaste of the kind of crisis which could arise and which evangelical inter-denominational unity would be ill-prepared to withstand.

Whatever personal weakness Spurgeon may have shown in this controversy, he cannot be fairly charged – as was the case at the time – with the 'singularity of bigotry'. His over-all concern was for the future of Protestantism; he had no ill will for evangelical clergymen, nor did he have any patience with dissent for dissent's sake. And at the height of the controversy he never abandoned his fundamental conviction that England's greatest need was for the preaching of the whole counsel of God. Lobbying Parliament or stirring agitation in denominational papers was never his method of encouraging men to seek reform; rather he held fast to the proclamation of the Word as the divinely-appointed way. Referring to the verse,

[23] The embarrassment of evangelicals at division within the Alliance is reflected in the conflicting statements which appeared on the cause of Spurgeon's resignation. A spokesman for the Alliance held that it was not due to any demand on their part, but Spurgeon asserted that he was asked by the secretary to retract his harsh language or withdraw, and in 1870 he still considered himself 'under the ban of the Evangelical Alliance'. Feelings had obviously run high in 1864, as illustrated by the words of a prominent lay Anglican member of the Alliance, Lord Shaftesbury, who told Spurgeon, 'You are very ignorant; to say the truth, you are a very saucy fellow.' From the Alliance in 1870, however, came a statement that the secretary's letter had never been authorized. Subsequently Spurgeon re-entered the Alliance though evidently retaining his belief that the Alliance could not deal effectively with church issues. Complying with a request to announce at the Tabernacle a week of prayer-meetings organized by the Alliance in London in 1874, Spurgeon noted that the subject for prayer one night would be 'Confessions of the sins of the Churches', upon which he commented, 'If anyone should dare to confess one-half of the darling sins of the Episcopal Church, he would be kicked out of the meeting for his pains!' (cf. *Autobiography*, 3, 86; Pike, 4, 338, and 5, 126.)

'God is a Spirit, and they that worship Him must worship Him in spirit and in truth', he says: 'that one truth, if it were to come with power from heaven into men's minds, would shiver St Peter's and St Paul's from their topmost cross to their lowest crypt.'[24] When he felt called to warn evangelicals who were in the State Church, it was not from any desire to score in public debate, and he invariably maintained a desire for co-operation and unity with such men: 'I can never forget the many gracious and faithful men who remain in this Church, nor can I cease to pray for them. Towards these brethren, as earnest adherents and promulgators of evangelical truth, I sincerely cherish the warmest love . . . May the Providence of God and the power of His Spirit render the way to the visible fellowship of believers more plain.'[25]

[24] 18, 428.
[25] Pike, 4, 372. For some general thoughts on this subject see his shrewd article, 'Unity and how *not* to promote it' in *The Sword and the Trowel*, 1886, 513–18. His last words are: 'Above all, we must not aim at unity by setting ourselves up as *the Church*, and styling all others "sectaries". This is to cement our walls with dynamite, and lay the foundations of peace upon barrels of gunpowder.'

BOOK REVIEW BY C.H.S. FROM
THE SWORD AND THE TROWEL, 1879

Church Principles and Church Comprehensiveness. Two Papers –
one read at the Derby Church Association Conference, and the
other at the Sheffield Congress. With Introduction. By Rev. J. C.
Ryle. London: W. Hunt & Co.

There is no party within the Church of England with whom we are
more nearly agreed than the Evangelical, and yet they excite far
more our wonder and pity than our sympathy. We wonder they are
not ashamed of being connected with men who openly defy the law
and preach the worst form of Popery. We pity them because, while
they remain in the Establishment, their protests against its errors
have but little power. The writer of the present papers is an evangelical champion, for whom we entertain a profound regard. The first of
his papers is a strong protest against the superstitious practices of the
Anglicans; but yet in the second paper he pleads hard for a compre-
hension which shall include believers in doctrines which are dia-
metrically opposed to each other. Such is the sad influence of a false
position. One of the bravest and best of men is found temporizing
in a way which grieves thousands even in his own denomination.
Congresses in which Christ and antichrist are brought together
cannot but exercise a very unhealthy influence even upon the most
decided followers of the truth. We wish Mr Ryle could review his
own position in the light of the Scriptures rather than in the darkness of ecclesiasticism; then would he come out from among them,
and no more touch the unclean thing.

Churches have summers, like our gardens, and then all things are full; but then come their winters, and, alas, what emptyings are seen! Have we not all seen the flood when the tide has come up far upon the beach, and have we not all marked the ebb when every wave has seemed to fall short of that which preceded it? Such ebbs and floods there are in the history of the kingdom of Christ. One day, 'The kingdom of God suffereth violence, and every man presses into it'; at another time men seem to be ashamed of the Christian faith, and they wander off into a thousand delusions, and the church is minished and brought low by heresy, by worldliness, by lukewarmness, and by all sorts of evils.

C.H.S., February 19th, 1882, SERMONS, 28, 110

Long ago I ceased to count heads. Truth is usually in the minority in this evil world. I have faith in the Lord Jesus for myself, a faith burned into me as with a hot iron. I thank God, what I believe I shall believe, even if I believe it alone.

C.H.S., October 16th, 1887, SERMONS, 33, 575

6: The Down-Grade

In the light of his over-all concern for the future of Protestant-ism it might have been expected that Spurgeon would have been prominent in the leadership of the movement which aimed at bringing the Free Church denominations closer together – the movement which resulted in the Manchester Congress of 1892 and which had among its objectives re-sistance to Anglo-Catholicism. But it was not so. Spurgeon not only took no part in these developments but five years before that date he had even withdrawn from his own denom-inational Union. He no longer believed that the Noncon-formist bodies would provide any bulwark against this evil. Few agreed with him. All over the country the coming together of the Free Churches was welcomed with enthusiasm, and thousands of pounds poured into a central fund from the denominations: 'Everywhere the response was indicative of the resolve to make the Christianity of the 20th century simpler and purer, aggressive, unsacerdotal, and free'; so wrote Silvester Horne in 1903.[1] To Spurgeon this expectation was a delusion, and the sermon published in the *Metropolitan Tabernacle Pulpit* for January 17, 1892, conveyed his own outlook under the title, 'Is God in the Camp'?

The explanation of Spurgeon's attitude is to be found in his assessment of the rise of Higher Criticism within the Pro-testant Churches. In many spheres of knowledge the 19th century witnessed spectacular advances: in science, philo-sophy, languages, and history there appeared to be a renais-

[1] *A Popular History of the Free Churches*, C. Silvester Horne, 1903, 425.

sance of learning and a new concern for accuracy and progress. In this effort to advance, traditional concepts were questioned, old sources were critically examined, and genuine progress was made. But if in all these spheres advances were possible, then why should man's spiritual knowledge be static? What gains might be made by Christianity if the Church was willing to adopt a less rigid and less uncritical attitude to the contents of Scripture? Indeed, was not a new approach to the interpretation of Scripture and a new definition of its inspiration essential if Christianity was not to lose touch with the onward march of science? And might it not be the case that some of the 'harder' aspects of Scripture – aspects which were already receiving a diminishing emphasis in preaching – could be explained with greater facility if the old outlook which justified them by reference to the character of God was abandoned?

Questions like these were being asked as early as the 1850's. Nonconformists met with them in the famous 'Rivulet Controversy' of 1856, in which the questionable character of a new book of hymns composed by Thomas Lynch was disputed. They came openly to the fore within the Establishment in 1860 with the publication of *Essays and Reviews*, a volume in which various writers sought to give new expression to truths which had been liable to suffer from 'conventional language and traditional methods of treatment.'

The general attitude to this new spirit in the Church was that it would produce no revolutionary change and that the benefits resulting from a new intellectual emphasis would be gradually assimilated by an unchanged but progressive Faith. Consequently there was a general unwillingness to confront the new teaching: and those who regarded the circulation of the new ideas as an incipient danger found little support. When a serious controversy broke out in the Lancashire Congregational College between two professors over the inspiration of Scripture, it was settled by a compromise in the retirement of both men. A similar failure to deal directly with the issue showed itself in connection with the notorious case of Colenso, Bishop of Natal. For a volume published in 1862, impugning the authenticity of the Pentateuch, Colenso was deposed in South Africa, yet when he returned to England the validity of his deposition was not upheld. This was the kind of thing Spurgeon was referring to in 1864 when he said:

'God's Word, in this age, is a small affair; some do not even believe it to be inspired; and those who profess to revere it set up other books in a sort of rivalry with it. Why, there are great Church dignitaries now-a-days who write against the Bible, and yet find bishops to defend them. "Do not, for a moment, think of condemning their books or them; they are our dear brethren, and must not be fettered in thought." How many days ago is it since a bishop talked in this way in convocation?'[2]

An outstanding attempt to preserve orthodoxy by the use of discipline was in the Free Church of Scotland where W. Robertson Smith, Professor of Old Testament at the Aberdeen College, was dismissed in 1881. But by that time, even in Scotland, the new critical 'appreciation' of Scripture was firmly established, and when Robertson Smith came south to a professorship at Cambridge his views were not regarded as heresy in an influential section of English Presbyterianism. W. G. Elmslie, who had been trained in the Higher Critical approach by A. B. Davidson of Edinburgh, inculcated the same approach to Scripture in the English Presbyterian College and far from regarding the influence of this teaching as producing apostasy he welcomed it as giving 'new light.' This was also the general standpoint of the influential Nonconformist paper, *The British Weekly*, founded in 1886 and edited, as we have noticed earlier, by William Robertson Nicoll.[3]

[2] 10, 372.
[3] The part played by Robertson Nicoll (1851–1923) in the controversies of his day can only be explained in terms of his mistaken belief that the higher critical approach to Scripture is not inimical to the preaching of the gospel:

By the 1880's the new school was dominant in Congregationalism. R. W. Dale had in 1874 declared against the eternal punishment of sinners, preferring the theory of annihilation. He went on to declare that a doctrinal acceptance of the Deity of Christ was not essential to the experience of saving faith in His Person, and in his book *The Living Christ and the Four Gospels* (1890) he argued that Christ is not lost to us though we discard the old belief in the inerrancy of Scripture. Indeed, greater honour, he claimed, was now given to the Saviour. Speaking to ministers Dale declared: 'There is now no authority to come between *us* – to come between the *congregations* to which you and I have to minister, and Him who is the very truth of God.' Alexander MacKennal, the chairman of the autumn session of the Congregational Union in 1887, summed up the new mood when he distinguished between dogma as a final statement, and doctrine which is something always progressing. Congregationalists rejected dogma, but retained doctrine. One of the 'dogmas' they rejected was underlined the next year when R. F. Horton, a minister of 'progressive' views, published his *Inspiration and the Bible*.

It was to this situation that Spurgeon publicly addressed himself in 1887 in the columns of his magazine, *The Sword and the Trowel*. In his first article in August he drew attention to the consequences already attendant upon the new teaching:

'Attendance at places of worship is declining, and reverence for holy things is vanishing; and we solemnly believe this to

he was a warm admirer of Spurgeon's sermons. In the Down-Grade, Nicoll took the opposite side to Spurgeon, yet on a number of occasions in later years he came to observe with deep regret signs of a growing scepticism in the churches. To Professor A. S. Peake he wrote in 1898: 'I am also extremely impressed by the heathenish manner in which certain Nonconformist "Settlements" are carried on. There is, it is true, a certain pretence of Christian teaching, but what is taught is not Christianity.' In 1908 he wrote to Professor H. R. Mackintosh of his concern over the position of James Denney whose theological teaching was popular in Scotland. Denney, he says, 'objects to the statement that Jesus claimed to be God. . . . There is a singular vein of scepticism in him, for all his apparent orthodoxy. For instance, he does not believe in the existence of the devil and of evil spirits. Nor does he believe in the Second Advent'. *William Robertson Nicoll*, 345, 364.

be largely attributable to the scepticism which has flashed from the pulpit and spread among the people. . . . Have these advanced thinkers filled their own chapels? Have they, after all, prospered through discarding the old methods? . . . In meeting-houses holding a thousand, or twelve hundred, or fifteen hundred, places once packed to the ceiling with ardent hearers, how small are the numbers now!'

In closing he raises an issue which others had declined to face: 'It now becomes a serious question how far those who abide by the faith once delivered to the saints should fraternize with those who have turned aside to another gospel. Christian love has its claims, and divisions are to be shunned as grievous evils; but how far are we justified in being in confederacy with those who are departing from the truth?'

In the September magazine Spurgeon continued to press the issue, replying to critics and adding evidence to prove that 'A chasm is opening between the men who believe their Bibles and the men who are prepared for an advance upon Scripture.' The time had come for Christians to stir: 'The house is being robbed, its very walls are being digged down, but the good people who are in bed are too fond of the warmth, and too much afraid of getting broken heads, to go downstairs and meet the burglars. . . . Inspiration and speculation cannot long abide in peace. Compromise there can be none. We cannot hold the inspiration of the Word, and yet reject it; we cannot believe in the atonement and deny it; we cannot hold the doctrine of the fall and yet talk of the evolution of spiritual life from human nature; we cannot recognize the punishment of the impenitent and yet indulge the "larger hope". One way or the other we must go. Decision is the virtue of the hour.'

These words were written shortly before the autumn meetings of the Baptist Union at Sheffield and Spurgeon evidently hoped for action. S. H. Booth, the secretary of the Union, had already consulted on several occasions with Spurgeon, expressing his concern at the decline in orthodoxy and furnishing Spurgeon with facts. Before the meetings Spurgeon had written, 'We trust that the Baptists are by no means so far gone as the Independents: indeed, we feel sure that they are not.' Later he had to admit, 'The error in the Baptist denomination is ten times more widely spread than we knew of . . . We did not at first aim at the Baptist body, for we thought most hopefully of it, but the controversy has revealed what we little dreamt of.'[4] The truth is that at Sheffield the 'Down-Grade' question was entirely avoided. On October 28th, Spurgeon withdrew from the Union, and in the November, 1887, issue of *The Sword and the Trowel* he gave his reason. The Union was preferring denominational peace to the duty of dealing with error and thus, by tolerating sin, they made the withdrawal of Christians unavoidable:

'Believers in Christ's atonement are now in declared union with those who make light of it; believers in Holy Scripture are in confederacy with those who deny plenary inspiration; those who hold evangelical doctrine are in open alliance with those who call the fall a fable, who deny the personality of the Holy Ghost, who call justification by faith immoral, and hold that there is another probation after death. . . . Yes, we have before us the wretched spectacle of professedly orthodox Christians publicly avowing their union with those who deny the faith, and scarcely concealing their contempt for those who cannot be guilty of such gross disloyalty to Christ. To be very plain, we are unable to call these things Christian Unions, they begin to look like Confederacies in Evil. . . .

'It is our solemn conviction that where there can be no real spiritual communion there should be no pretence of fellowship. *Fellowship with known and vital error is participation in sin.*'

After Spurgeon's resignation the controversy as it was linked with Spurgeon's own relationship to the Union took the following course. In November, 1887, when he was in

[4] *Sword and Trowel*, 1888, 249.

Mentone, he explained in correspondence with ministers belonging to the Pastor's College Conference, that his decision
to leave was not a sudden one; it came rather, he says, after
'my private remonstrances to officials, and my repeated
pointed appeals to the whole body, had been of no avail'.[5]
Nevertheless when the Council of the Baptist Union met on
December 13th, the officers, and notably S. H. Booth, the
secretary denied having received from Spurgeon any charge
of laxity of faith 'such as would have justified them in laying
it before the Council'.[6] The Council considered that the
scriptural procedure was to seek a personal interview with
Spurgeon. Spurgeon was amazed at Booth's denial: the
latter's protest that he had received, as secretary, no *formal*
charge from Spurgeon was an evasion, for he and others had
ample knowledge of Spurgeon's mind long before his resignation. Distrust grew on Spurgeon's side and he had no
respect for the so-called 'scriptural' procedure advocated:
'What a farce about my seeing these brethren, privately,
according to Matt. xviii. 15! Why, I saw the Secretary and the
President again and again; and then I printed my plaint, and
only left the Union when nothing could be done. Now,
something will be done. Not until I took the decided step
could I effect anything.'[7] At this point Spurgeon could have
summarily proved the extent of his prior consultation with
Union officials by producing correspondence from Booth, but
Booth privately insisted that these were confidential and
should not be disclosed. Spurgeon's assent to Booth's wish
was magnanimous, especially as the December 13th meeting
had cast doubt upon Spurgeon's honesty by apparently denying that any such communications had taken place. In general
terms Spurgeon cleared himself of this aspersion in a letter to
The Baptist on December 19th, 1887.[8]

[5] Pike, 6, 290.   [6] ibid., 292.   [7] *Autobiography*, 4, 256.
[8] Pike, 6, 292–293. To the co-pastor and deacons at the Tabernacle he wrote
from Mentone, 'It is not possible for me to communicate to anyone all that has

146

When Spurgeon returned from Mentone, four doctors of divinity, deputed by the Council, met him at the Tabernacle on January 13th, 1888. The purpose of this meeting, as stated in a telegram of the Council's to Spurgeon, was 'to deliberate with you how the unity of our denomination in truth, and love, and good works may be maintained'. To this point Spurgeon gave his visitors a straight answer, namely, that the object could only be achieved by the adoption of a definite evangelical basis of faith (such as that of the Evangelical Alliance), the existing basis being no more than the belief that 'the immersion of believers is the only Christian baptism'. But Spurgeon felt that there was a subsidiary and unstated purpose in the visit of the Council's representatives; he feared it might be designed to fix on him 'the odium of being implacable'[9] and this suspicion was confirmed in his own mind when, a week later, the Council on January 18th, having heard from the deputation that Spurgeon would not withdraw his resignation, proceeded to pass a vote of 'censure' upon him. His charges of doctrinal laxity, being unsupported by the names of those whom he considered offending parties, 'ought not to have been made'.[10]

This action on the Council's part, before they had dealt with his appeal for the drawing up of an evangelical basis, confirmed Spurgeon in his view that it was hopeless to expect firm action: 'I would like all Christendom to know,' he wrote in *The Sword and the Trowel* in February, 'that all I asked of the Union is that it be formed on a Scriptural basis.'[11] It remained to be seen how the Union itself at its Assembly in April would deal with the issues which the restricted membership of the Council had so far debated. The Council at a meeting on February 21st adopted a declaration to be presented to the Assembly and many considered that this would

passed under my knowledge; but I have had abundant reason for every step I have taken, as the day of days will reveal.' *Autobiography*, 4, 261. On the correspondence with Booth, cf. Carlile, 247–51.

[9] *Autobiography*, 4, 258.   [10] Carlile, 251.   [11] 1888, 82.

provide grounds for reunion. On the face of it the document was evangelical – in fact not far removed from the basis of the Evangelical Alliance. But Spurgeon, who was apparently allowed to see it in confidence before April, entirely distrusted it.[12] His attitude at this point needs clarifying for at first sight it seems as though, having asked for an evangelical basis, he was not satisfied when one was presented. Says Carlile: 'while at the beginning Spurgeon asked for a simple declaration of what the Baptist Union taught, some of his later utterances gave the impression that he wanted a definite theological authority'. The explanation is that Spurgeon was dissatisfied with the whole spirit in which the declaration was drawn up. He wrote to *The Baptist*:

'Whatever the Council does, let it above all things avoid the use of language which could legitimately have two meanings contrary to each other. Let us be plain and outspoken. *There are grave differences* – let them be avowed honestly. Why should any man be ashamed to do so? Policy must not be our guide, nor the wish to retain this party or that. Right is safe, and compromise by the use of double meanings can never in the long run be wise.'[13]

This was almost precisely the policy which the Council did not follow. Spurgeon had asked them for a resolution which would set forth 'that it rejected the dream of future probation and restoration as unscriptural';[14] instead the statement on future judgment clearly left room, in its own words, for 'brethren in the Union' who did not hold 'the common interpretation'. Spurgeon wanted a declaration which would be a real means of finding out the respective numbers of those standing for the old faith and those advocating the new:[15] such a test and consequent disruption the strong middle party in the Council desperately wanted to avoid. Spurgeon

[12] Pike, 6, 296.　　　　[13] *Sword and Trowel*, 1888, 148.
[14] ibid., 1888, 91.
[15] *Sword and Trowel*, 1888, 198.

sought a basis which, as far as possible, would not permit men to 'say one thing and mean another', a basis which would decidedly answer the question, 'Is the Union an assemblage of evangelical churches, or is it an indiscriminate collection of communities practising immersion?'[16] Writing for *The Sword and the Trowel* before the April Assembly, Spurgeon expressed his pessimism on the outcome; the denominational body, while not wanting to refuse the demand that it should declare its faith, 'balances sentences, discusses everything except the main question, and proffers a base imitation of a declaration in lieu of that which is sought from it. Writing before the Annual Meeting,' he continues, 'we write hopelessly. . . . What is said of us is nothing; but shall truth be sold to keep up a wider fellowship?'[17]

These words did not appear in print until after the Assembly was over. If they had appeared earlier there might have been a slight alteration in the voting figures, but as it is, the extraordinary fact must go down in history that when the adoption of the Council's 'evangelical' declaration was put to the vote it was accepted by 2,000 votes against 7! Without question a number of evangelicals voting could not have understood what they were voting about: both they and the liberals thought the motion was to their advantage and Spurgeon's own brother, James, who seconded it, regarded the vote as 'a great victory'.[18] Few saw it in the same light as Spurgeon, they naively thought that with such a massive vote for 'the Gospel' the controversy over the evangelical standing of the Union 'was closed for ever'.[19] For Spurgeon, far from being a basis for reunion it but confirmed him in his conviction that his resignation must be irrevocable. His comments

[16] Pike, 6, 294.   [17] *Sword and Trowel*, 1888, 249.
[18] 'My brother thinks he has gained a great victory, but I believe we are hopelessly sold. I feel heart-broken. Certainly he has done the very opposite of what I should have done. Yet he is not to be blamed, for he followed his best judgment. Pray for me, that my faith fail not.' C.H.S. in a letter to a personal friend on April 26th, quoted in Fullerton, 313.
[19] Pike, 6, 301.

in *The Sword and the Trowel* for June, on the Assembly's adoption of the declaration tell us his feelings:

'The resolution, with its footnote, with the interpretation of its mover, and the re-election of the old council, fairly represent the utmost that would be done when everybody was in his best humour. Is it satisfactory? Does anybody understand it in the same sense as anybody else? Does not the whole virtue of the thing lie in its pleasing both sides a little? And is not this the vice and the condemnation of it?

'I am not, however, careful to criticize the action of a body from which I am now finally divided. My course has been made clear by what has been done. I was afraid from the beginning that the reform of the Baptist Union was hopeless, and therefore I resigned. I am far more sure of it now, and should never under any probable circumstances dream of returning'.[20]

We conclude this brief narrative of the Down-Grade controversy with the words of an eye-witness who was present at the Assembly meetings on that memorable April 23rd, 1888. Henry Oakley wrote the following words in 1934 and from that vantage point in history he saw the overwhelming vote of the Union for what it was – an implied censure on the position Spurgeon had taken up, but it needs to be understood that many were far from seeing it in that light at the time:

'I was present at the City Temple when the motion was moved, seconded, and carried. Possibly the City Temple was as full as it could be. I was there very early, but found only a "standing seat" in the aisle of the back gallery. I listened to the speeches. The only one of which I have any distinct remembrance was that of Mr Charles Williams. He quoted Tennyson in favour of a liberal theology and justification of doubt. The moment of voting came. Only those in the area were qualified to vote as members of the assembly. When the

[20] *Sword and Trowel*, 1888, 299.

motion of censure was put, a forest of hands went up. "Against," called the chairman, Dr Clifford. I did not see any hands, but history records that there were *seven*. Without any announcement of numbers the vast assembly broke into tumultuous cheering, and cheering and cheering yet. From some of the older men their pent-up hostility found vent; from many of the younger men wild resistance of "any obscurantist trammels,' as they said, broke loose. It was a strange scene. I viewed it almost with tears. I stood near a "Spurgeon's man," whom I knew very well. Mr Spurgeon had welcomed him from a very lowly position. He went wild almost with delight at this censure of his great and generous master. I say it was a strange scene, that that vast assembly should be so outrageously delighted at the condemnation of the greatest, noblest, and grandest leader of their faith.'[21]

[21] *The Witness*, 1934. Reprinted in the July-September, 1934 issue of *Our Outlook*, from which source I quote. E. J. Poole-Connor, who died in 1962 and who wrote one of the few faithful 20th-century accounts of the Down-Grade, is mistaken when he says that the resolution which put the basis of faith to the Assembly was understood to be a censure on Spurgeon 'and that it was on this understanding they voted in favour of it'. *Evangelicalism in England*, 1951, 248. Some could not have seen at the time that there was in the adoption of this inadequate basis and declaration of 'the evangelical character of the churches of the Union' a censure on Spurgeon's action, cf. *Autobiography*, 4, 255. The Down-Grade has put subsequent writers on Spurgeon to a test which few have come through creditably: Pike seeks to give an objective record, but writing near the time there was much he left unsaid. Fullerton and Carlile show little theological insight and both are inaccurate. Fullerton dates Spurgeon's letter of resignation from the Union October 8th, instead of October 28th, 1887, and Carlile is a year out in his dating of Spurgeon's meeting with the four doctors of divinity on January 13th, 1888.

It is a great grief to me that hitherto many of our most honoured friends in the Baptist Union have, with strong determination, closed their eyes to serious divergencies from truth. I doubt not that their motive has been in a measure laudable, for they desired to preserve peace, and hoped that errors, which they were forced to see, would be removed as their friends advanced in years and knowledge.

But at last even these will, I trust, discover that the new views are not the old truth in a better dress, but deadly errors with which we can have no fellowship. I regard full-grown 'modern thought' as a totally new cult, having no more relation to Christianity than the mist of the evening to the everlasting hills.

C.H.S., November 23rd, 1887, PIKE, 6. 291

Let us see to it that we set forth our Lord Jesus Christ as the infallible Teacher, *through His inspired Word. I do not understand that loyalty to Christ which is accompanied by indifference to His words. How can we reverence His person, if His own words and those of His apostles are treated with disrespect? Unless we receive Christ's words, we cannot receive Christ; unless we receive His apostles' words, we do not receive Christ; for John saith, 'He that knoweth God heareth us; he that is not of God heareth not us. Hereby know we the spirit of truth, and the spirit of error.'*

C.H.S., AN ALL-ROUND MINISTRY, 373

7: The Down-Grade and its Lessons

There are many aspects from which the Down-Grade controversy can be studied. The one we are here concerned with is the question of denominational loyalty and this was central to the whole controversy. There were undoubtedly genuine evangelical Baptists who would have been glad to see the spreading error arrested, but to achieve this at the cost of the disruption of the Union was a possibility they could not bring themselves to face. Booth, the Secretary, was typical of those who at the crisis drew back, and as has been said, "Booth no doubt believed until the last that Spurgeon would not withdraw from the Union.' When Spurgeon now spoke plainly against the condition of Nonconformity, he was chided for giving material to Anglicans to strengthen their position. In Spurgeon's statements, observed one critical Nonconformist, Anglicans generally found abundant evidence of the decadence of evangelical truth in Free Church communities. But Spurgeon now held to what he had declared more than twenty years before in the great controversy of 1864:

'Whether it be the Baptist Church, or the Episcopalian, or the Presbyterian Church which errs from Christ's way, it is nothing to any one of us which it may be; it is Christ we are to care for, and Christ's truth, and this we are to follow over all the hedges and ditches of men's making.'[1]

At the very outset of the Down-Grade controversy Spurgeon declared that what evangelicals had to meet was a 'policy which would urge us to subordinate the maintenance of truth

[1] 10, 372.

153

to denominational prosperity and unity.'[2] And there can be little doubt that the ultimate human reason for his failure to obtain disciplinary action was the strength of this policy. As Dr Payne writes, the factor which retained the multitude in the Union which he left was that 'the great majority of Baptists had come to regard a national organization of their churches as essential to their well-being.' 'In the early stages of the controversy Spurgeon had perhaps failed to realize the way in which the Union had rooted itself in the life of the Churches.'[3] The pastor of the Metropolitan Tabernacle might counsel the duty of withdrawal, but, continues the same writer: 'For the minister of the average Baptist church the situation was different. The Augmentation and Annuity Funds, Home Missions and the Board of Introduction were drawing together and supplementing the resources of the individual churches, carrying out tasks they could not otherwise fulfil.'

In other words, a Union originally intended as a fellowship to propagate the truth, was now unwilling to check error which sapped the vitals of the Gospel, and yet it was a power (from which many could not easily extricate themselves) holding together congregations whose only avowed agreement consisted in their common view of baptism.

Before the end of 1887, Spurgeon came to question the whole character of the Union, as he believed that the flimsy nature of its original foundations had been thoroughly exposed:

'The Union, as at present constituted, has no disciplinary power, for it has no doctrinal basis whatever, and we see no reason why every form of belief and misbelief should not be comprehended in it so long as immersion only is acknowledged as baptism. There is no use in blaming the Union for harbouring errors of the extremist kind, for, so far as we can see, it is powerless to help itself, if it ever wished to do so. Those who originally founded it made it "without form and

[2] *Sword and Trowel*, 1887, 400.
[3] E. A. Payne, *The Baptist Union: A Short History*, 1958, cf. 127–143.

void", and so it must remain. At least we do not see any likelihood of a change. A large number have this state of things in admiration, and will go on with it; we have no such admiration, and therefore have ceased from it. . .[4]

'Every Union, unless it is a mere fiction, must be based upon certain principles. How can we unite except upon some great common truths? And the doctrine of baptism by immersion is not sufficient for a ground-work. Surely, to be a Baptist is not everything. If I disagree with a man on ninety-nine points, but happen to be one with him in baptism, this can never furnish such ground of unity as I have with another with whom I believe in ninety-nine points, and only happen to differ upon one ordinance . . . To alter the foundation of a building is a difficult undertaking. Underpinning is expensive and perilous work. It might be more satisfactory to take the whole house down, and reconstruct it. If I had believed that the Baptist Union could be made a satisfactory structure, I could not then have remained in it; because to do so would have violated my conscience. But *my* conscience is no guide for others. Those who believe in the structure, and think that they can rectify its foundation, have my hearty sympathy in the attempt.'[5]

Later, in July, 1889, he spoke even more decidedly: 'The day will come when those who think they can repair a house which has no foundations will see the wisdom of quitting it altogether. All along we have seen that to come out from association with questionable doctrines is the only possible solution of a difficulty which, however it may be denied, is not to be trifled with by those who are conscious of its terrible reality.'[6]

The Down-Grade controversy did not arrest the apostasy

[4] *Sword and Trowel*, 1887, 560. In a letter to Dr Culross on November 26th, 1887, he writes: 'The good men who formed the Union, I fancy, had no idea that it would become what it now is, or they would have fashioned it otherwise. It has, by its centralization and absorption of various societies, become far other than at the first. This is a good thing, but it involves a strain on the frail fabric which it is ill adapted to bear.' *Autobiography*, 4, 263.

[5] *Sword and Trowel*, 1888, 82–3.   [6] ibid., 1889, 389–90.

in Nonconformity; rather it gave concrete evidence of the existence of new attitudes – attitudes which were to dominate the Free Church denominations for several generations to come. We may describe some of these attitudes as follows:

1. An unwillingness to define precisely any doctrinal issue, a readiness to reduce what constitutes the content of orthodox Christianity to a minimum, and a 'charity' which made men unwilling to question the standing of any denomination in the sight of God so long as it *professed* the 'Evangelical Faith'. The Congregational Union, while error was becoming widespread amongst its ministers, had made such a profession at its 1877 Assembly, affirming the loyalty of Congregationalists to 'The Evangelical Faith revealed in the Holy Scriptures'. When, as we have already seen, the Baptist Union made a similar declaration, coupled with a brief list of six doctrines, at its April Assembly in 1888, there were few who stood with Spurgeon when he regarded this profession of the Union as useless.

As we look back now on the last decades of the 19th century we cannot exonerate orthodox ministers who allowed the term 'evangelical' to become debased: they had not the strength to declare that men were not ministers of Christ who, while professing the 'Evangelical Faith', either never preached that Faith or practically repudiated it in the details of their teaching. This compromise was the start of a process which has since often made the word 'evangelical' a cover for doctrinal laxity. The present century is full of examples of the evil which has resulted from this perversion of terminology. For instance, we read that when the advanced liberal, Arthur S. Peake, was appointed to the Methodist College at Manchester – a college which 'had stood for the most rigid orthodoxy' – the students came to recognize in their new teacher 'a unique combination of the higher critic and the evangelist; while he led them into unexplored fields of knowledge they were not less amazed at his evangelical fervour.' This kind of use of the term 'evangelical', which the authors of a book on *The Methodist Church* applied to Peake in 1932, is by no means unique. As for the Baptist denomination, we are told concerning T. R. Glover (1869–1943) that 'those who knew him best were aware of the depth of his evangelical experience';[7] yet it was Glover who spent a considerable part of his life attempting an intellectual demolition of historic Christianity, and who, in 1932, gloried in the fact that there were no colleges left adhering to the position of the old evangelical confessions. It may be surprising that at this date, when men like Glover were given such honour in the Baptist Union, another Baptist, J. C. Carlile, could write, 'The denomination is today more Evangelical in spirit than at any period of its history',[8] but this is only indicative of the extent to which spiritual confusion and obscurity had come to prevail in England before the Second World War. Henry Oakley, writing at the same time as Carlile, was a lone voice when he said: 'The Baptist Union ceased to be a union of likeminded men and churches, and became the union of men and churches widely separated in faith and practice – a kind of theological Woolworth's, where variety is the principal thing. All that Mr Spurgeon saw, and much more, has come to pass.'[9]

2. The Down-Grade movement revealed that the Scriptures were no longer the rule of faith and practice within Nonconformity.

Spurgeon acted decisively because he believed it was the only course consistent with the Word of God. But many would not recognize this. They could not see that 'the prince of the power of the air is loosed in an extraordinary manner

[7] A. C. Underwood, *A History of the English Baptists*, 1947, 258.
[8] *C. H. Spurgeon: An Interpretative Biography*, 257.
[9] Quoted in *Our Outlook*, 1934, 51. Oakley wrote a good deal on the spiritual condition of the Baptist Union; his charges were too true to be answered, but the tide was so strong against the position he represented that his words were probably read by few.

for a season, misleading even the godly, and triumphing greatly in those whose willing minds yield full assent to his deceitful teachings.'[10] Consequently they were not ready to apply the New Testament's instructions concerning resistance to demonic influences. They discerned that the Higher Criticism was modifying the doctrinal content of the old confessions, but to say that the liberals were introducing 'another gospel' and that 'there is an essential difference in spirit between the old believer and the man of new and advancing views,'[11] was more than they could bring themselves to do. The denominational association with those known to be either sympathizers with or advocates of the new teaching, men whose faith was paraded as eminently 'Christocentric', was also a powerful factor in blurring the issues. Would it not be a breach in unity to separate from those who had been baptized and who shared in the same denominational life? Some with more discernment could see that fellowship with the new school of liberals was wrong, but if the liberals were only a minority, why should the orthodox leave the Union in their hands by withdrawing from it? And as each congregation belonging to the Union was able to preserve its own faith and self-government, was there any compromise involved in staying within?

The tragedy of the Down-Grade was that there were many who could not see that Scripture spoke definitely on the existing situation. Spurgeon was in a lonely position, because unlike most of his fellow-ministers, he saw the main points clearly:

For Christians to be linked in association with ministers who do not preach the gospel of Christ is to incur moral guilt.

A Union which can continue irrespective of whether its member churches belong to a common faith is not fulfilling any scriptural function.

The preservation of a denominational association when it is

[10] *Sword and Trowel*, 1888, 160.   [11] ibid., 1888, 610.

powerless to discipline heretics cannot be justified on the grounds of the preservation of 'Christian unity'.

It is error which breaks the unity of churches, and to remain in a denominational alignment which condones error is to support schism.

'As to a breach of unity,' says Spurgeon in reply to the charge often brought against him, 'nothing has ever more largely promoted the union of the true than the break with the false.'[12] An article in *The Sword and the Trowel*, entitled 'Separation not Schism', takes up the same point: 'Separation from such as connive at fundamental error, or withhold the "Bread of life" from perishing souls, is not schism, but only what truth, and conscience, and God require of all who would be found faithful.'[13]

The crisis at the end of the last century revealed the weaknesses in the foundations of the Unions which had been established earlier in the century. The founders of the Unions had been concerned with the immediate practical benefits of closer association between congregations of the same church polity. They had not concerned themselves so much with the long-term prospect. They had largely given up the Puritan endeavour to see the unity of Christ's Body, which is the Church, being visibly manifested throughout the nation, and resigned themselves for the time being at least, to the preservation of their own distinctive principles within denominations. Necessary though this may have been, it was an expedient rather than a fully Scriptural course, for the permanent separation of Christians, that is, those who are faithful to the one apostolic Gospel, can hardly be justified simply in terms of differences over the externals of church polity. The New Testament does not minimize the importance of sound church order and government, but whatever the difficulties connected with the subject, it can never be conceded that the Scripture warrants the permanent division of *true* churches,

[12] *Sword and Trowel*, 1888, 249.   [13] ibid., 1888, 127.

existing in the same geographical locality, into distinct groups. As, however, the prestige and strength of the Nonconformist denominations developed during the last century, the consideration became obscured that no man could equate his denomination with the one Church of the New Testament, and the confusion developed to the point where leaving a denomination was treated as though it meant leaving 'the Church.' Thus the liberals castigated Spurgeon's withdrawal from the Union as 17th-century Bishops had denounced Puritans – as though he had committed some offence. 'Those who are so exceedingly liberal, large-hearted, and broad,' Spurgeon observed, 'might be so good as to allow us to forego the charms of their society without coming under the full violence of their wrath.'[14] Others of more orthodox persuasion were far too confused in their own minds over the relationship between loyalty to denomination and loyalty to Scripture, either to censure Spurgeon or to agree with him. They were caught in a paralysis of indecision and fell easy victims to a policy of expediency.

3. The Down-Grade controversy showed a readiness on the part of many ministers to justify their lack of firm action on the grounds of the greater good to be gained by a more accommodating policy. This was the attitude of those who sympathized with Spurgeon's concern, but regretted his withdrawal as they balanced it over against the influence he might have exerted had he stayed in the Union. Newspapers reflected the same outlook. *The Scotsman* asked, 'Ought he not rather to remain within it, and use all his great influence to stay it on its downward course?' Likewise *The Standard* of Chicago, 'Better to resist all this drift, so far as it exists, where we are face to face with it, than from any position outside.'[15]

This argument was not new to Spurgeon. Preaching from Daniel, chapter 6, in 1868, and referring to the probable temptation which came to Daniel in the form of a suggestion

[14] *Sword and Trowel*, 1888, 620.　[15] Pike, 6, 288.

that he would be of more assistance to true religion if he adopted a prudent policy and stayed alive in Darius's Court, Spurgeon declared: 'That argument I have heard hundreds of times when people have been urged to come out of false positions and do the right. But what have you and I to do with maintaining our influence and position at the expense of truth? It is never right to do a little wrong to obtain the greatest possible good. . . . Your duty is to do the right: consequences are with God.'[16] There is no doubt that in the Down-Grade controversy, Spurgeon was well aware (without the advice of 'judicious' friends and newspapers) that his decision to stand against the prevailing current of opinion might greatly weaken his position as a leader. In the months of comparative isolation following his withdrawal from the Union in October, 1887, he had plenty of time to observe that he was not carrying men with him as in former days, but he was convinced that a Scriptural principle was involved which placed all personal considerations out of the reckoning. 'I care for no man and for no newspaper, but only for God,' he told an assembly of pastors in April, 1888. Later in the same year a short passage from his pen in *The Sword and the Trowel* narrates a temptation which he may himself well have felt at this crisis:

'Failure at a crucial moment may mar the entire outcome of a life. A man who has enjoyed special light is made bold to follow in the way of the Lord, and is anointed to guide others therein. He rises into a place of love and esteem among the godly, and this promotes his advancement among men. What then? The temptation comes to be careful of the position he has gained, and to do nothing to endanger it. The man, so lately a faithful man of God, compromises with worldlings, and to quiet his own conscience invents a theory by which such compromises are justified and even commended. He receives the praises of 'the judicious'; he has, in truth, gone over to the enemy. The whole force of his former life now tells upon the wrong side. . . . To avoid such an end it becomes us ever to stand fast.'[17]

In 1891, the last year of his life, there was another sermon from the Book of Daniel, this time on the resolution of Daniel's three companions who were thrown into the fiery furnace for their refusal to submit to Nebuchadnezzar. In the first division of the sermon he lists the kind of excuses the three men might have used to justify a compliance which would have kept them out of the furnace. They might have said, 'We can do more good by living,' dying would 'cut short our opportunities of usefulness.' Upon which Spurgeon enlarges:

'Ah, my dear brethren! there are many that are deceived by this method of reasoning. They remain where their conscience tells them they ought not to be, because, they say, they are more useful than they would be if they went "without the camp". This is doing evil that good may come, and can never be tolerated by an enlightened conscience. If an act of sin would increase my usefulness tenfold, I have no right to do it; and if an act of righteousness would appear likely to destroy all my apparent usefulness, I am yet to do it. It is yours and mine to do the right though the heavens fall, and follow the command of Christ whatever the consequences may be. "That is strong meat," do you say? Be strong men, then, and feed thereon . . .

> *For right is right, since God is God,*
> *And right the day must win;*
> *To doubt would be disloyalty,*
> *To falter would be sin.*'[18]

The Down-Grade struggle was one which Spurgeon was not to outlive. After spending the first weeks of 1891 at Mentone in the sunny south of France – a place which had

[17] *Sword and Trowel*, 1888, 620.   [18] 37, 426.

long been his favourite retreat when health fled him – Spurgeon was back in the London frosts and fogs by February and continued his regular daily work until Sunday, May 17th, when he was overtaken by sickness and pain before the evening service. After what was wrongly diagnosed as an attack of influenza he did not preach again until the morning of Sunday, June 7th, and this service proved to be the end of the thirty-eight years of ministry in the congregation which, since that far-off spring in 1854, had encircled him with their love and prayers. The following week he spent in his beloved Essex among the scenes of his childhood, his object being to guide a photographer who was to take pictures for inclusion in his little book, *Memories of Stambourne*. Men said of James Spurgeon, the old Independent minister of Stambourne, that after being a martyr to gout in middle life, he later got over the malady and lived to the age of ninety. The hope was that his grandson might have the same experience. But it was not to be. Besides gout he now had a deadly disease in his kidneys. Returning to London, there were three months of desperate illness before he could take a few steps in the warmth of September sunshine. Of reading, writing and thinking he could now do little, though the burdens of the controversy of the past five years were still upon his heart, Standing on the platform at Herne Hill station on October 26th, 1891, before he went to Mentone for the last time, his parting words to his friends were, 'The fight is killing me.'

Yet at the Hotel Beau-Rivage, Mentone, where he stayed with Mrs Spurgeon, he still hoped for a return of strength to end his 'dumb Sabbaths'. On the last evening of the year and on January 1, 1892, when, though disease of his kidneys was far advanced there was a deceptive appearance of returning health, he gave two addresses to a company in his bedroom. The next day he wrote to Archibald Brown: 'Debtors to free and sovereign grace, we will together sing to our Redeeming Lord, world without end.' His last song on earth was in the words of Samuel Rutherford in the hymn, 'The sands of time are sinking', sung at the close of a short bedroom service on January 17th. By the end of that week Spurgeon had said to his faithful friend and secretary, J. W. Harrald,[19] 'My work is done.' The greater part of the last week in January was spent in unconsciousness until, in the last hour of the last day of the month, he went across the shining bridge to glory. His personal testimony to the Gospel of his Saviour was complete. Years before he had testified:

'Ah! the bridge of grace will bear your weight, brother. Thousands of big sinners have gone across that bridge, yea, tens of thousands have gone over it. I can hear their trampings now as they traverse the great arches of the bridge of salvation. They come by their thousands, by their myriads; e'er since the day when Christ first entered into His glory, they come, and yet never a stone has sprung in that mighty bridge. Some have been the chief of sinners, and some have come at the very last of their days, but the arch has never yielded beneath their weight. I will go with them trusting to the same support; it will bear me over as it has borne them.'

On Monday, February 1st, on the railings outside the Metropolitan Tabernacle there were fixed printed copies of the telegram which told the news:

[19] J. W. Harrald, born at Bury St Edmunds in 1849, was himself a minister of the gospel and able to fill the Tabernacle pulpit if need arose. Theologically he was of one mind with Spurgeon. From the spring of 1878 onwards he devoted his literary and shorthand gifts in the post of private secretary. The value of this indispensable and unfailing service appears to have been overlooked by the Spurgeon biographers but in his slender life of *Joseph William Harrald*, A. Harwood Field is probably not exaggerating when he says: 'With the death of his beloved chief Mr Harrald lost the zest of living. He had lived for Spurgeon, thought for him, acted for him, been strength for him'. It was largely due to Harrald that Spurgeon's sermons continued to be revised as carefully for the press in the twenty years following his death as they had been before. While in the act of revising one such sermon, Harrald was quietly called home to Christ on July 1st, 1912. Thereafter others prepared from the diminishing stores of manuscripts the weekly Spurgeon sermon until the great series terminated in 1917. Spurgeon's other secretary and literary assistant was J. L. Keys (died 1899), through whose hands all Spurgeon's publications passed from 1867 to 1891. *Autobiography*, 3, 201.

'Mentone 11.50

Spurgeon's Tabernacle, London.

Our beloved pastor entered heaven, 11.5 Sunday night. Harrald.'

A week later the coffin, bearing the earthly remains, stood in silent state in the Tabernacle with a simple inscription, the relevance of which those who had stood with him in the Down-Grade could understand:

In Loving Memory of

CHARLES HADDON SPURGEON

Born at Kelvedon, June 19th, 1834.

Fell asleep in Jesus on Sunday, January 31st, 1892.

'I Have Fought A Good Fight, I Have Finished

My Course, I Have Kept The Faith.'

The opinion became current that Spurgeon had used Paul's verse as his own last words, but his 'armour-bearer', J. W. Harrald, who was with him to the end, denied it: 'He did not utter them: it would have been contrary to the whole spirit of his life for him to have done so; he had far too humble an opinion of his own work, and worth to use the inspired language.'[20]

[20] *Sword and Trowel*, 1892, 131.

On February 5, 1882, preaching on the words, 'From that time many of his disciples went back, and walked no more with him' (John 6:66), Spurgeon said:

The defection in this case was on account of doctrine ... The truth was too hard for them, it was not to be borne with. 'It is a hard saying. Who can hear it?' A true disciple sits at the feet of his Master, and believes what he is told even when he cannot quite comprehend the meaning, or see the reasons for what his Master utters; but these men had not the essential spirit of a disciple, and consequently when their Instructor began to unfold the innermost parts of the roll of truth, they would not listen to His reading of it. They would believe as far as they could understand, but when they could not comprehend they turned on their heel and left the school of the Great Teacher. Besides, the Lord Jesus Christ had taught the doctrine of the sovereignty of God, and of the need of the Spirit of God, that men should be led to Him, 'for Jesus knew from the beginning who they were that believed not, and who should betray him. And he said, Therefore said I unto you, that no man can come unto me, except it were given unto him of my Father.' Here our Lord uttered a bit of old-fashioned free-grace doctrine, such as people nowadays do not like. They call it 'Calvinism', and put it aside among the old exploded tenets which this enlightened age knows nothing of. What right they have to ascribe to the Genevan reformer a doctrine old as the hills I do not know. But our Lord Jesus never hesitated to fling that truth into the face of His enemies. He told them, 'Ye believe not because ye are not of my sheep, as I said unto you.' 'No man can come to me, except the Father which hath sent me draw him.' Here he tells them plainly that they could not come unto Him unless the Father gave them the grace to come. This humbling doctrine they could not receive, and so they went aside.

C.H.S., SERMONS, 28, 111–2

8: Free Grace and the Down-Grade in Perspective

We have sought in the preceding pages to trace Spurgeon's convictions in the three main controversies of his life – the controversy arising out of his strong proclamation of Gospel 'Calvinism' in the New Park Street ministry, the Baptismal Regeneration controversy of 1864, and finally the Down-Grade which drained the energies of his closing years. Contemporary and later writers have alike expressed regret that Spurgeon should have given his strength to these disputes: 'It pains me unspeakably,' said John Clifford in 1888, 'to see this eminent "winner of souls" rousing the energies of thousands of Christians to engage in personal wrangling and strife, instead of inspiring them, as he might, to sustained and heroic effort to carry the good news of God's Gospel to our fellow-countrymen.'[1] Spurgeon, the controversialist, was not the true Spurgeon, argued Clifford. And as a rule these three controversies have been very superficially treated (if treated at all) on the grounds that they do not represent the 'real' Spurgeon: at New Park Street he was young and his views immature, or, in the Down-Grade he was ill and lapsing in his judgment!

This is certainly a summary way of dealing with controversial subjects, but it is directly opposed to the deepest convictions of Spurgeon himself to whom these three controversies were major events in his long ministry. Undoubtedly he regarded the issues at stake as of vital significance to Protestantism and to the future welfare of England, for he saw the

[1] Pike, 6, 297.

bearings of the subjects which were in dispute casting shadows far into the future – 'trimming now, and debasing doctrine now, will affect children yet unborn, generation after generation'.[2] The antithesis which Clifford drew between evangelism and controversy was utterly false.

Spurgeon never moved from the belief expressed so forcefully in his early ministry that the doctrines of grace are the only basis for sound evangelism and a Biblical faith, and for the sake of clarity in debate he was prepared to accept the common designation of these doctrines as Calvinism. From this position he never withdrew. An announcement in the *Brighton Examiner* in 1859 that he was giving up his Calvinistic doctrines drew forth the reply: 'The statement you have made with regard to my recantation of Calvinistic doctrine is a fabrication from beginning to end. . . . I am the same in doctrine as I have ever been, and I hope to remain faithful to the same grand truth until death.'[3] In 1884, he could still declare: 'If all men that live or ever shall live should throw up the old Calvinism, there remains one that will hold it, for this reason – that he could not hold any other. I must be crushed out of existence before my convictions of the truth of the doctrines of grace in the old-fashioned form can ever be taken from me.'[4]

Admittedly when Spurgeon had a more settled congregation at the Metropolitan Tabernacle, where he preached for thirty-one years, certain of the emphases of his New Park Street and Surrey Music Hall days were not so prominent, and the blending of the Calvinism in the all-roundness of his ministry was more maturely exercised than formerly. But if the mode of its presentation was refined, the doctrine was unaltered; the same convictions underlay all his preaching, and instead of thinking he had gone too far in his early Calvinism he looked back to the manifest blessing of God upon that message.

[2] *An All-Round Ministry*, 360.   [3] Pike, 2, 327.
        [4] 30, 672–83.

Speaking in 1872 he said: 'Nearly twenty years ago our ministry commenced in this city, under much opposition and hostile criticism ... everyone of our sermons was full of the old-fashioned gospel. ... We brought out before the world the old Reformers' doctrines, Calvinistic truth, Augustinian teaching, and Pauline dogma. We were not ashamed to be the "echo of an exploded evangelism", as some wiseacre called us.'[5]

Near the close of his life, when he had re-examined the early sermons prior to their re-publication, he wrote, 'I was happy to find that I had no occasion to alter any of the doctrines which I preached in those early days of my ministry.'[6]

In the three decades between Spurgeon's first controversy and his last, great religious changes had occurred in England. On the one hand there was the rise of the higher-critical movement of which we have already spoken, and on the other a new spate of evangelical activity. The years around 1859 — the time of the great revival in Ulster — saw a vast stirring of energy amongst evangelicals: evangelists like Brownlow North filled theatres in London's West End, Protestant Societies packed the Exeter Hall with great meetings, devotional literature and tracts poured from the press, and missionary societies, old and new, were sending out men into all parts of the Empire upon which the sun never set. In all this activity Spurgeon was prominent. His own well-supported agencies such as Stockwell Orphanage, the Colportage Association and the Society of Evangelists were in harmony with the general spirit of endeavour and much of Spurgeon's time was given to practical deeds and vigorous organization.

[5] 18, 559. As a result of this manner of gospel preaching, Spurgeon says, those who applied for Church membership gave 'clear evidence that they were well instructed in the doctrines that cluster around the covenant of grace'. He adds, 'I believe that one reason why our church has been, for these many years, so signally blessed of God, is that the great majority of those who have been added to our ranks have been well established in the old-fashioned faith of the Puritans and the Covenanters'. *The Early Years*, 530.

[6] *The Early Years*, 396.

But as the years passed, there were indications that the popular and widespread Evangelicalism which was stirring the land was not producing in the churches a deeper commitment to those historic creeds and confessions which evangelicals (excepting the Wesleyans) had hitherto commonly regarded as definitive statements of Biblical Christianity. On the contrary, a trend away from the older doctrinal position was developing amongst those who were in the forefront of evangelistic work and apparent success. Observing this change, Dr. R. W. Dale, the Birmingham Congregational leader, was one of the first to point out that Spurgeon's doctrinal convictions were no longer representative of Free Church Evangelicalism as a whole. Writing in the *Daily Telegraph* on Christmas Day, 1873, Dale welcomed the new evangelicalism, which he frankly admitted differed from the old orthodoxy, and he gave it as his opinion 'that Calvinism would be almost obsolete among Baptists were it not still maintained by the powerful influence of Mr. Spurgeon.' This led Spurgeon to write an editorial in *The Sword and the Trowel*, entitled 'The Present Position of Calvinism in England', and it is full of interest as a statement of his assessment of the situation in February, 1874. His verdict was very different from that of Dale: 'We are persuaded that the Calvinism which it is our delight to preach, so far from being an obsolete theory, is growingly operative upon the minds of a large section of Christian people. ... What our Calvinism regards as sound views of truth are in the ascendant.'[7]

Spurgeon's mood on the prospects of the Calvinistic truths remaining an abiding force in evangelicalism were thus optimistic. At the same time as this exchange with Dale, however, events were taking place in the North of Britain which, in the outcome, were to give a powerful acceleration to the change which Dale had already observed. In the Summer of 1873, D. L. Moody and Ira D. Sankey had arrived in

[7] *Sword and Trowel*, 1874, 49–53.

England with the avowed object of winning 'ten thousand souls for Christ'. Almost unknown at first, their campaigns in York, Newcastle and Sunderland brought them into notice. Then, arriving in the Scottish capital, by the invitation of some ministers, near the end of November, 1873, they began nine months of evangelism which roused the hopes of Christians all over Britain. The response to Moody's straight preaching and Sankey's singing was great and it seemed to indicate that a new age of revival had begun. An address by Archibald Brown in the March 1874 issue of *The Sword and the Trowel*, entitled 'The Coming Revival,' spoke of 'the revival spirit' and 'the rolling tide of religious enthusiasm in Edinburgh.[8] In the same issue there appeared 'A Few Words Upon Objections to Revivals' by Spurgeon and without naming the two Americans he expressed the conviction 'that the present gracious visitation which many parts of England and Scotland are enjoying is of the Lord'.[9] The April number contained the account of a fervent eye-witness on 'The Awakening in the North', with news of converts being 'added to the church by hundreds' in the Scottish capital.[10]

There was much in Moody to draw Spurgeon's affection. He liked the plainness of the Yankee. He sympathized with the enterprising spirit which made Moody go out after men in compassion for their souls, and with Moody's readiness to put his foot through musty traditions. Above all, he was behind him in his proclamation of immediate salvation through faith in the blood of Jesus. Spurgeon had long been critical of American 'revivalists', but in Moody's work in Scotland he believed there was something different. There was a power present greater than the man and not a few of Scotland's spiritual leaders saw what they believed was a genuine Divine visitation. They regarded Moody as being a servant of the Gospel in an awakening which was wider in its scope than the

[8] *Sword and Trowel*, 1874, 113.   [9] ibid., 139.   [10] ibid., 153.

areas reached by the two Americans; and the fact that the work could spread and deepen in places comparatively untouched by Moody confirmed their belief in a movement of the Spirit of God.

It is not surprising, then, that when Moody and Sankey came to London in 1875 they had the firm support of the pastor of the Metropolitan Tabernacle. The work in the South, however, did not parallel what had been witnessed in the North. An attempt by some ministers to use their visit to spread evangelistic endeavour failed because there was an 'almost instantaneous collapse of the meetings' as soon as the evangelists removed to another district.[11] Of the mission meetings which were held, Spurgeon wrote: 'The large halls were crowded with Christians, and so the unconverted were kept out, and the work was quite distinct from all places of worship, and so many who were converted have not yet found their way to regular houses of prayer. The state of affairs in London was very different from that in Scotland and if (as we fear) the result is different, the honoured men of God are none the less accepted of their Master.'[12]

Such is the background to the Moody missions of 1873–75. Our purpose in introducing the subject is not to assess the spiritual fruitfulness of the work but to relate it to the emerging pattern of doctrinal change. Spurgeon accepted Moody as being in the Calvinistic tradition. Speaking of the reaction to Moody in Sunderland in 1873, he comments, 'Having scented

[11] Pike, 5, 154.
[12] *Sword and Trowel*, 1876, 87. 'We met with few decided conversions, after the London missions', Spurgeon said. This view he later revised (ibid., 530), though his final opinion seems to be, 'Messrs. Moody & Sankey are two blessed men of God, and if their converts on that occasion vanished, it was no fault of theirs'. *Letters of C. H. Spurgeon*, 1923, 219. Moody's missions were not church-based but relied on the loose co-operation of all denominations. For Spurgeon, noting the increasing defection from the truth in the Church of England, this policy was a serious hindrance to united action, and he spoke emphatically against co-operation with 'an established semi-Papal Church'. This is honestly recorded in *The Sword and the Trowel* and is hardly a 'new sidelight on Spurgeon' as a recent biographer of Moody supposes, *Moody Without Sankey*, J. C. Pollock, 1963, 139.

his "Calvinistic theology" the Wesleyans would have found reason for justifying a determined opposition, had not the wise counsel of Dr Punshon led them to adopt an opposite course.' Moody went to Scotland, he says, with 'unimpeachable testimony that all was orthodox'.[13]

The subsequent unfolding of events as now known to us, has made it impossible for us to agree with Spurgeon in putting Moody down on the Calvinistic side. Yet it was not easy to see the theological direction that Moody's evangelism was taking at the time. For one thing, except for the need of immediate salvation, theology of any kind was not prominent in the preaching. 'Moody's sermons were certainly not intellectual,' wrote a close sympathiser, 'they were plain, honest, somewhat blunt appeals.'[14] Doctrine as such was not Moody's realm. But the backing of Calvinistic Presbyterians and the apparent touch of genuine revival served to assure people of the pureness of the preaching.

At least one contemporary of Spurgeon, and a man who was one of the greatest evangelical preachers Scotland has ever raised, did dissent from the popular view. This was John Kennedy (1819–84) of Dingwall, who, in a stirring pamphlet entitled *Hyper-Evangelism*, criticized some of the principal features of Moody's teaching and practice. The barrage of rebukes which Kennedy received placed Spurgeon in some difficulty, as the two men were firm friends. Believing Kennedy was mistaken, Spurgeon nevertheless came to the defence of his character:

'We are sorry to read every now and then the most bitter reflections on Dr Kennedy, as though he were an enemy of

[13] These words appear in Spurgeon's longest comment on Moody's work, being a review article of *D. L. Moody and His Work*, by W. H. Daniels, *Sword and Trowel*, 1876, 84–7.
[14] *W. G. Blaikie*, An Autobiography, 1901, 334, Blaikie, in whose Edinburgh home Moody lived for most of the winter of 1873–74, also adds: 'It is a significant fact that Mr. Moody found his most impressionable and sympathetic people among members of our godly families and godly congregations.'

the gospel. Now, we know him to be one of the best and holiest of men, and quite undeserving of severe upbraiding. Nothing but zeal for the truth has moved him, we are quite sure. He is fearful lest the doctrines of grace should be forgotten, and he is jealous for divine sovereignty. He is also fearful that the work owes more to music than to the force of truth, and is more the work of fleshly excitement than of the Holy Spirit. Is it altogether an unpardonable sin to feel such a sacred anxiety?'[15]

Moody seemed to be a good example of a man who, unlike most previous evangelists, could preach the simple gospel of conversion and forgiveness without being distinctly Calvinistic or Arminian. Whereas, in the case of Brownlow North or Charles G. Finney, their evangelism at once displayed their theological system, it was different with Moody. Hence many Calvinists accepted Moody as an evangelist while conscious that he had deficiencies as a teacher. Kennedy, however, could not accept this analysis. He did not believe there is such a thing as a simple gospel, half-way between Calvinism and Arminianism; rather, a man in preaching the centralities of salvation *must* be either Calvinistic or Arminian even though at first sight, he might *appear* to be neither. Kennedy opposed Moody, not merely because Moody left out certain truths, but because in doing so he was quietly yet inevitably promoting a type of gospel preaching which in its general tendency was bound to weaken both the orthodoxy and the evangelism known to Scotland since the Reformation.[16] 20th-century

[15] *Sword and Trowel*, 1875, 142. J. C. Pollock's *Moody Without Sankey* repeats the old caricatures of Kennedy, 118–20.
[16] The difference between contemporary Calvinists in their assessment of Moody is full of interest. Horatius Bonar, known for his opposition to Arminianism in earlier years, replied to Kennedy's *Hyper-Evangelism*. Kennedy responded with *A Reply to Dr Bonar's Defence of Hyper-Evangelism* (1875). Like Spurgeon, Bonar did not differ from Kennedy over basic theology, but over the question, whether, in point of fact, the Moody missions were Arminian in tendency. My own tentative impression of this disagreement is that Bonar was indisposed, on account of the fruitfulness of the missions, to countenance theological criticism, while Kennedy probably did not give sufficient

Scottish writers on the influence of the Moody missions –
whether for or against Kennedy's theology – have agreed with
his view of the trend of the new evangelism. Carnegie
Simpson, in his *Life of Principal Rainy*, observes how the old
Calvinism was in decline in Scotland before 1873 ('it was no
longer Hodge or Cunningham the men chiefly read, nor
perhaps even Augustine or Calvin'), and he goes on to state
how the Moody mission hastened the change in the theological climate – a change which Simpson regarded as being in
the right direction: 'Moody's preaching of a "free gospel" to
all sinners did more to relieve Scotland generally – that is to
say, apart from a limited number of select minds – of the old
hyper-Calvinistic doctrine of election and of what theologians
call "a limited atonement" and to bring home the sense of the
love and grace of God towards all men, than did even the
teaching of John MacLeod Campbell.'[17]

The late Principal John MacLeod of the Free Church College, Edinburgh, writing from the opposite standpoint, refutes
the charge that Kennedy did not preach the offer of the gospel,
and he proceeds to give this assessment of why Kennedy
raised a warning in relation to Moody's teaching. Speaking
first of Kennedy, he says:

'No man in his generation made conscience more than he
did of proclaiming as the gospel a message that was as full as
it was free and as free as it was full. It was, however, the day of
ebb-tide and the definite out-and-out Calvinism of another

weight to the immediate benefits attending Moody's work in Scotland. Bonar
looked at the immediate blessings and saw no need for caution; Kennedy
looked first at the long-term doctrinal implications and in so doing he arrived
at far more critical conclusions. Spurgeon's approach was much the same as
Bonar's. He had no thought of conniving at Arminianism (indeed Charles G.
Finney was strongly criticized at this time in *The Sword and the Trowel*,
1876, 213–218); it was only that he did not see the danger which Kennedy discerned. Kennedy's pamphlet, *Hyper-Evangelism*, may be read in *The Banner
of Truth*, No. 6.
[*17*] *The Life of Principal Rainy* (popular edition), 1, 408. Campbell (1800–
72) was deposed from the Church of Scotland ministry in 1831 after a heresy
charge.

day was going out of fashion and yielding place to a presentation of the gospel which, without being pronouncedly Arminian, avoided the emphasis which the older Evangelicals
laid on the new birth as a Divine intervention. This modified
message put its emphasis on the need the sinner has of forgiveness to the eclipse of the equally urgent need that he has
of regeneration. It stressed the rectifying of his standing and
did not give sufficient prominence to his need of a change of
heart. In this connection the newer Evangelicalism said less
of the Spirit and His work, and of the provision made in
Christ for a walk in newness of life, than did the fuller message which brought home as equally urgent the need of
having a man's nature renewed with that of having acceptance for his person.'[18]

It appears to us that Spurgeon's views on the state of
Calvinism in 1874 were not well-founded. Unchanged himself
in his beliefs, he was optimistic in believing that the evangelical trend was towards rather than away from his position.
With this hope he refuted Dale's references to Calvinism
becoming obsolete, and unlike Dr. Kennedy, he did not
consider that the Moody missions contained a serious tendency
towards doctrinal defections.

One thing is certain. By the 1880's Spurgeon came to
see that the tide was not for Calvinism but against it. When
Dale, in 1881, repeated his belief that 'Mr. Spurgeon stands
alone among the modern leaders of Evangelical Nonconformity in his fidelity to the older Calvinistic creed', Spurgeon did
not attempt to refute it.[19] Speaking to the editor of the *Pall
Mall Gazette*, in June, 1884, Spurgeon made the following
significant statement:

'In theology I stand where I did when I began preaching,
and I stand almost alone . . . Even those who occupy Baptist

[18] *Scottish Theology*, 1943, 328–9. For J. C. Ryle's penetrating analysis of
the type of theology popularized by the Moody missions, cf. *Holiness*, 1952,
74–75.
[19] *Sword and Trowel*, 1881, 85.

pulpits do not preach exactly the same truths that I preach. They see things differently; and, of course, they preach in their own way. Although few will deny the wonderful power of the truth as it has been preached at the Tabernacle, it is not according to their methods; yet it is the Calvinistic way of looking at things which causes my sermons to have such acceptance in Scotland, in Holland, and even in the Transvaal, where a recent traveller expressed his astonishment at finding translations of them lying beside the family Bible in a great many of the farmsteads of the country. I am aware that my preaching repels many; that I cannot help.'[20]

The same consciousness of the growing rejection of the old theology is also apparent in his later sermons. Preaching at Upton Chapel, Lambeth, he said:

'*We believe in God's Covenant.* That is a strange, uncouth word, to some people's ears. We have friends about who have never heard it; and if their pastors were asked why they never preached about the covenant, they would reply, "Covenant! that is a Scotch thing, is it not? Something to do with the Puritans, and men of that ilk? They are all dead now; at least, nearly all; there are just a few of them left, like fossils of the olden time; they cling to this obsolete form of religion, but there are so few of them that they will soon be quite extinct!" *So they say* brethren; but we shall see; and meanwhile, we poor fossils *do* believe in the covenant; we are almost as absurd as David, who said, "He hath made with me an everlasting covenant, ordered in all things, and sure." He who understands the covenant has reached the very core and marrow of the Gospel; but how few do care about it nowadays![21]

Aware though he was by the 1880's of the rising hostility to the doctrines of grace, Spurgeon could not have anticipated the hurricane of criticism and abuse directed against his Calvinism as soon as the Down-Grade controversy com-

[20] *Autobiography*, 4, 240–241.　　　[21] *Sword and Trowel*, 1892, 391.

menced. Indeed he had a right to be surprised for at first sight Calvinism had no connection with the Down-Grade controversy and he had taken care to emphasize at the outset that the issue concerned the modern denial of those basic Christian truths which had long been the common possession of both Calvinist and Arminian evangelicals. Addressing fellow-Baptist pastors in 1888 he declared, 'I do not wish to impose any doctrine of my own, not even the grand old Calvinism; but it is not a question of Calvinism, but rather of the divinity of Christ'[22]. Again, speaking on 'The Evils of the Present Time', he said, 'We used to debate upon particular and general redemption, but now men question whether there is any redemption at all worthy of the name.'[23]

Nonetheless, no sooner was Spurgeon's charge against religious disbelief made in the summer of 1887, than he was assailed for those 'narrow' doctrines which distinguished him from others. He was out of step with everyone else, men said, because John Calvin's ghost 'rode him like a nightmare.' According to *The Birmingham Daily Post*, the key to Spurgeon's resignation from the Baptist Union was that he was 'a convinced and vehement Calvinist.'[24] *The Sunday School Chronicle* blamed Spurgeon for 'making the precise lines of his own theology the standard by which he measures fidelity to the Gospel.' 'He is a Calvinist,' continued the same paper, 'but it is not fair to judge of a man's attachment to the teaching of Christ and His Apostles by the standard of even so revered an authority as the Assembly's Catechism.'[25] A minister wrote in *The Congregational Review*: 'What has been given up is not faith, but mainly Calvinism ... A former generation was

[22] Pike, 6, 301.
[23] *An All-Round Ministry*, 285. See also *Sword and Trowel*, 1888, 563.
[24] Quoted by Pike, 6, 288.
[25] This quotation, and the many from other religious journals and papers which follow, I have taken from the scrap-books originally belonging to Spurgeon and now housed in the Heritage Room at Spurgeon's College, London. These little-used scrap-books must be a primary source for any future biographers of C.H.S.

Calvinistic to the backbone. Indeed. there were not wanting those who treated Calvinism as the essential creed of Congregationalists. This is so no longer ... as it seems to me not the younger men only, but the bulk of Congregational ministers, have moved far from that Calvinistic standpoint which Mr. Spurgeon still courageously holds.' *The Methodist Times* thought the same: 'It can no longer be concealed that Mr. Spurgeon is out of touch with the new democracy and the younger generation of devout evangelicals. He is standing still, but the Church of God moves on ... old-fashioned Puritan formulae are driving him into a reactionary and vanquished camp.'

Others used less moderate language. A non-Christian writing in *The National Reformer* asserted, 'If any such terrible being as Mr. Spurgeon's God existed, I would not worship him.'[26] Similarly statements came from those within the Church. A Baptist minister in Leicester wrote in *The Christian World*, September 22, 1887; 'I *hope* I love the Holy Book, but I do not read it as Mr. Spurgeon reads it. The God of Mr. Spurgeon's theology is not my God.' In the same issue of this paper, J. P. Williams, a Yorkshire Congregational minister wrote, 'I fully endorse the late Henry W. Beecher's view that the old Calvinistic form of stating Christian truth is at the root of a great deal of the scepticism of the age. Rather, then, than fear, I hail with delight the desire that prevails in the pulpit and pew of today for a restatement of Christian truth.' A Glasgow periodical, *The Theological Reformer*, carried an article in October, 1887, entitled 'Calvinism and Mr Spurgeon.' The writer approved of Charles G. Finney and of John 3.16 but protested: 'Calvinism, however, is at an infinite remove from this evangelical conception of things. *John Calvin (Mr Spurgeon's infallible Pope) never was converted*, but all his life was an ungodly man ...'

The Rev. T. R. Stevenson, a member of the Baptist Union

[26] 'A Word to Mr. Spurgeon,' June 1, 1890.

Council in 1887, thought it necessary to send his strictures of Spurgeon's belief to the *Derby Daily Telegraph*:

'The Rev. C. H. Spurgeon is a noble man. We all admire him. His generosity and self-abnegation are notorious. To love and to value him amount to a duty. *But he is not infallible.* Much of his theology is unworthy of him. It is out of joint with the Bible: it is also opposed to the best instincts of humanity.

'To be plain, Calvinism has had its day. It is sick unto death. All the restoratives so diligently administered by its friends will not save it. Thank heaven, the world has outgrown it, and has nothing for it but a smile of pity on account of its ignorance. One leg is in the grave; where will the other be in fifty years? There let it lie for ever.

I am, sir, your obedient servant, T.R. Stevenson – Apr. 7, 1887.

The same writer wrote in *The Christian World* for February 16, 1888: 'The prevailing dissatisfaction, not to say disgust, with Calvinism is most obvious. Nothing strikes one more. Press and pew, in nine cases out of ten, display an utter recoil from the hateful doctrines of Geneva.'

Notwithstanding all that Spurgeon asserted to the contrary, the accusation was repeated on all sides that what he really wanted was to commit the Baptist Union to Calvinism. And when the Association of his former college students was dissolved in order to be re-aligned on a basis which included three points, the doctrines of grace, believers' baptism, and earnest endeavours to win souls to Christ, there was a further cry of outrage over the first point. George Hill, a Baptist minister in Leeds, wrote: 'Mr Spurgeon desires to exclude from the Conference all the ministers who since their College days have learned anything about the ways of God with men, unless their new learning agrees with what is found in Hodge's *Outlines of Theology*, and Coles on *Divine Sovereignty*. Another incensed writer in *The Christian World*, after quoting

Hodge and Coles together with Calvinistic passages from Spurgeon's own sermons, deplored what he alleged was Spurgeon's intention, 'In order to make these terrible dogmas once more the Credal basis of the Baptist Union, the Annual Assembly is to be stormed, the Association cleft in twain.'

These quotations indicate the storm of opinion which there was against Calvinistic belief within Nonconformity in the 1880's. They also reveal something of the hostility shown towards the only Free Church leader who remained true to what had once been the historic faith of Presbyterians, Congregationalists and Baptists alike. Sometimes the criticism touched depths which could be well forgotten and yet if we are to understand Spurgeon's closing years and, more important, the theological revolution of that age, the whole record should be heard. In 1890 *The Christian World*, a paper which had done so much to attack orthodoxy, represented Spurgeon as 'wasting in despair.' The description was false, yet there was certainly enough cruelty and dishonesty in some of Spurgeon's opponents to induce despair in any man unsupported by the grace of God. To the astonishment of not a few it was the professedly evangelical journal, *The British Weekly*, which went the furthest in publishing on April 25, 1890, an 'Open Letter to Spurgeon' from Joseph Parker – a London Nonconformist leader who was probably second only to Spurgeon in pulpit influence in the capital. Among Parker's biting words were the following:

'When people ask me what I think of Spurgeon, I always ask which Spurgeon – the head or the heart – the Spurgeon of the Tabernacle or the Spurgeon of the Orphanage? The kind of Calvinism which the one occasionally represents I simply hate, as I hate selfishness and blasphemy. It is that leering, slavering, sly-winking Calvinism that says, "Bless the Lord we are all right, booked straight through to heaven first-class" ... But when I turn to the Orphanage all is changed. All is beauty. All is love. . . .'

Scarcely could enmity to the truth go lower than this caricature of the grace of God wrapped in the language of partial admiration for its spokesman!

In the light of the above it is not surprising that newspapers outside the Nonconformist circle also regarded the Down-Grade as an unavailing protest by Spurgeon at the passing of Calvinism.

From the Anglican side, *The Church Review* for April 12, 1889, contained an article, 'The Revolt Against Calvinism, And After – ?':

'The dead-set against the Westminster Confession seems to grow apace ... even the redoubtable Dr Parker's fiercest attacks on the Creed-bound Church are but veiled protests against the document by which he, like so many of his brethren, is bound ...

'As to the Westminster Confession, of course it is unnecessary for us to say that we have not the smallest sympathy with it. That gloomy epitome of Calvinism was framed expressly against the Church in troublous times, and, like most weapons directed against her, it is now, nearly 300 years after, beginning to recoil against those who have hitherto held to its provisions ... With regard to the recoil from Calvinism, we see nothing but cause for congratulation.'

The general view was ably summarized by *The Unitarian Herald*, on November 11, 1887. The writer concurred with the judgment that Spurgeon's withdrawal from the Baptist Union was due to his insistence on Calvinism. He continued:

'There can be no doubt whatever as to the direction in which the broad stream is flowing. The thoughts which people entertain about the character of God, and the destinies of man in the world to come, have of late years been undergoing a vast transformation ... What is preached and believed at the present time is greatly in advance of what our pious grandparents were wont to listen to as the Word of God. Mr Spurgeon and his friends form a mere back-current or eddy in the stream of religious progress. One might be tempted to say, looking at the immense personal following Mr Spurgeon has, their numbers and the energy of their faith, – "Why, this man has got the people with him"; but that would be a grievously incorrect conclusion to arrive at. The breaking up of orthodoxy is not affected without some struggling survivals in an age that is surely leaving it behind. There can be no doubt about the issue. The authorities of the Baptist denomination are perfectly well aware of what is taking place; and powerful as the name of Mr Spurgeon has always been among them, they know they must not take his side against the younger men who have the spirit of the age with them . . . The big man must go; the big man is nothing before the march of the spirit of the age.'

Many were thus united in asserting that Spurgeon's theology was unsuited to the needs and the spirit of modern times. Yet despite the confidence engendered amongst themselves by the strength of their numbers, these critics were not unaware that the history and continuing unparalleled influence of the Metropolitan Tabernacle gave too much weight to the rejoinder that it was *they* who did not know how to help men. In the light of the effects of Spurgeon's ministry, could his doctrine be as antiquated and as unhelpful as they wished to represent it? The credibility of the critics' case therefore depended, as they frequently realized, on a demonstration that Spurgeon's success could not be related to the Calvinism which he preached.

Sometimes the demonstration consisted of 'proof' that other preachers who fed on the Puritans were utter failures. A Baptist minister, eager to persuade his colleagues not to be misled, took up this subject in the course of an address to a meeting of the Midland Baptist Union. One of his fellow-students at Bristol, he told them, had given four hours a day to 'Puritanic theology'. After this 'surfeit' doubts arose in his mind as to the value of such studies. 'In his perplexity he consulted an eminent minister [C.H.S.], who re-assured him by a post-card on which was written, "By all means read the Puritans, they are worth more than all the modern stuff put together."' So for four years the student proceeded to saturate himself in Puritan literature and, the speaker claimed, with disastrous results! 'No congregation would look at him, and he had serious thoughts of resuming his secular calling. In his despair a happy thought occurred. In desperation he sold every bit of Puritan paper he possessed, and with the proceeds bought Stopford Brooke, Robertson, and a few others of the same school, and in a few weeks he got a church.' For such words of wisdom the speaker was voted a unanimous vote of thanks by the large number of Baptist ministers who were present.[27]

In a letter to *The Christian World*, September 22, 1887, W. Copeland Bowie resorted to straight assertions in denying any connection between Spurgeon's theology and his influence:

'Mr Spurgeon professes to despise or ignore the science and criticism and the progressive life and thought of the present day. He is an orthodox Calvinist, and yet people crowd in their thousands to hear him. Are we to conclude, then, that Calvinism is what the indifferent and the unchurched need and desire? Are all the churches and chapels in which the fire and blood theology is plainly and loudly proclaimed quite full? Mr Spurgeon lives under a delusion in regard to himself. It is his oratory and his fame, his genuine earnestness and goodness, and not his Calvinism, that make it so difficult to obtain a seat at the Tabernacle on Sunday ... In spite of his own personal success there is nothing to show that Calvinism is capable of saving the world of to-day from its sin and its doubt.'

We turn now to make some general observations on the connection between Calvinism and the Down-Grade contro-

[27] Reported in *Word and Work*, February 24, 1888.

versy. Some questions immediately present themselves: How was it that evangelicals who were not Calvinists so singularly failed to support Spurgeon in the controversy within the Baptist Union? Further, why was Spurgeon's church, with its distinctly Calvinistic confession, ever in the Union if opposition to the old doctrinal outlook was so strong? A glance back is necessary at this point. At the first meeting of the Baptist Union in 1812, Spurgeon's predecessor, John Rippon was chairman, and a doctrinal declaration was drawn up which, by specifying personal election and particular redemption, limited the association to Calvinistic Baptist churches – then known as 'Particular Baptists'. In the interests of a wider association this declaration was dropped in 1832, and thereafter 'General' Baptist churches (Arminian evangelicals) gradually entered the Union. In 1863 these General Baptist churches only constituted a third of those in the Union, being considerably outnumbered by those professedly Calvinistic. Ten years after that date we noted Spurgeon's view that Calvinism was 'growingly operative' and he therefore saw no reason for concern lest the old theology should disappear in the Baptist Union.[28] It was the Down-Grade controversy which brought out not only the extent of liberal belief in the Union but the general wish that the old Calvinistic creeds might be obliterated. By the time that John Clifford, a General Baptist, had become President of the Baptist Union in the critical years 1888–89, the one-time minority had become a powerful majority!

If, as he first hoped, Spurgeon had succeeded in uniting all evangelicals within the Union on a basis of those truths which were held in common, some liberals might have been forced to withdraw. Yet even supposing that an association of Baptist evangelical churches had emerged there is reason to

[28] In a letter to a correspondent who had drawn his attention to a Baptist minister preaching error, Spurgeon replied on Dec. 29, 1877, 'There are not above a dozen loose men among us to my knowledge, but an attack upon one might make a martyr of a party, and cause a world of trouble to the many faithful ones among us.' (Copy in Heritage Room, Spurgeon's College.)

believe that such a union could not have lasted; the old Calvinistic evangelicalism, with its long heritage and distinctive literature, belonged to an ethos too widely different from the anti-credal evangelicalism then in the ascendancy to admit of a lasting union.

In one sense it was unfair that both liberals and evangelicals blamed Spurgeon's Calvinism for his withdrawal from the Union, for he was honest in his protest that it was not that standard of doctrine which he sought to have imposed in the Union.[29] In another respect, however, those who differed with Spurgeon were right in regarding his judgments and actions as inseparably bound up with his doctrinal standpoint. Believing as he did that Calvinistic Christianity is Biblical Christianity, his critics regarded him as inevitably prejudiced in his assessment of the contemporary religious scene. In this they were right. Spurgeon's theology consistently governed his total outlook: 'Calvinism means the placing of the eternal God at the head of all things. I look at everything through its relation to God's glory. I see God first, and man far down the list. We think too much of God to please this age.'[30]

Arminian evangelicals tended to see the struggle with Higher Criticism as a difference over particular doctrines rather than as a difference in attitude and spirit. The strength of Spurgeon's opposition to liberal thought was not only that he held it to be erroneous, it was fundamentally wrong in *spirit*. At the heart of the new theology was disbelief in divine revelation and thus, for Spurgeon, its pretensions, its intellectual brilliance, and its claims made in the name of 'progress' or 'science', were all nothing more than evidence of the pride of unregenerate man. His charge, in a word, against the Down-Grade movement was that it was man-centered;

[29] *Sword and Trowel*, 1888, 563.
[30] *An All-Round Ministry*, 337.

instead of submission to God's Word, it urged accommodation to human wisdom: 'The new religion practically sets "thought" above revelation, and, constitutes man the supreme judge of what ought to be true.' The spirit of Higher Criticism was its condemnation, and its teachers, far from possessing superior knowledge, would, if they persisted in unbelief, show that they were not the taught and chosen of God.[31]

Few Arminian evangelicals at the time of the Down-Grade cared to endorse such an assessment of the situation. Spurgeon took higher ground. He judged things from their God-ward aspect and there can be little question that it was this theological viewpoint which was primarily responsible for his isolation at the end.

Not only, however, did the vague and non-Calvinistic evangelicalism of the 1870's and the 1880's generally fail to make a firm stand against Higher Criticism, it may even be argued that it served the interest of that movement. Sometimes tacit support was given by professed evangelicals as, for instance, by Dr John Clifford who could associate with those who denied the deity of Christ because he believed that 'evangelicalism' and theological liberalism could be combined.[32] More often aid to the Higher Critical movement was given *unconsciously* by men who at heart had no sympathy with disbelief in Scripture. We noted earlier how the ascendent evangelicalism of the 1870's was non-doctrinal in emphasis and disinterested in the historic creeds. Strong in earnestness, and faithful in preaching the need of a conversion experience, it was nevertheless especially vulnerable to the old error of Deism which the teachers of Higher Criticism had revived,

[31] cf. his sermon on John 6:45, entitled 'Choice Teaching for the Chosen' 45, 38.
[32] Clifford's position clarified in the Down-Grade; prior to that Spurgeon had taken services for Clifford. Once, in the latter's vestry, before service, Spurgeon had opened his mind: 'I cannot imagine, Clifford, why you do not come to my way of thinking,' he said, referring to his own Calvinistic beliefs. 'Well, you see, Mr Spurgeon,' came the smart answer, 'I only see you about once a month, but I read my Bible every day.' Fullerton, *op. cit.* 255.

namely, that a man can have true Christian experience apart
from what he may or may not believe.

It was a serious weakness in the ministry of D. L. Moody
that he was not sufficiently alive to this danger. His popular
type of preaching, replete with anecdotes and notably thin in
doctrinal content, suited those who wanted to forward the
view that the gospel and the new critical views were not
incompatible. Liberals found they could praise Moody and
associate with him. Henry Drummond, one of the evangelist's
most prominent supporters in Scotland, reckoned this to
Moody's credit:

'No other living man has done so much to unite man with
man, to break down personal grudges and ecclesiastical
barriers, bringing into united worship and harmonious co-
operation men of divers views and dispositions. . . . No other
evangelist has kept himself so aloof from fads, religious or
otherwise; from 'isms, from special reforms, from running
specific doctrines, or attacking specific sins; has so concen-
trated his life upon the one supreme endeavour.'[33]

Drummond, whose book, *The Greatest Thing in the World*,
was a Victorian best-seller, appears to have departed from all
the central doctrines of the faith, yet at his early death at the
age of forty-five Moody spoke of him as 'the most Christlike
man I ever met'.[34]

This was precisely the attitude which Spurgeon had to fight
against in the Down-Grade. The mood of the age was against
creeds of any sort, and evangelicals, with their already diluted
Faith, succumbed in large numbers to the idea that clear-cut
doctrinal positions were 'unchristian' in their tendency.

[33] *Life of Moody*, Henry Drummond, 123.
[34] Spurgeon commends a criticism of Drummond's book, entitled *The
Strangest Thing in the World*, by Charles Bullock. 'Mr Charles Bullock thinks
that the strangest thing in the world is "*The Gospel with the Gospel omitted*" —
and he rightly judges that the Drummond teaching is precisely *that* . . . Mr
Bullock has done grand service by laying bare the device of deleting the atonement of Christ with the idea of promoting the imitation of Jesus.' *Sword and
Trowel*, 1891, 340.

Moody weakened Calvinism, and in so doing he left the churches more exposed to the Higher Criticism which the non-doctrinal evangelicals were unprepared to combat. The tendency, as we have said, was in the churches before Moody's missions, but it gained rapidly in strength after the 1870's. John Aldis, Joseph Angus and Alexander Maclaren, all Baptist evangelical leaders, taking opposite sides to Spurgeon in 1887, declared: 'We feel that the imposition of theological tests or a human creed would ... defeat the objects of the Union.'[35] In doing so they did not intend to shelter liberals, yet that, in effect, was what they did, and subsequently in scores of churches higher critical views were to replace the evangelical faith.

The decline of Calvinism was thus clearly related to the growth of liberal theology. Arminianism had 'softened-up' evangelicals so that Higher Critical views could permeate the Nonconformist denominations with little opposition. For Spurgeon history was repeating itself as his generation re-enacted what 18th century Nonconformists had done when the Confessions and catechisms of the 17th century had been abandoned: 'There followed an age of drivelling, in which our Nonconformity existed, but gradually dwindled down, first into Arminianism, and then into Unitarianism, until it almost ceased to be. Men know that it was so and yet they would act it all over again. They read history, and yet demand that the old doctrine should again be given up ... oh, fools and slow of heart! Will not history teach them? No, it will not if the Bible does not ... Surely evil days are near, unless the church shall again clasp the truth to her heart.'[36]

As we have said, Spurgeon did not make Calvinism the issue in the Down-Grade controversy, but neither did he hide his personal committment to the old faith which he knew

[35] Pike, 6, 289.
[36] 29, 394. This argument from history was used more fully by Robert Shindler in his articles entitled 'The Down-Grade' which preceded the controversy. See *Sword and Trowel*, 1887, 122–6, and 166–72.

190

would in God's time come back into its own: 'The doctrine
which is now rejected as the effete theory of Puritans and
Calvinists will yet conquer human thought and reign supreme.
As surely as the sun which sets tonight shall rise tomorrow
at the predestined hour, so shall the truth of God shine forth
over the whole earth.'[37]

[37] 23, 514; 32, 91. Calvinistic material in *The Sword and the Trowel* at the
time of the Down-Grade included 'John Bunyan on Election' and 'A Plea for
Calvin'.

We admire a man who was firm in the faith, say four hundred years ago ... but such a man today is a nuisance, and must be put down. Call him a narrow-minded bigot, or give him a worse name if you can think of one. Yet imagine that in those ages past, Luther, Zwingle, Calvin, and their compeers had said, 'The world is out of order; but if we try to set it right we shall only make a great row, and get ourselves into disgrace. Let us go to our chambers, put on our night-caps, and sleep over the bad times, and perhaps when we wake up things will have grown better.' Such conduct on their part would have entailed upon us a heritage of error. Age after age would have gone down into the infernal deeps, and the pestiferous bogs of error would have swallowed all. These men loved the faith and the name of Jesus too well to see them trampled on ...

It is today as it was in the Reformers' days. Decision is needed. Here is the day for the man, where is the man for the day? We who have had the gospel passed to us by martyr hands dare not trifle with it, nor sit by and hear it denied by traitors, who pretend to love it, but inwardly abhor every line of it ... Look you, sirs, there are ages yet to come. If the Lord does not speedily appear, there will come another generation, and another, and all these generations will be tainted and injured if we are not faithful to God and to His truth today. We have come to a turning-point in the road. If we turn to the right, mayhap our children and our children's children will go that way; but if we turn to the left, generations yet unborn will curse our names for having been unfaithful to God and to His Word.

C.H.S., SERMONS, 1888, 83–84

9: 'Though the Heavens Fall...'

In our last chapter we sought to show the relationship between Spurgeon's first and last great controversies. The convictions which he held on free grace in the first, underlay the final struggle, and because the mood of a declining Evangelicalism was against those convictions, Spurgeon stood comparatively alone amongst Free Church leaders in the Down-Grade. We turn now finally to ask how the middle controversy – the Baptismal Regeneration debate – fits into this picture and where resurgent Catholicism stands in relation to evangelicalism on the one hand and the liberalism of the Higher Critical movement on the other.

E. B. Pusey, the Anglo-Catholic leader in the Establishment, who died in 1882, made the significant forecast that the two final combatants in what he saw to be the coming religious struggle would on the one hand be Rome, with a faith claiming to be authoritative and supernatural, and on the other, theological liberalism as held by the rationalistic schools of thought dominant in Continental Protestantism.[1] In other words, evangelical Protestantism was already so weakened, in Pusey's view, that it was on the point of abandoning the arena and would play no decisive part in determining the Christianity of the future. The extent to which evangelicalism was eclipsed in the major English denominations before the end of the 19th century was confirmation of this assessment.

[1] 'Two systems are now, and probably for the last time, in conflict – the Catholic and Genevan.' Quoted from a letter by Pusey to the Archbishop of Canterbury, by J. H. Merle d'Aubigné, *Discourses and Essays*, 1846, 174. Geneva was then a centre of the rationalism which Pusey ably opposed.

Yet Pusey was wrong in presenting Catholicism and liberalism as necessarily in permanent opposition. The publication of *Lux Mundi*, a book written by younger disciples of the Tractarian movement, in 1889, indicated that rationalistic thought and a sacramental religion were not as incompatible as Pusey supposed. The two sides did not destroy each other; indeed, liberals such as H. E. Ryle gave support to the move to legalize Romish vestments in the Establishment,[2] while, *pari passu*, Anglo-Catholic bishops sheltered liberals from the charge of heresy. And in the 20th century, despite the theological liberalism of many of the clergy, Anglo-Catholic sympathies have come to permeate the Church of England.[3] A direct confrontation never materialized and, in the wider scene, the co-operation of liberals and pro-Catholics in the ecumenical movement gives clear evidence that the final struggle will not be as Pusey anticipated it.

Nor is there the slightest likelihood that Nonconformity, in its present condition, will provide a final antidote to the resurgent power of Rome. The most striking contrast is observable between the mood which seventy years ago

[2] *Herbert Edward Ryle*, Maurice H. Fitzgerald, 1928, 164. Herbert Ryle, the son of the great evangelical, is a tragic example of the outworking of the Higher Critical influence. An early exponent of the new views, he is described by his biographer as being one of the company who live 'to see the "heresy" of their youth accepted as the "orthodoxy" of their old age'. But the same writer also reveals that in his last illness, when he was Dean of Westminster, H. E. Ryle 'never spoke either to Mrs Ryle or to his son about the future or about religion'.

[3] Professor Norman Sykes has noted the difference between the Lambeth Conferences of 1920 and 1948 in connection with the prevalence of distinctly Anglo-Catholic views on Episcopacy and sacraments. *Old Priest and New Presbyter*, 1956, 243. The 1958 report of the Lambeth Conference gave an explicit affirmation of Tractarian doctrine: 'It must . . . be recognized as a fact that Anglicans conscientiously hold that the celebrant of the Eucharist should have been ordained by a bishop standing in the historical succession, and generally believe it to be their duty to bear witness to this principle by receiving Holy Communion only from those who have thus been ordained'. Evangelical weakness in the Establishment was revealed in 1964 when vestments associated with the mass were legalized by a vote of 214 against 30 in the House of Clergy and a unanimous vote of 31 bishops. Was the late Lord Alexander of Hillsborough not right in declaring that no true Protestant bishops were to be found in the Church of England?

brought Free Churchmen together in the National Free Church Council, and the present position of leaders in the Nonconformist denominations. Speaking of the above Council, Silvester Horne wrote in 1903, 'The Free Churches came together under the shadow of a great common peril. Everywhere it was felt and recognized that the maintenance of the sturdy Protestant character of English life and worship rested mainly on them.'[4] The words are pathetic in the light of subsequent history. The great characteristic of 20th-century Nonconformity has been its decline into a state of pernicious anaemia[5] and today its leaders are so enfeebled that the claims of Episcopacy are not only listened to with docility but the warrant for any continued existence of Nonconforming denominations is openly doubted.

Yet the cause of the changed attitude in the Free Churches to Rome and to Anglo-Catholicism is to be sought before and not after the year 1903 when Horne wrote the above words. Though Horne himself was blind to it, the change was the inevitable outworking of the liberal view of Scripture which, as the Down-Grade showed, was rampant in the churches before the end of the 19th century. By 1900 the generality of Free Churchmen were Nonconformist by the inherited traditions of birth and education rather than by loyalty to Scripture, and while these traditions may take a long time to die, they have abundantly proved their impotence in the contest with deep-seated convictions – even though those convictions be false and unscriptural. This was precisely what Spurgeon foresaw. He deplored the readiness to cling to the outer shell of Nonconformity when the inner kernel, namely, loyalty to its basic principles, had been abandoned: 'Conformity, or nonconformity, *per se* is nothing; but a new creature is everything and the truth upon which alone that

[4] Horne, op. cit., 424.
[5] Professor D. W. Brogan wrote in 1943, 'In the generation that has passed since the great liberal landslide of 1906, one of the greatest changes in the English religious and social landscape has been the decline of Nonconformity'.

new creature can live is worth dying a thousand deaths to conserve. It is not the shell that is so precious, but the kernel which it contains; when the kernel is gone, what is there left that is worth a thought? Our nonconformity is beyond measure precious as a vital spiritual force, but only while it remains such will it justify its own existence'.[6]

Today, neither in the major Nonconformist denominations nor in the Establishment, is there any bulwark against the pressure from the re-union of all 'Churches' in a comprehensiveness speciously friendly but actually resolutely inimical to true Christianity. Inter-denominational Evangelicalism likewise has no backbone against this kind of pressure: compromise and a diluted theology have reduced evangelical witness to a point where crusades which have liberals and Anglo-Catholics sharing in the sponsorship are not regarded as being any denial of our message. Arminianism, experience-centred rather than truth-centred, has shown itself far more compatible with non-evangelical and non-Protestant traditions than the old Reformed Evangelicalism which because of its definite formulation of the Biblical doctrines of sin, grace, and justification could not be so amalgamated. A striking characteristic of modern thought is that the triumvirate of evils which Spurgeon fought – 'free-will', sacramentalism, and liberalism – are frequently no longer regarded as evils at all. One-time opponents have become 'camp-followers'. It is therefore not surprising that many evangelicals today would reject Spurgeon's standpoint as an appalling anachronism.

Our own belief is that Spurgeon was led, in the three great controversies we have sketched, to stand against errors which were to dominate the coming generations. He engaged in his controversies of deliberate purpose with the deep conviction that he was not mistaken in his recognition of the importance of what was in dispute. Many old debates which once electrified the churches would not now raise a spark of interest, but

[6] *Sword and Trowel*, 1887, 399.

this is not true of these three controversies. They are still explosive, and that because the errors involved have become so prevalent.

Spurgeon's approach to controversy can teach us much.

First, there is evident in all the major controversies in which he was involved a pastoral concern for the spiritual welfare of men and women. Thus in the first great controversy, while accepting the Christian standing of some who could not receive the doctrines of free grace, Spurgeon saw how a general toleration of errors respecting those doctrines injured the prosperity of the Church and the progress of the gospel. He spoke accordingly. Similarly in 1864, his fundamental objection to the Establishment was its support of a comprehensiveness which confused the difference between the regenerate and the unregenerate. But his pastoral motive came out supremely in the Down-Grade. He regarded the attitude of current religious thought which treated central Biblical doctrines as mere opinions or theories and argued that disbelief in 'dogmas' does not affect a person's relation to Christ, as fraught with spiritual peril. For his part an acceptance of the new views was tantamount to the abandonment of a saving interest in Jesus Christ and he believed that if liberalism took possession of the pulpits in the name of Christianity then ministers and congregations would go to the judgment seat of Christ lost and undone. So to him it was no exaggeration to point to the tremendous destruction of Pompeii under volcanic lava and to parallel with it the danger of the Church 'being buried beneath the boiling mud-showers of modern heresy'.

It was because Spurgeon linked salvation with faith in a definite body of Biblical truth, and questioned the Christian standing of those who denied that truth, that the Down-Grade controversy was marked by strong feeling on both sides. For this Spurgeon has often been blamed, as he failed to recognize, it is said, that an underlying spiritual oneness in

Christ may exist along with wide differences of opinion on 'dogma'. According to this viewpoint, both sides were really Christian and it was a tragedy Spurgeon could not see it. Richard Ellsworth Day, an exponent of this attitude, after a brief sketch of the Down-Grade, concludes, 'it is tragic to find that one has been fighting an ally, Mr Divergent-opinion, mistaking him for the enemy, Mr Different-heart'.[7] Spurgeon, Day implies, was guilty of careless thinking in failing to realize that true 'faith' need not be identified with any particular set of theological opinions. We mention this because, if the criticism were true, Spurgeon's words in the Down-Grade would reveal the very opposite of a pastoral spirit – they could, with justice, be held to be unnecessarily harsh. Precisely because the kind of distinction which Day makes has been accepted as a premise, Spurgeon has been charged with falling into bitterness and bigotry in the Down-Grade controversy. It was intolerable that he should suggest that eminent religious leaders might be adversaries of the Lord.

The only way to judge Spurgeon's spirit is by reference to Scripture. Does Scripture permit a dichotomy between true spiritual experience and belief in the doctrinal truths of the Gospel? Does it give any support to the liberal idea that men may receive 'grace and truth from God in ways uncharted by Christian theology?' Spurgeon believed that Scripture decisively answers these questions and that the broad definition of a 'Christian' implied in the ideas of the new school was scripturally false. Nevertheless, he was far from supposing that all who did not stand where he did in the Down-Grade were non-Christians. He would have agreed with the words of one of his favourite Puritan authors, George Hutcheson, in his comment on John 12:42, 'Nevertheless among the chief rulers also many believed on him; but because of the Pharisees

[7] *The Shadow of the Broad Brim*: the Life Story of Charles Haddon Spurgeon, Heir of the Puritans, 1934, 150.

they did not confess him, lest they should be put out of the synagogue.' Says Hutcheson, 'There may be true faith and grace where yet there is much infirmity to smother and bear it down', and so he continues, we should be charitable and not think men 'are graceless because they are weak'. There was plenty of evidence in the Down-Grade of Christian ministers who through weakness kept silence: 'Ostracism seems to be dreaded so much that good men and true hold their tongues'.[8]

But there were other men and 'leading religionists', as Spurgeon calls them, whose position was very different. They publicly and persistently professed their disbelief in cardinal truths and consequently could not be, in Spurgeon's mind, regarded as Christians at all. Here lay the great divide; is there any definite gospel which men must believe in order to be saved? If the testimony of Scripture is dependable, then the faith which is required of sinners is an undivided committal to Christ – to His person, to His Word, to His work. And these things are inseparable, for faith in His person as God at once requires submission to the authority of His Word: accordingly we find that Christ treats not receiving His words as the same as rejecting Him (John 12:48), while conversely, true discipleship is proved by continuing in His Word (John 8:31).[9] Belief in His Divine majesty is, from his own lips, declared to be the only alternative to 'dying in your sins' (John 8:24). For a Christian these statements are final, because Christ's authority as Lord is meaningless unless we accept Him as an infallible teacher. To receive the Saviour without receiving the truth which He came into the world to

[8] *Sword and Trowel*, 1891, 249.
[9] R. C. H. Lenski rightly comments on the words 'He that rejects me and receives not my sayings': 'This man does not need to attack Jesus or rage against His sayings; simply not to receive them is fatal and insures his judgment.' *Commentary on John*, 1963, 896. 'If we abide in Christ as "the truth",' writes John Murray, 'we abide in His Word, and there is no abiding in Him apart from continuance in His Word. . . . To speak of knowing God and the truth that He is apart from the word of revelation which is incorporated for us in the Scripture is for us men an abstraction which has no meaning or relevance.' *Principles of Conduct*, 1957, 129.

bear witness to, is an impossibility (John 18:37). For Spurgeon this was fundamental, 'Unless we receive Christ's words, we cannot receive Christ; and unless we receive His apostles' words, we do not receive Christ; for John saith, "He that knoweth God heareth us; he that is not of God heareth not us. Hereby know we the spirit of truth and the spirit of error".'[10]

On the same grounds there can be no benefit from the work of Christ for those who do not believe His testimony concerning the purpose of that work. Personal faith in His death in the place of sinners is represented as indispensable to salvation: 'Except ye eat the flesh of the Son of man, and drink his blood, ye have no life in you' (John 6:53). At the cross the Son of God 'died a death in which all the weight of divine vengeance for sin was compressed into a few hours of bodily and spiritual anguish', and to renounce the truth that Christ was 'smitten of God' as our surety is to renounce Jesus altogether. Preaching on 'The Sine Qua Non' Spurgeon says:

'If thou receive not His perfect, unrivalled, Godlike blood-washing, thou art no Christian. Whatever be thy profession whatever thy supposed experience, whatever thy reformation, whatever thou mayst have attempted or accomplished, if thou hast never come as a guilty one, and seen thy sin laid upon the bleeding Son of God, thou art in the gall of bitterness and in the bond of iniquity. . . . Without faith in the atonement thou canst have no part in Christ . . . Jesus Christ will be either acknowledged the anointed Saviour, or He will be nothing to you. If you will not take Him to be an expiation for your sins . . . you refuse Him altogether.'[11]

Because the new religious views being popularized in the

[10] *An All-Round Ministry*, 373.
[11] 16, 220 & 223. On the doctrine of the atonement as it is related to the command to 'try the spirits whether they are of God', see R. S. Candlish's valuable chapter 29 in his *Lectures on The First Epistle of John*, 1870. The confession that Jesus Christ is come in the flesh, he shows, when truly and fairly admitted, means that He came to redeem by substitution those whose flesh He shared. The assurance of present victory for Christians over antichristian spirits and men (1 John 4:4) is rendered needful in the terms of the

last quarter of the 19th century cast doubt upon both the trustworthiness of Christ's words and upon the value of His blood, Spurgeon had no hesitation in regarding the movement as basically non-Christian. 'An unregenerate heart lies at the bottom of "modern thought".'[12] His protests in the Down-Grade were not made in the spirit of bitterness, but in a spirit of compassion towards those who, not only in his own generation but in ages to come, might be fatally deceived in receiving a gospel which is not a gospel. (Gal. 1:7).

In the consideration of how the very meaning of 'Christian' was involved in the Down-Grade, the position of Marcus Dods may be cited. Dods, an eminent Scottish Doctor of Divinity of the same school of thought as his friend Henry Drummond, deplored Spurgeon's words in the Down-Grade and would have recommended Aristotle more readily to his students than the writing of the pastor of the Metropolitan Tabernacle. He believed that Christ 'has in some mysterious fashion found entrance for His thought into many minds that know little or nothing of Himself.' Writing of Buddhism and Christianity in 1907, he says to a correspondent: 'It is amazing on the one hand to see how little Christians understand Christ; and on the other hand to see how instinctively men of all religions adore what is good, and how often they seek to possess it. It's a strange, unintelligible world, and the one fixed point on which hope can rest is that God is Father of all. If it is not so, then the solid firmament truly is rottenness, and "earth's base built on stubble".'[13]

constant warfare waged by the spirit of antichrist and in this warfare one central truth is always attacked: 'From the day when Cain slew his brother – it might be seen to turn upon the question of the worship of God by atoning sacrifice. Is there, or is there not, to be the shedding of blood for the remission of sins? That, more or less clearly, with variations suited to the varied aspect of the church and the world, has ever since continued to be in substance the point at issue.' Candlish, op. cit., 2, 82.   [12] *An All-Round Ministry*, 375. [13] *Later Letters of Marcus Dods* (late Principal of New College, Edinburgh), edited by his son, Marcus Dods, 1911, 153 & 256. For an interesting letter to Dods by Robertson Nicoll in 1892 in defence of Spurgeon, see *William Robertson Nicoll*, 103–4.

The whole theology of a generation which had rejected a supernatural gospel was built on the false hope that sinners could find shelter in God without faith in the propitiation offered on Calvary. Spurgeon had not exaggerated the magnitude of what was involved.

Secondly, Spurgeon engaged in controversy with great faith in God, and with a sense of his duty to do God's will whatever the outcome. 'I have had to lean on the bare arm of God,' he wrote to a friend in a dark hour during the Down-Grade. Spurgeon did not base his actions on any calculations about the probable measure of human support he would receive if he took a lead in opposing error. In the Baptismal Regeneration controversy he won considerable support from many he had expected to oppose him, while in the Down-Grade he expected sympathy and instead suffered heavy disappointment, yet in neither case did this affect his position. 'He went out to the fray in both cases assured of result,' says Fullerton, 'but in neither did he foresee what the result would be.'[14] This was the man of faith; he would do his duty 'though the heavens fall'. The same faith bound him to the promises of Scripture in an hour of general defection. He looked prophetically at the threatening possibilities, he saw ahead years of barrenness and decline, and he came, by faith, to a firm conclusion: 'My Lord will revive His buried truth as sure as He is God.'[15]

It was this same faith in God which enabled Spurgeon to esteem the approval of God above all human commendation. Indeed he repudiated the latter when it came from those who showed no zeal for God. 'When Spurgeon died,' wrote J. C. Carlile, 'leaders of the Baptist Union without exception were loud in their praise of the man.'[16] But Spurgeon had such 'praise' before his death and to him it was 'lighter than vanity'. In 1888, referring to those leaders who spoke of him as an 'honoured friend' and yet opposed what he held most dear, he wrote, 'The harsh language of more outspoken opponents has

[14] op. cit., 304.   [15] 30, 680.   [16] op. cit., 257.

more music in it than such idle compliments'.[17] Another incident in an earlier year illustrates the same feature in Spurgeon's character. Having had occasion to speak against the sayings of a certain bishop, it had come to his ears that this same bishop had referred to his book *The Treasury of David* as *the* book on the Psalms. Spurgeon, says Pike, 'was not at all conciliated by this compliment, but on the contrary he seemed to be all the more incensed, and remarked that the man said fair things of everybody, and then did what he could to oppose those whom he hated'.[18]

Thirdly, the various controversies of Spurgeon's life are unified when we see them as parts of his total commitment to the Word of God. This perhaps is his greatest legacy. Some might follow him with zeal in his assault on Anglo-Catholicism, only to recoil, alarmed, at his attitude to the Baptist Union when the latter body refused to impose discipline. But in both cases he was acting on the same Biblical principle. Others might espouse his presentation of the doctrines of grace but fail to see that a theology which puts God first cannot, in areas of church alignment and practice, be true to itself if it descends to the level of the expedient. A zeal which is confined to certain aspects of scriptural teaching is the consequence of an unworthy view of the Word of God, and from such an inconsistency Spurgeon continually sought to escape.

The irreconcilable conflict does not lie between liberalism and Catholicism as Pusey thought, but between a Christianity which appeals solely to Scripture for its warrant and a Catholicism which refuses to receive Scripture as its sole guide. And if it be asked where such a Christianity can be found, Spurgeon would point us to that system of truth which, handed on from apostolic days, through Reformers and Puritans, has come down to us under the name of Calvinism. We need be neither enamoured with the name nor ashamed of it. It merely serves to characterize a position and a creed which is the only

[17] *Sword and Trowel*, 1888, 249.   [18] Pike, 6, 223.

final alternative to Rome. Arminianism obscures the nature of grace in salvation, while liberalism assails the inerrancy of Scripture and teaches the insufficiency of the written Word. Clinging fast, as she does, to works and human authority in her doctrine of salvation, Rome can accommodate both the Arminian error and the liberal error into her system. The only sure ground of consistent evangelicalism which can never be circumvented by heresy is that on which Spurgeon stood in the controversy of New Park Street days, in the Prayer Book controversy of 1864, and finally in the Down-Grade.

Fourthly, along with the thoroughness of Spurgeon's adherence to Scripture in all matters of controversy went his desire for true union with all evangelical Christians. He expressed this desire in the great Baptismal Regeneration controversy and it appeared again strongly in his last lacerating years. Forced by the Down-Grade into 'the isolation of independency' his spirit longed for something else: 'Oh, that the day would come when, in a larger communion than any sect can offer, all those who are one in Christ may be able to blend in manifest unity!'[19] It is a common argument that the Puritan stress upon total submission to the Word of God, along with its sense of accountability to 'obey even in the jots and titles, at all hazards', has a disruptive and dividing tendency. To Spurgeon the truth of the matter was far otherwise. Disunity, he argued, is not caused by a too thorough attachment to Scripture, but by the intrusion and toleration of beliefs and practices which are the products of human wisdom alone: the Lord's 'will is in the Scriptures: and if we searched them more and more, and were determined, irrespective of anything that may have been done by the church, or the world, or by government, or by anybody else, that we would all follow our Lord's will, we should come to closer union. We are divided because we do not study the Lord's will as we should.'[20] This is not to deny that men even in

[19] Sword and Trowel, 1887, 560.   [20] 19, 354-5.

their best state are subject to prejudice and fallibility in their interpretation of the Word. But though human weakness makes our obedience to Scripture imperfect, it in no way excuses the necessity of such total committal, nor does the record of human infirmity as it appears in Church history, invalidate the great truth that spiritual unity and prosperity cannot be attained along any path except that of submission to the Word of God. 'The statutes of the Lord are right . . . in keeping of them there is great reward.' (Psalm 19. 8–11).

Lastly, Spurgeon reminds us that piety and devotion to Christ is not a preferable alternative to controversy, but rather that it should – when circumstances demand it – lead to the second. He was careful to maintain that order. The minister who makes controversy his starting point will soon have a blighted ministry and spirituality will wither away. But controversy which is entered into out of love for God and reverence for His Name, will wrap a man's spirit in peace and joy even when he is fighting in the thickest of the battle. The piety which Spurgeon admired was not that of a cloistered pacificism but the spirit of men like William Tyndale and Samuel Rutherford who, while contending for Christ, could rise heavenwards, jeopardizing 'their lives unto the death in the high places of the field'. At the height of his controversies Spurgeon preached some of the most fragrant of all his sermons. One such sermon, preached during the Down-Grade and entitled 'Something Done for Jesus', reveals the mainspring of Spurgeon's motives and is a fitting summary to conclude a record of his labours:

'We love our brethren for Jesus' sake, but He is the chief among ten thousand, and the altogether lovely. We could not live without Him. To enjoy His company is bliss to us: for Him to hide His face from us is our midnight of sorrow . . . Oh, for the power to live, to die, to labour, to suffer as unto Him, and unto Him alone! . . . If a deed done for Christ should bring you into disesteem, and threaten to deprive you of usefulness, do it none the less. I count my own character, popularity, and usefulness to be as the small dust of the balance compared with fidelity to the Lord Jesus. It is the devil's logic which says, "You see I cannot come out and avow the truth because I have a sphere of usefulness which I hold by temporizing with what I fear may be false." O sirs, what have we to do with consequences? Let the heavens fall, but let the good man be obedient to his Master, and loyal to his truth. O man of God, be just and fear not! The consequences are with God, and not with thee. If thou hast done a good work unto Christ, though it should seem to thy poor bleared eyes as if great evil has come of it, yet hast thou done it, Christ has accepted it, and He will note it down, and in thy conscience He will smile thee His approval.[21]

[21] 36, 53–58.

I sometimes think if I were in heaven I should almost wish to visit my work at the Tabernacle, to see whether it will abide the test of time and prosper when I am gone. Will you keep to the truth? Will you hold to the grand old doctrines of the gospel? Or will this church, like so many others, go astray from the simplicity of its faith, and set up gaudy services and false doctrine? Methinks I should turn over in my grave if such a thing could be. God forbid it! But there will be no coming back ... We cannot return to save the burning mass, nor to rebuild the ruin, but we shall, doubtless, see and know what comes of it.

C.H.S., SERMONS, 23, 514

10: The Aftermath at the Metropolitan Tabernacle

If the conviction that lay behind the writing of this book is true, namely, that the real character of Spurgeon's ministry faded because in some of its essential features it differed too markedly to co-exist with the school of evangelical belief which prevailed almost universally in England in the first half of this century, one question remains to be considered: How was it that such a change took place in Evangelicalism after Spurgeon's lifetime? In this concluding chapter I want to show not only that there was a revolution in evangelical thought and practice but that Spurgeon's own church played a prominent part in the movement away from Puritan belief and practice. As the Metropolitan Tabernacle had stood for one outlook through thirty years – 'we are set for a sign and token of the power of the old-fashioned Gospel' – so it was to stand for another. I will not argue that the Tabernacle simply lost its influence. Were that the whole story it could be accounted for in terms of the church's inability to find anyone to succeed to such a unique structure as Spurgeon had built around him. The case is more serious; it is that the Tabernacle gave its weight to a *different* influence, it gave leadership to an Evangelicalism comparatively new to England, and its history in the twenty and more years after Spurgeon's death in 1892 provides an example, in microcosm, of the change which was affecting the whole evangelical tradition in the British Isles.

Before Spurgeon left London for the last time in the autumn of 1891, he had arranged for a Presbyterian minister from

Philadelphia, Arthur T. Pierson, to occupy his pulpit. The two men had made each other's acquaintance some three years earlier and Pierson had first preached in the Tabernacle in December, 1889. He was then fifty-two years of age and had recently resigned his pastorate in the interests of a wider ministry. Being available when Spurgeon's health broke down so seriously in 1891, he offered his help and Spurgeon welcomed it. Pierson's stature and personality were such that he could be expected to hold the Tabernacle congregation, while his adherence to Scripture, his union with Spurgeon in opposition to contemporary religious disbelief, and his missionary vision were well known.

At that date no one thought of him as Spurgeon's successor; Spurgeon encouraged his congregation in the expectation that he would be able to return from Mentone[1] where he had convalesced so often before, and, in any case, Pierson was a paedo-baptist. The outcome with regard to Spurgeon we have already noted; he died less than four months after Pierson's arrival. The American was now, in the eyes of man, even more urgently needed at the Tabernacle, and he continued to minister without interruption until June, 1892. By that date, Spurgeon's brother, James, who was still co-pastor of the Tabernacle, had proposed that Pierson be called permanently to occupy the pulpit while he himself would continue to discharge many of the pastoral duties. The matter was temporarily left in abeyance as Pierson had to return briefly to the States in the summer of 1892. Meanwhile, Spurgeon's son, Thomas, who was just home from New Zealand, was asked to supply the Tabernacle.

Speaking of the months of Pierson's ministry, W. Y. Fullerton, in his *Thomas Spurgeon*, a biography, writes: 'That year had done much for the people, but it was a very different type of ministry they had enjoyed. When the New Zealand

[1] cf. his words relating to Pierson in his letter to the congregation published in *The Metropolitan Tabernacle Pulpit*, 37, 552.

son came, many of the congregation began again to detect the authentic Spurgeon note, and their hearts warmed to the younger preacher'.[2] When Pierson resumed at the Tabernacle, in November, 1892, the congregation was by no means as harmonious as it had been twelve months earlier. A division – described by newspapers as the 'Tabernacle tempest' – emerged between those wanting to call Pierson and those who wished the son to succeed the father. Thomas Spurgeon had gone back to New Zealand, but in March, 1893, by a vote of three to one, over two thousand members called him to occupy the pulpit for twelve months, with a view to the pastorate. Consequently James Spurgeon resigned and Pierson terminated his ministry in June, 1893. Eight months after Spurgeon's twin-son took up the work he was elected to the pastorate. It seems that even then the disagreement over who would be the best successor at the Tabernacle was not entirely ended and when Pierson was re-baptized by immersion at James Spurgeon's Baptist Chapel in West Croydon in February, 1896, there were those who unjustly questioned his motives. The truth is that Pierson had been very moderate in his attachment to paedo-baptist belief for some years and there is no reason to doubt that his ultimate decision was a conscientious one.

Before anyone judges that the controversy at the Tabernacle in 1892–93 is simply another of those unedifying episodes in Church history when Christians are divided by an over-zealous attachment to 'Paul' or 'Apollos', it needs now to be shown that what was taking place was altogether more far-reaching in its significance. Dr Pierson had a better mind than Thomas Spurgeon and was a magnetic personality; Spurgeon's son, on the other hand, was in the family tradition in so far as his preaching was more to the heart than was the American's, and, to the pleasure of many, he had his father's voice. Yet all these things were comparatively inconsequential compared

[2] *Thomas Spurgeon.* 1919, 152.

with the main issue. Under C. H. Spurgeon's ministry the Tabernacle had consciously stood for the old Evangelicalism; by the ordinary services of the Sabbath and the mid-week, by worship conducted in the scriptural simplicity of the Puritan tradition, by the definite Pauline theology of the Reformed tradition, and by the evangelism of holy-living – by these means, and without any other – the Tabernacle congregation had remained a witness to the power of a Christianity which was everywhere disappearing in the late nineteenth century. The tragedy of the Metropolitan Tabernacle after Spurgeon's death was that the public discussions which disturbed its life did not centre on what was most fundamental.

The long-drawn-out discussion over Pierson's possible call to the pastorate ought to have been ended much earlier by the evidence that his was not the evangelical Calvinism which had been Spurgeon's. One who heard Pierson at the Tabernacle said, 'He is like a Puritan risen from the grave', a reference, however, only to his appearance![3] Pierson's biography does not reveal that he had the slightest interest in the Puritans. The books which had been the staple of Spurgeon's spiritual upbringing were not his reading.

There is no doubt that Pierson himself recognized that his coming to occupy Spurgeon's charge had brought him into a tradition rather different from his own. Commenting later on what was required of him when he arrived in London he wrote: 'I was to preach to an immense concourse of people who had been trained in different modes of construing not a little, both of Scripture teaching and of primitive practice of the Apostolic Church.'[4] Again, in one of Pierson's first descriptions of the Metropolitan Tabernacle congregation as he found it in 1891, he wrote: 'Here is nothing to divert the mind from the simplicity of worship and the gospel ... A precentor leads congregational song without even the help of a cornet; prayer,

[3] *Arthur T. Pierson*, A Biography, D. L. Pierson, 1912, 232.
[4] *James Archer Spurgeon*, G. Holden Pike, 1894, 6 [Preface by A. T. Pierson].

and praise and the reading of the Word of God with plain putting of Gospel truth – these have been Mr Spurgeon's lifelong "means of grace".'[5]

This commendation of the Tabernacle's primitive simplicity would mislead us if we supposed it evidenced a proper understanding of the underlying theological significance. For within a short time of Pierson's arrival there was a significant *addition* made to the above 'means of grace', namely, the inquiry-room method of separating a congregation at the end of a service – the preacher counselling all under concern to remain behind to be addressed collectively or individually. It was, as experience had elsewhere already proved, a short step from this to the announcement of the number of 'converts' – that is to say, those who were judged to have passed satisfactorily through the 'inquiry-room'.

Writing in his diary on January 2nd, 1892, Pierson recorded: 'Three months of uninterrupted health and happiness. Everybody cordial and sympathetic and responsive. Fifty souls gathered in in December and many more inquiring. Immense after-meetings in the Tabernacle. Prayer-meetings of the profoundest interest.'[6] If Pierson did not at this date make appeals for immediate public professions of faith at the end of his gospel preaching that was later to follow. Writing to his children of a preaching engagement at the Tabernacle in 1909 [his first visit there after sixteen years] he says:

'It was so plain that the Holy Spirit was moving mightily that I felt led to put the test to the congregation. When those who were willing to take salvation as offered in the Gospel were asked to rise, a few stood up at first, then more followed until in the vast audience not one person remained sitting. The emotion was intense. The officers afterwards approached me with reference to holding a series of services in the building'.[7]

The proposed services were not held, for this proved

[5] *Sword and Trowel*, 1892, 81.   [6] *Arthur T. Pierson*, op. cit., 241.
[7] *Ibid*, 271.

to be Pierson's last visit to Britain before his death in 1911.

In the light of the words of Fullerton which contrast Pierson unfavourably with Thomas Spurgeon it might be assumed that once the son was established at the Tabernacle the 'authentic' Spurgeon tradition would be secure. This, unhappily, was not the case. Thomas Spurgeon had a simple evangelical faith, he loved art and poetry, and had, like his father, the gifts of humour and imagination. In his pulpit use of anecdotes and illustrations Fullerton speaks of him as masterful.[8] Yet he did not have the structure of theological thought, nor the spirit accompanying it, which were the essence of his father's ministry. In regard to evangelism it was Thomas who was to establish the new ethos at the Tabernacle, an ethos which was none other than the one in which Pierson himself worked. In the case of both men the source of the new influence was the same: back in the 1870's D. L. Moody and Ira D. Sankey had ushered in a new era, and after Spurgeon's death these two men remained, without any doubt, the best-known evangelical figures in the English-speaking world.

In October, 1892, when Thomas Spurgeon was supplying the pulpit during Pierson's absence in America, he held a mission with Moody in the Tabernacle. The November issue of *The Sword and the Trowel* reported its success – 'some hundreds professed to find Christ and salvation' – but it did not report that the Tabernacle had now endorsed the method which C. H. Spurgeon would never receive. For this we must turn to an eye-witness, E. J. Poole-Connor, present at the mission. His account, written in 1941, has long been out of print and we therefore give it in full:

[8] Fullerton tells us that Thomas Spurgeon's address to the Pastors' College Conference in 1896 was on the subject of 'Antidotes', 'suggested by the saying of a woman, who stayed at home on Sundays and read Spurgeon's sermons, instead of attending her chapel, saying of the preacher, "It was antidotes, antidotes, antidotes, from beginning to end, nothing but antidotes".' The old woman's complaint on the multiplicity of anecdotes in the new style sermons was probably far too near the truth to be a subject for amusement.

'It may be of interest to record some personal memories of a mission meeting conducted by Mr Moody in the Metropolitan Tabernacle in 1892. The present writer and two friends – one of them now his wife – were just able to squeeze in about an hour before the meeting was advertised to begin, and as the building was now filled to capacity the doors were closed and the service commenced. There was a very large choir, and Mr Stebbins was the soloist. He sang "It may be at morn when the day is a-waking." Mr Moody's text was Luke 23. 51, and his subject was the moral courage often required to confess Christ. "I guess there are as many cowards to the square foot in England as in Amurrica," he said. He was, as we recall him, stout, very thick-set, bearded, his head rather humping down into his shoulders. His general appearance was that of a keen, rather prosperous business man, very intent on the job before him. He did not seem in the least ministerial, the somewhat Gladstonian collar that he wore heightening the "lay" effect of his dress; and the absence of all rant or undue pietism contributed to the business-like directness of his manner. His speech was alert, racy, and straight to the point, and enlivened with interesting anecdotes. We do not recall noticing any grammatical errors, such as are sometimes related of him. There seemed no great power in his words while he was speaking, but the effect at the close of his address was electrical. When he asked for those of his hearers – particularly men – that were prepared to confess Christ for the first time to stand up and say, "I will, Sir.' a wave of intense emotion swept the great audience, and from every quarter men rose to respond. "I will, Sir." "I will, Sir," "I will, Sir." Nearly everyone around us was in tears, and murmured prayers could be heard all over the building. We learnt that some three hundred professed conversion that night.'[9]

Thomas Spurgeon returned to New Zealand just before this mission concluded. On his last Sunday with Moody at the

[9] *Evangelical Unity*, E. J. Poole-Connor, 1941, 98–99.

Tabernacle he tells us how the American evangelist 'had a talk with me in the vestry in which he said, "You are yet to come back to this place, and I am going to pray God here and now that it may be so."[10] When the call did come to Thomas from the Church the following year he decided to travel via America and visit Moody *en route*. The general prevalence of Moody's methods which he found in the large evangelical congregations of the United States did nothing to give him second thoughts on whether a wrong turn was being taken with the innovations at the Metropolitan Tabernacle.

How much the mood changed at the Tabernacle can be judged by the meetings held to commemorate the opening of the new Tabernacle in October, 1900, after the old had been ruined by a disastrous fire in April, 1898. Let the reader compare these meetings with those held at the time of the opening of the original building in 1861, and he will find a whole world has passed away. At the meetings in 1861 Spurgeon declared, 'The controversy which has been carried on between the Calvinist and the Arminian is exceedingly important,' and thus he had the opening of the Tabernacle marked by five addresses on the leading doctrines of grace, including the doctrines of election and particular redemption.[11] Of music there was none save the solemn praise of God by the united worship of the whole congregation. In contrast, reporting the opening of the new Tabernacle, Fullerton writes, 'A great feature at the opening services was the presence of Mr Ira D. Sankey.'[12] He goes on to name the speakers who addressed the gatherings on the second day, they were the Rev F. B. Meyer and the Rev J. H. Jowett, both men decidedly not in Spurgeon's theological tradition. At the time of the Down-Grade controversy Meyer had moved a resolution in the London Baptist Association *against* the adoption of a

[10] *Thomas Spurgeon*, op. cit., 158.
[11] 7, 294–328.
[12] *Thomas Spurgeon*, op. cit., 197.

doctrinal statement and, while evangelical himself, it was the new school evangelicalism which was to prove itself wholly Arminian in sympathy. Another speaker was Dr Alexander McLaren who as we noted in an earlier chapter singularly failed to support Spurgeon at the time of the Down-Grade. 'Mr Sankey sang at several of these meetings,' says Fullerton, 'and on the Saturday evening, to a crowded Tabernacle, gave a service of song.'

Practically the only early twentieth-century history of the Metropolitan Tabernacle which Fullerton gives us in his life of Thomas Spurgeon concerns the various missions or evangelistic campaigns which were then playing such a part in the life of the church. In the special meetings of 1905 – referred to in *The Sword and the Trowel* as a 'revival' – seven hundred names of those who 'confessed Christ' were registered. By the time Thomas Spurgeon resigned on grounds of ill-health in 1908, 2,200 persons had been received into the church during his fourteen happy years. Despite the figures just given Fullerton speaks guardedly of 'decreasing membership'.[13] In a private letter to a friend in 1902, Spurgeon's son wrote: 'There have been many and sore trials, and I have been depressed beyond measure. Truth to tell, I am at this present time not altogether jubilant. The difficulties are enormous and they seem to increase . . . My one dread is of remaining in a post of honour longer than I should.'[14]

After Thomas Spurgeon's resignation the pastoral charge was undertaken by A. G. Brown. Though ten years younger than C. H. Spurgeon, Brown had been close to him and had conducted his funeral. He probably had a better understanding of Spurgeon's ministry than any of the other occupants of the pulpit after 1892 and in T. L. Edwards, an assistant appointed in 1908, he had a like-minded colleague. This was, however, to last only three brief years. Brown resigned in 1910, and the following year, with the appointment of Amzi Clarence

[13] Ibid., 211   [14] Ibid., 211

Dixon, the Tabernacle succumbed to the full impact of American Fundamentalism and its own brand of evangelicalism. Dr Dixon came straight from five years' ministry at Moody Memorial Church, Chicago, where, his biographer tells us, 'in the course of each year from five hundred to a thousand professions of conversion had been noted on the books of the Moody Church.' With his coming any lingering distinction between Spurgeon's ministry and the Moody ethos seems to have been obliterated. A grand piano was installed, and 'singing the gospel', along with public appeals for 'decision' and the inquiry-room system, all became part of the every-day life of the church. The occasional and the irregular had at last become the common-place.

Dixon himself was aware that he was inaugurating changes. Before he took up the regular pastorate in London he had spent some weeks preaching at the Tabernacle early in 1911 and gave the following interview on his return to the United States:

' "Did you hold an after-meeting, as you do in Chicago?" asked *The Advance* representative.

"Yes," replied Dr Dixon, "and I want to tell you a remarkable thing about it. I conducted the first after-meeting ever held in Spurgeon's Tabernacle, and continued every Sunday night as long as I was there. Had fifteen conversions the first night, thirty the second, and the number ran as high as thirty-five to forty some evenings.'

"Didn't they take to your methods?"

"I can't say that they did, at first. My methods were too American: but they warmed up to them later."

"What were your first impressions of a London audience?"

"At first they seemed rather stolid. The weather was chilly; perhaps that had something to do with making the people seem chilly. But after the ice was broken they were the most enthusiastic lot you ever saw." '15

[15] Reported in *The Christian Age*, May 4, 1911.

Enthusiasm could be taken as the key-word for the opening of Dixon's London ministry and the spirit was soon conveyed to others. One Christian paper, commenting on the Tabernacle, wrote on 'Signs of a Revival', giving the information that the lower gallery was once more in use on Thursday evenings. To a representative of the *South London Press*, who interviewed Dr Dixon in his vestry, he disclosed the hope that there would be a revival that would 'Shake South London' – apparently supporting his feeling by a statement on the number of inquirers who had recently confessed faith. In the summer of 1912, when Dixon was one of the speakers at Keswick, there was further excitement over great advances to be made at the Tabernacle. *The Christian Age* for July 5, 1912, commented on Dr Dixon's amazing proposal for the conversion of 'The Elephant and Castle' into an evangelical bee-hive. But there was a trace of scepticism in the reporter's words: "All credit to Dr Dixon for his big ideas. The £100,000 he wants, however, does not include the great buildings which would take the place of the "Elephant", or the maintenance of them, and one wonders whether another expensive central mission here is really necessary.'

It is not easy to assess the spiritual fruit of Dixon's eight years in London. The great rebuilding project never materialised; it is indeed unmentioned by Dixon's biographer, his second wife, Helen C. A. Dixon. But according to Mrs Dixon there was certainly revival. In a campaign in 1912 'more than three hundred confessed their decision for Christ';[16] in 1915 Dixon covenanted with some of his members 'to try to win at least one soul for Christ every week',[17] and in a service in May of that year for Continental refugees, 'In a single meeting twenty-seven French people decided for Christ.' The next year Dixon helped to lead the six-months-long 'Jubilee Campaign' of the London Baptist churches and he wrote of

[16] A. C. Dixon, *A Romance of Preaching*, 1931, 212.
[17] Ibid., 218.

'tokens of great revival at the Tabernacle.'[18] In 1912, when there was a five months' 'Trench Campaign' and a 'Gospel Picture Mission', 'more than seven hundred people accepted Christ'.[19] 'The Tabernacle', wrote Dixon towards the end of 1918, 'was never in a more prosperous condition'.[20] Yet at that same date, Charles Noble, an old member at the Tabernacle wrote a very different account of the condition of the church[21] – an account which the present writer has heard confirmed by others who also belonged to the congregation and whose memory went back to that period.

Dixon's ministry illustrates how different from Spurgeon's was the new evangelical outlook. In the vocabulary of the Puritan school, revivals were extraordinary manifestations of the power of God, and, by definition, not produced by human labour. But under C. G. Finney, and later Moody, so many 'results' attended campaigns that these also came to be spoken of as 'revivals'. Indeed Finney deliberately treated evangelistic endeavour and revivals as synonymous, and encouraged the philosophy of 'the more effort the more revival.' This was the thought-pattern of Dixon's background, put into words by his own father in the advice he gave him on going to his first pastorate, 'My son, have as many prayer-meetings and revivals as you can, and as few church meetings as possible.'[22] But unlike the old revivals, the yard-stick of campaigns was not primarily the evidence of the changed lives – admitting men and women to the discipline and duties of church membership – it was, more simply, the number of 'decisions'. To obtain 'decisions' an opportunity for a public response to the

[18] Ibid., 222.   [19] Ibid., 233.   [20] Ibid., 237.
[21] See the Appendix to this volume. There is no suggestion in Dixon's biography that criticism existed of his pastorate at the Tabernacle though in a letter of 1917 to his first wife, discussing whether he should remain at the Tabernacle, he wrote: 'It looks as if God wants me to stay right here and witness for Him, though I can see it will mean opposition, if not persecution and suffering.' *A. C. Dixon*, 228, The meaning of this statement his biography does not explain.
[22] Ibid., 275

message was essential and this practice thus became the practically universal hallmark of 'evangelistic preaching'. 'He always closed his sermon with an appeal to accept Christ,' wrote one observer of Dixon,[23] and another accorded him this testimony; 'Evangelism was the passion of his life. Even after lecturing on "Abraham Lincoln", I heard him close with an appeal, and souls came to Christ.'[24]

Mrs Dixon, speaking of her husband's evangelistic preaching, refers to a criticism made by a deacon in one 'historic church' where her husband was pastor. The phrase and nature of the story point to Spurgeon's Tabernacle. The deacon's criticism was allayed, we are told, in this manner: 'Next Sunday the Spirit of God touched his heart, and the dew of heaven fell upon the church. For the first time in the memory of anyone present, there were conversions at the morning service. Five persons responded to an appeal for decisions.'[25] To write in this fashion indicates how oblivious Mrs Dixon appears to have been to Spurgeon's oft-repeated warning that 'decisions' and 'conversions' might well be two different things.

The evidence of the frequently large number of supposed 'converts' under the new type of evangelism whose Christianity proved short-lived ought to have been sufficient proof of this[26], but such was the evangelizing fervour, and the im-

---

[23] Ibid., 264   [24] Ibid., 282.   [25] Ibid., 273
[26] A writer who belonged to the old evangelical school gave this report in *The Signal*, July 1, 1884, on the common results of the new methods in Scotland: 'An Evangelist gave as the report of two weeks' meetings, in connection with a Church, "sixty saved". Might I ask the reader, how many he supposes of these sixty, three months after, made even a profession of Christianity? We are sorry to say, not one. We suppose while the Church on earth lasts we must look for the fulfilment of the Lord's parable, of the four kinds of ground or rather the four samples of ground, in different states of preparation for the seed, but we never saw the stony ground, and the trodden ground, and the shallow ground, in such proportions as we see these now.' Those Scottish church leaders who gave their approval to Moody never foresaw this consequence of his public appeal, though they had misgivings about it at the time. John Cairns, for example, commenting on Moody's work in Scotland, wrote: 'The only feature that all might not approve of has been the coming forward

patience with doctrinal definitions, that few stopped to question whether the numbers responding to 'appeals' were a true indication of spiritual realities.

We have thus considered something of the history of the Tabernacle after 1892. It remains now to be asked how such a change was possible at the very centre of Spurgeon's work? To the present writer there are three reasons which stand out.

First, the influences which brought the change were at work in Spurgeon's own life-time. Even in the wider circle of some of the institutions which he had commenced, practices and methods had gained a footing which he had not authorized and yet which he did not forbid. The most notable instances occurred in the Pastors' College Society of Evangelists, an organization which began as an offshoot of the College in the 1870's for special evangelistic effort in needy parts of the country. Among the men who served in this Society the most prominent were 'C. H. Spurgeon's evangelists, Fullerton and Smith'.[27] According to Fullerton's later account, he was the main speaker in the mission services while J. Manton Smith's gifts lay in the telling use of anecdotes, in his skill with the cornet and in his singing. 'I recognize that it was Manton Smith who attracted the people to whom I preached ... At first we used to rest on Saturday evening, but at length, resting on the Friday, we invented "Song Services", selecting a number of pieces with a consecutive bearing on one subject. This made a great popular appeal, and gave my colleague ample opportunity to use his special talents ...'[28]

W. Y. Fullerton has given us his autobiography in his volume, *At The Sixtieth Milestone*. Converted as a 'teenager in the old-fashioned Presbyterian Church of his Belfast child-

of persons to be prayed for, yet I have become used to this, and everything else is so decorous that I am satisfied and even thankful.' *Life and Letters of John Cairns*, A. R. MacEwan, 1895, 721.
[27] See *Autobiography* 4, 335
[28] *At the Sixtieth Milestone*, W. Y. Fullerton, no date, 77 and 96.

hood he 'discovered' his life's work when Moody and Sankey came to that city in 1874. Of their mission at that time he writes, 'Those to whom such movements are familiar can have no conception of the revolution that can be made in a young life by such a ministry.'[29] Thereafter, going to London and to Spurgeon's College he took up itinerant evangelism himself, and was whole-hearted in his adoption of the new methods. The belief that music is an essential attractive influence, the appeal for public decisions for Christ, the apparatus of the inquiry-room and the subsequent announcement of numbers – all these were features of Fullerton's ministry, as the reader of his autobiography will soon discover. It is not altogether clear how far all these things were common in the Society of Evangelists before Spurgeon's death. Significantly a recommendation of the methods of C. G. Finney did not appear in the columns of *The Sword and the Trowel* until the year after Spurgeon's editorial pen was laid down, when A. A. Harmer, another member of the same Society, wrote, 'The evangelist of today may learn much from the methods adopted in revival work by Mr Finney.'[30] Nonetheless, some evidence of a departure from Spurgeon's own position is to be found in the Notes of the same magazine which report the work of the Society of Evangelists before 1892. The Secretary of the Bradford Y.M.C.A., for instance, informs the readers of *The Sword and the Trowel*, December, 1890, that in Fullerton and Smith's recent services '350 anxious inquirers were personally dealt with in the after-meetings.' Of another Fullerton mission in the same year we read, 'Every night of the mission souls were saved, and such a scene as that witnessed last Sunday night, when about a hundred filled the inquiry-room, made our hearts sing for joy.'

Why then did Spurgeon permit these things in the circle

[29] Ibid., 60.
[30] *Sword and Trowel*, 1893, 188. One is not surprised to find A. C. Dixon's biographer giving Finney unqualified commendation, op. cit., 6.

where his word might have been decisive? Without doubt one consideration which made him tolerant was that the evangelists were earnestly set upon soul-winning: their motives he did not doubt, and if their theological understanding was not strong he remembered that God gives different gifts to men. Furthermore, much of this 'special' evangelistic work was not regarded as public worship. The age in which mission halls, theatres and other buildings were the venue for evangelism had begun and Spurgeon always had sympathy with attempts to reach the masses by any means; in a sense he had done this himself in earlier years. In what was plainly a reference to Moody and Sankey, he had said in 1873: 'I do not hesitate to say that a great deal of church order, and a great deal of propriety and decorum, and regulation, and "As-it-was-in-the-beginning,-is-now,-and-ever-shall-be," -ism, are only so much spices and linen for a dead Christ, and Christ is alive, and, what is wanted is to give him room! I do not say this for my own sake – am I not always proper? – but I say it for the sake of earnest brother Evangelists . . .'[31]

Spurgeon was prepared to caution men against the too-frequent employment of special services but, in principle, he accepted their usefulness; what was left unclear by all parties at the time was the question how far such meetings should be regulated by the same principles which governed the regular worship and activities of the Church. If the new evangelistic methods had, at the outset, been proposed for introduction into the regular services of the churches there can be little doubt that they would have been widely opposed. The fact is that they gained their ascendancy in another sphere. The work of Moody's friend, F. B. Meyer, pastor of Christ Church, a congregation not far from the Tabernacle, illustrates the common pattern. In an effort to reach non-church-goers Meyer began at the end of 1893 to hold special meetings for men designated 'A Pleasant Sunday Afternoon'. Here, unlike his church services, there was band, choir and organ! In addition, the meeting was regarded as 'informal' and even 'applause' was not out of place. Nonetheless, there was an order which Meyer tells us was as follows:

3.30   Hymn
3.35   Reading of Scripture; about ten verses by a selected Brother.
3.38   Anthem, or Hymn with Chorus, by the Prize Choir.
3.43   Prayer, followed by the Lord's Prayer, led by a Brother.
3.45   The first Solo.
3.50   The Notices, by the Secretary.
3.53   The Chairman; always, when at all possible, myself.
4.00   Hymn.
4.05   Our Speaker for the Afternoon.
4.25   The second Solo.
4.30   Exhortations to sign the Pledge and decide for God, followed by the last hymn.
4.35   A short Prayer.[32]

Those willing to become Christians, Meyer writes, were exhorted to go to an area of the church named 'Consecration corner'.

It is not the case, however, that Spurgeon's attitude to these things was simply one of forbearance. He gave repeated warn-

[32] *Reveries and Realities: or, Life and Work in London*, F. B. Meyer, 51. When Meyer went to Christ Church, W. Y. Fullerton was appointed to his former charge, Melbourne Hall, Leicester. Fullerton subsequently became Meyer's biographer. In that volume, as in his biography of Spurgeon, Fullerton fails to give any indication of how far the Evangelicalism of the early twentieth century had drifted from Spurgeon's position. When the Spurgeon biography came out in 1920, H. Tydeman Chilvers, who was then pastor at the Tabernacle, criticized Fullerton for writing in such non-committal terms of the Down-Grade Controversy and not 'boldly in advocacy of Mr Spurgeon's attitude' [quoted in *A Centennial History of Spurgeon's Tabernacle*, Eric W. Hayden, 1971, 43] but Fullerton's whole printed treatment of Spurgeon, in its poverty of theological understanding, merits censure. Some of the things Spurgeon cared for most, Fullerton, by his silence, allowed his readers to forget.

ings against the new trend. As early as 1875 he expressed concern lest the Moody and Sankey practice should create a new traditionalism: 'We are all too apt to get into fine harness and tie ourselves up with rules and methods ... Why, dear me, if we are to have a special service, one brother must have it conducted on the Moody method, and another can only have Sankey hymns. Who, then, are we that we must follow others? Do not talk to us about innovations, and all that; away with your rubbish!'[33] The readiness to regard music as a vital part of evangelism he also condemned. 'Dear friends, we know that souls are not to be won by music,' if they were, he goes on to say, it would be time for preachers to give way to opera singers.[34] In 1882 he declared, 'The heaving of the masses under newly invented excitements we are too apt to identify with the power of God. This age of novelties would seem to have discovered spiritual power in brass bands and tambourines ... The tendency of the time is towards bigness, parade, and show of power, as if these would surely accomplish what more regular agencies have failed to achieve.'[35] Again, in 1888: 'Jesus said, "Preach the gospel to every creature." But men are getting tired of the divine plan; they are going to be saved by the priest, going to be saved by the music, going to be saved by theatricals, and nobody knows what! Well, they may try these things as long as ever they like; but nothing can ever come of the whole thing but utter disappointment and confusion, God dishonoured, the gospel travestied, hypocrites manufactured by thousands, and the church dragged down to the level of the world.'[36]

Equally strong were his words against the system of getting those under concern to make some *public* step which would 'commit' them or bring them to the attention of 'personal workers'. He never adopted the practice himself because he believed that sinners must deal *directly* with God; once the

[33] 21, 515.   [34] 18, 239.
[35] 28, 377.   [36] 40, 199.

gospel was plainly preached all the counsel which seeking souls needed could be given in such words as these: 'You have not far to go to find him. Cover your eyes and breathe a prayer to him. Stand behind one of the columns outside, or get into the street and let your heart say, "Saviour, I want peace, and peace I can never have till I have found thee. Behold, I trust thee. Manifest thyself to me at this moment and say unto my soul, 'I am thy salvation.' "37

Even so, if others would occasionally appoint an after-meeting or an inquiry-room he did not condemn it, provided that it was not treated as a *necessary* part of evangelism.

In the closing years of Spurgeon's life he was alarmed lest some of his own men were not seeing the dangers. Speaking to his students and to the members of the Pastors' College Society of Evangelists he said: 'In our revival services, it might be as well to vary our procedure. Sometimes shut up that inquiry-room. I have my fears about that institution if it be used in permanence, and as an inevitable part of the services.'38 And again to the same men:

'It is a fact that thousands of persons live close to our notable sanctuaries and never dream of entering them. Even curiosity seems dulled.

'Why is this? Whence this distaste for the ordinary services of the sanctuary? I believe that the answer, in some measure, lies in a direction little suspected. There has been a growing pandering to sensationalism; and, as this wretched appetite increases in fury the more it is gratified, it is at last found to be impossible to meet its demands. Those who have introduced all sorts of attractions into their services have themselves to blame if people forsake their more sober teachings, and demand more and more of the noisy and the singular. Like dram-drinking, the thirst for excitement grows. At first, the fiery spirit may be watered down; but the next draught of it must be stronger, and soon it is required to be

[37] 24, 84.   [38] *An All-Round Ministry*, 372.

overproof. The customary gin-drinker wants something stronger than the pure spirit, deadly though that draught may be. One said, as she tossed off her glass, "Do you call *that* gin? Why, I know a place where, for threepence, I can get a drink that will burn your very soul out!" Yes, gin leads on to vitriol; and the sensational leads to the outrageous, if not to the blasphemous. I would condemn no one, but I confess that I feel deeply grieved at some of the inventions of modern mission work.'[39]

From the preceding paragraphs it may be seen that there was a certain ambivalence in Spurgeon's attitude to the new evangelistic approach. His warnings were clear and their emphasis strengthened towards his death, but he was generously prepared to overlook a good deal in some of his workers, and as he had not insisted on a stop to the methods which troubled him, those who were using them were not publicly seen to be in disagreement with their leader. The popular current was running strongly in favour of the methods which claimed for gospel preaching results more immediate and more numerous. In his later years Spurgeon was becoming increasingly isolated in his adherence to the simplicity of the old approach. To most people the change from the old to the new seemed as natural as a change from gas-light to electricity, and once the pastor of the Metropolitan Tabernacle was gone, there was no prominent voice left to tell them why the old was better.

A second reason for the failure of the Metropolitan Tabernacle to stand by Spurgeon's position may be found in the prevalence of American influence between 1891 and 1919, that is, from the time of Pierson's arrival to the date of Dixon's resignation. Even in the pastorate of Thomas Spurgeon we have noted how strong was the influence of D. L. Moody, and

[39] Ibid., 296–7. His Sermons contain many similar warnings. 'If you want to get up a revival, as the term is, you can do it, just as you can grow tasteless strawberries in winter, by artificial heat.' 17, 499.

it was the same son who heartily approved of Dixon's call to the Tabernacle. Dr Pierson had likewise urged Dixon's appointment, sending to Deacon Olney the message, 'Trust God, and call Dixon to the pastorate.'[40]

There is an explanation for the ascendancy of this United States leadership in Spurgeon's charge and it is related to the way in which the last years of his life were dominated by the Down-Grade Controversy. In that controversy the abject weakness of many of the English Free Church leaders was plainly revealed and Spurgeon's distrust of the Baptist Union had been openly registered. The circumstances of this painful situation encouraged Spurgeon to put a premium on friends whom he trusted to stand by the Bible as the Word of God, and in men such as Pierson and Moody he saw sympathetic allies in the battle against infidelity. With the survival of supernatural Christianity itself at stake in the pulpits of England, Spurgeon was ready to welcome help from men who, though they might not be committed to historic evangelical Calvinism, were upholding 'fundamentals'. His emphasis, in the face of the threat from Higher Criticism, was for 'unity of those free from rationalism and superstition'. Partly in the interests of this wider union of Bible-believers, Spurgeon insisted, as we have noted, that the Down-Grade Controversy was not over the truths of Calvinism. This opened the way to the American alliance. It is hard to assess how far Spurgeon was conscious of the fact that the American preachers who followed Moody to England were closer to the school of Finney than to the classic American evangelicalism of Jonathan Edwards and the Princeton men – after all, generally, he never heard them preach – yet notwithstanding any measure of doubt which he may have had respecting their intelligent commitment to the Reformed Confessions, he wanted their fellowship in oppsoing the danger of the hour. Speaking of this trans-Atlantic link, Helen C. A. Dixon wrote, 'A constant

[40] A. C. Dixon, op. cit., 193

interchange of preachers and evangelists was doing much in those days to weld the evangelical believers of England and America together in opposing the destructive teachings of the New Theology'.[41]

The encouragement which Spurgeon gave to the American alliance and to broader evangelical fellowship was not, however, an encouragement to *church* unity irrespective of Calvinism. In a letter to a ministerial friend in 1889 Spurgeon wrote of maintaining a common front with General Baptists who were evangelicals though perhaps Arminian: 'There is a vital difference between us and the Down-Graders, but there is a clear evangelistic platform upon which we can stand with G.B.'s.' However, in the same letter he also says, 'I do not see how we who are Calvinistic can become pastors of avowedly Arminian churches.'[42] In regular church work and teaching he recognized there was a serious objection to Calvinistic truth being weakened for the sake of unity. It would have been unthinkable for him to have approved an Arminian pastor at the Tabernacle. Little did he anticipate that in befriending the American visitors, and in giving the impression that in all important respects they were one, he was in some measure preparing the way for the establishment in his own pulpit of a tradition alien to his own. The catholic spirit in which Spurgeon welcomed fellowship with Christians of another evangelical school surely needs no defence; where he did, we believe, miscalculate, was in not foreseeing that out of this alliance, formed in a temporary crisis, a permanent new form of evangelism was to emerge. He regarded Moody as a man who was making a contribution to evangelicalism, he did not assess the extent to which the whole evangelical outlook for a long time to come was to be influenced by 'Moodyism'. In this misjudgment Spurgeon was not alone. As late as 1903,

[41] Ibid., 95 Dixon first visited England, and met Spurgeon at the Tabernacle, in 1889.
[42] Letter to Mr. Mills, March 1, 1889, copy at Spurgeon's College.

David R. Breed in an article on 'The New Era in Evangelism', in *The Princeton Theological Review*, a bastion of Reformed orthodoxy, took a similar line to Spurgeon. He commended Moody but criticized 'Moodyism': 'Moodyism' meant much that was intensely earnest, vital and evangelical; but it meant much also that was crude, mistaken and divisive . . . In course of time the defects began to involve its decay. Mr Moody himself seemed to realize this.' The same writer goes on to speak of 'Moodyism' as a thing of the past. This assessment was profoundly wrong.

Twentieth-century evangelicalism on both sides of the Atlantic was to be a movement in which all that was distinctive of Reformed Christianity dwindled out of sight – it was to be the evangelicalism of 'The Fundamentals' [the name of the twelve volumes which Lyman Stewart and A. C. Dixon started publishing in 1910], of Keswick,[43] of the Scofield

[43] Spurgeon regarded the 'higher spiritual life' teaching which inspired the Keswick Convention as founded upon an error and therefore productive of an unbiblical strain of piety. ' "Oh, wretched man that I am," said the apostle Paul, "who shall deliver me from the body of this death?" He said this, not because he was not a saint, but because he was so far advanced in the way of holiness.' *Met. Tab. Pulpit*, 24, 436. 'Some say that they live very near to Jesus. It is an evil sign when men speak of their own attainments . . . I like to be with God's people of the poorer class, and of the more struggling and afflicted sort. I like to be with God's people who wrestle hard with sins, and doubts, and fears. If I get spoken to by my superior brethren, I find I have very little pleasant fellowship with them, for I know nothing about their wonderful experience of freedom from conflict, and complete deliverance from every evil tendency. I have never lived a day but I have had to sorrow over my imperfections.' Ibid., 34, 623. 'I tell you solemnly that the talk which we have heard lately about perfection in the flesh cometh of ignorance of the law and of self.' Ibid., 25, 367. 'God's children sin, for they are still in the body. If they are in a right state of heart they will mourn over this, and it will be the burden of their lives. Oh that they could live without sin! It is this that they sigh after, and they can never be fully content until they obtain it. They do not excuse themselves by saying, "I cannot be perfect," but they feel that their inability is their sin. They regard every transgression and tendency to sin as a grievous fault, and they mourn over it from day to day. They would be holy as Christ is holy. The will is present with them, but how to perform that which they would they find not.'

In this respect also A. T. Pierson was in marked contrast to Spurgeon. His biographer writes: 'He had become familiar with "Keswick Teaching", as it is commonly called, before he ever visited Keswick. In the year 1895 he had

Bible,[44] and of the evangelistic campaign with its apparatus for 'decisions'. To the credit of this movement it must be said that it opposed Modernism and believed in taking the gospel to the masses, but on the debit side its condemnation is that it ignored so much of the historic Christian heritage; it went after new fads – for instance, dispensational premillenialism, and the teaching that the believer is, by faith, to receive the fulness of the Holy Spirit and thus pass from 'carnal Christianity' to 'victorious living'. In general it bred a generation in the evangelical churches who loved anecdotes, humour and music, but knew next to nothing of theology and Confessions of Faith. All this happened because the doctrine of God had been supplanted from its central position in the Biblical revelation and consequently the true Christian vision of the glorification of God – 'that God may be all in all' – passed from view. Evangelicals began to think and speak as though the message of salvation was not 'the gospel of God' and as though Christ alone is to be the object of faith. Spurgeon noted this danger as early as 1879: 'Nowadays there appears to be in some minds a forgetfulness of the Father. Christ is loved, for he died, but many seem to look upon the Father as having no share in the wondrous work of redemption'.[45] This lack of theocentric belief came to have a serious effect upon the content of the gospel message; too often forgiveness was presented as though that, rather than knowing and glorifying God, was the end of salvation. Similarly the manner in which the message was presented to men underwent a change. In their eagerness to

learned from experience the purpose and power of God to transform character and to give victory over every known sin.' Thereafter he was a popular speaker in Keswick circles on both sides of the Atlantic. *Arthur T. Pierson*, op. cit., 287ff.

[44] On the part which the interpretation of prophecy played in forming the Fundamentalist ethos see Ernest R. Sandeen, *The Roots of Fundamentalism*, British and American Millenarianism 1800–1930. The reader will also find more on the history of A. C. Dixon in this volume. Spurgeon's views on prophecy and his opposition to dispensationalism I have discussed in an appendix to my book, *The Puritan Hope*, 1971.

[45] 25, 170.

'win' men to Christ, evangelists tended to overlook the fact that for sin to be measured in its true light men must know that they are creatures – dependent upon and obligated to the Creator. In the interests of 'successful evangelism' the emphasis was no longer upon the declaration of the character of God and the claims of his holy law, but upon encouraging men to 'open their hearts' to Christ. The apostolic phrase 'repentance toward God' dropped out of common usage and 'deciding for Christ' became the new comprehensive term.

There is no more serious charge to be brought against the 'Fundamentalist' school of Christianity than that it bred a generation of evangelicals who were largely without reverence for God and whose familiarity with Jesus was too often the product of ignorance.[46]

One more thing needs to be said in explanation of the course the Tabernacle took after Spurgeon's death. For reasons which we will not now attempt to account for, Spurgeon left behind him few colleagues who stood where he did. In this respect the following passage in an obituary published in *The Daily Chronicle*, February 1, 1892, was largely accurate:

'In a sense, indeed, Spurgeon lived largely in the past. He cared nothing for new ideas, for modern refinements of faith and morals. His language, save for its characteristic turn of humour, and perhaps not even in that, differed little from that of some stout camp-preacher of Cromwellian days. His method of interpreting Scripture was largely theirs. His views of the future life, and its relations to the existence of to-day, were in no sense distinct from those of the authors of the Westminster Confession. It has, indeed, been one of the

[46] One preacher of the early 20th Century who saw the danger, G. H. Morrison of Glasgow, wrote: 'There never was a time when so much was spoken and written about Christian love. If we loved more, and said less about it, we might revive our dying reverence. O what a deal of our so-called love to Jesus is spurned and scouted by an infinite God because the feeling of reverence is not in it. It is so easy to talk of leaning on Jesus' bosom. It is so easy to forget that he who leaned on Jesus' bosom fell down at Jesus' feet as dead.' *Flood-Tide*, Sunday Evenings in a City Pulpit, 8th edition, 113.

wonders of the time that in the midst of our humanitarian, aesthetic, sensitive age, with its Universalist formulae, its shrinking from logical extremes, its leaning to optimist idealism, one powerful, insistent, strenuous voice has resolutely preached the old doctrines in the old style, illumined by the light which genius gives, but set uncompromisingly to the note which found favour with the 'rude forefathers' who made English Puritanism. And the voice has been a solitary one. Spurgeon leaves no heirs. The attempt to found a kind of Sacred College, of which he was head failed. His "young men" recall only the less desirable features of his ministry. Truly, the Last of the Puritans is gone from us.'

His brother James, who was called upon to give the address on 'Particular Redemption' at the time of the opening of the Tabernacle in 1861 was no longer of that conviction thirty years later. His confused thinking appeared in the uncertain part he played in the Down-Grade Controversy, and at length he resigned the Presidency of the College in May, 1896, 'on the ground', says Fullerton, 'of loyalty to the Trust Deed, which stated that the college existed to train men for the Particular [i.e. Calvinistic] Baptist denomination.' He died in 1899 in a railway carriage travelling to London.[47]

Thomas Spurgeon was only in England for two periods between 1877 – his first visit to Australia – and his father's death in 1892. We have no means of knowing how far this long absence may have influenced his later judgments. Certainly, judged by his father's standards, Fullerton's biography of Thomas Spurgeon is a very disappointing book.

Of those who did survive Spurgeon, and who thoroughly understood what he had believed, Joseph Harrald is possibly the most significant. He shouldered the burden of producing the great four-volume *Autobiography of Spurgeon* – the most

[47] It is a pity that G. Holden Pike's *Life of James Spurgeon* does not go beyond 1892. Spurgeon's father, John Spurgeon, lived until June 14, 1902; his son Thomas died in 1917 at the age of 61.

accurate of all works on the preacher – and he continued carefully to edit his sermons week by week until his death in 1912. Spurgeon had once laughingly paid tribute to his friend in rhyme, and one verse ran:

> *Too familiar we, forget that he,*
> *Is the Reverend Joseph Harrald;*
> *From Geneva he; his theology*
> *Is Calvinized and Farelled.*

To Harrald it was given to do the most to further the testimony of Spurgeon's life and ministry after his death! He was not, however, without his sorrows, as the reader of the preceding pages can imagine. In *The Sword and the Trowel* for April, 1892, there is a Note on Mr J. W. Harrald, which describes him as 'Mr Spurgeon's most trusted friend, and faithful ally.' The same Note continues; 'On several occasions he has occupied Mr Spurgeon's pulpit with acceptance; and many will be glad to know that, in future, he is to conduct the Lord's-day afternoon services, at the Tabernacle lecture-hall.' For reasons unstated arrangements broke down in the 'Tabernacle Tempest' which ensued later the same year. It seems extraordinary that a man so close to Spurgeon, and so one with him in belief, could have been set aside in the way that A. Harwood Field in his book *The Reverend Joseph William Harrald* tells us was the case:

'Then came stormy days at the Tabernacle, when the public Press exulted openly at the dissensions that had sprung up in the great church, and the want of family unity that was thus revealed. As was only to be expected, Mr Harrald had to bear much that was unpleasant, hard, and unfair at this time. It was said that he was forbidden to preach at the Tabernacle, and many voices were raised against him. Oh, the pain of these troubles in the churches! How they hold back the work of the Holy Spirit, and limit the purpose of God towards the sinning,

suffering world! Mr Harrald bore himself through this trial
with the quiet patience which was one of his noted characteristics. He stated in public that he himself had sent his resignation
as preacher for the afternoon services at the Tabernacle. So he
had, but he would not have felt impelled to this course had it
not been for the undercurrents of unpleasantness which
rendered it imperative for him to take the step he did. Even
then he had the satisfaction of knowing that it was because
of his loyalty that he had to suffer. Such pain has always secret
peace for its healing.'[48]

With his work at the Tabernacle done, and then, in 1902,
with the death of Mrs C. H. Spurgeon, whom he had so much
helped, which ended his need to be in London, Harrald returned to Shoreham on the Sussex coast – the scene of his first
pastorate. On July 1, 1912, he took his customary walk on the
beach, then died peacefully while in the act of revising one of
Spurgeon's sermons for the press. In tribute to him Harwood
Field says: 'He was always behind the curtain, as it were. He
did the work, yet had no recognition for it. Only the One who
sees in secret, could know and estimate the service of this most
devoted labourer in the harvest field.'[49]

Harrald was thus not permitted to play any part in the
shaping of the Tabernacle future after Spurgeon's death. But
what, it may be asked, became of all the elders and deacons
who steadfastly supported their leader in his life-time? We
can throw no light on their conduct except that which Harrald
gives us in two cryptic lines in the midst of the fourth volume
of *Spurgeon's Autobiography*, published in 1900. After a letter
from the church to Spurgeon about the year 1880, when the
pastor was absent on account of illness – his secretary tells us
that it was signed by fifteen deacons and elders – he then adds,
'It is significant that only two of the church-officers whose
signatures were appended to the letter – one deacon and one

[48] *Joseph William Harrald*, no date, 117.
[49] Op. cit., 118.

elder – still survive'.[50] Thus there were plainly great changes among the office-bearers before the end of the century and those who had done most to lead the work in former years were no longer at the helm.

It appears that during Dr Dixon's ministry the treatment which had earlier forced Harrald's resignation was repeated in the case of two other assistants, Benjamin Reeve who served as a second assistant pastor for two years from 1915, and T. L. Edwards, appointed, as noted earlier, in 1908 and compelled to withdraw by Dixon after seven years' service. Details of the injustice done to Edwards were given by Charles Noble, in the pamphlet referred to earlier. Noble's charge was that the root of the trouble lay in the fact that the Tabernacle had come to be ruled by a Pastor and office-bearers who did not believe in the constitution of the church: 'You have allowed many of its provisions to be ignored as to doctrine and order. The very first of these provisions is that the Pastor shall be a man holding and maintaining the doctrines commonly called Calvinistic, and he is only to hold office so long as he does so. The pulpit itself is denied him if he fails in this. But you allow these truths to be forgotten, and Arminianism to take their place.'

One year later Dixon resigned and a better man succeeded him. Yet damage had been done not only in the Tabernacle but in English evangelicalism as a whole which many generations would not be able to repair. Spurgeon's voice had not long been silent when the new evangelical spirit – intoxicated with all that era, impressive, modern and sensational – swept all before it. The age of 'Fundamentalism' had begun, and little else was remembered about Spurgeon save that he was a 'soul-winner'. When the Metropolitan Tabernacle was destroyed for the second time by enemy bombing in 1941, it was found that beneath the foundation stone the Confession of Faith of 1680 was still where Spurgeon had laid it in 1860. There was in

1941 no influential congregation in England known to stand for the theology which that document contained; nor was there any College preparing men to preach that Faith. Yet, as those who read this book will know, despite the history of the last eighty years, Calvinism has not come to the sorry end which its 19th-century opponents predicted. In different buildings, in younger lives, in pulpits and in pews, the truth which gives all glory to the grace of God is today speaking to the world and as long as it does so, the preaching of Spurgeon, who spoke so much of Him who is 'the same yesterday, and today, and for ever', will surely not be forgotten.

Appendix

AN OPEN LETTER

TO THE MEMBERS OF THE CHURCH OF CHRIST WORSHIPPING AT THE METROPOLITAN ::: TABERNACLE.

BY AN OLD MEMBER.

"Thus saith the Lord, Stand ye in the ways, and see, and ask for the old paths, where is the good way, and walk therein, and ye shall find rest for your souls."

Jer. vi. 16.

ISSUED IN THE FOURTH YEAR OF THE GREAT WAR, JULY, 1918.

A WORD IN SEASON.

BELOVED FRIENDS, CHURCH OFFICERS, AND FELLOW MEMBERS

As I address a few words to you, I want you to remember that we make it our boast that we believe and follow the Word of God, and that 'if a man speaks not according to this rule' it is 'because there is no light in him.' I am sorry that the time has come when to be silent with respect to the state of the Church is to my mind a crime, and I hope that you will give your careful, honest and conscientious consideration to what is here said. Had there been an opportunity of speaking at any of our recent Church Meetings, I could have expressed myself there by word of mouth, but we had no opportunity, so that I am driven to speak to you by letter. I feel greatly concerned for the present and future well-being of the Church, and feel that upon us all, and especially upon the Deacons, there rests a great responsibility. If what I have to say moves you to return to the good old paths, I shall rejoice, and no doubt the Lord will go before us in the pillar of fire and cloud as of old.

At the outset let me say that, as a Church member, I am a constitutionalist: I stand by our Church Deeds and the constitution of the Church as declared therein – to its Doctrine, its Church Order, its demands, its rights and privileges and responsibilities. It is in agreement with the Word of God, and is built upon it. It is therefore sacred, and may not be changed, trifled with, nor evaded. Whosoever departs from it wilfully is a backslider and should be ashamed.

When I joined the Church I did so because I approved of its constitution. Did you not? Surely every member should be a constitutionalist. If I had not believed in the doctrines and responsibilities and rights and order and privileges of the Church, I should not have sought membership; I should have had no right to seek admission, nor should I have been admitted. To admit a person into a Church or Society who does not agree with its principles, doctrines, rules and aims, is to corrupt it. No honourable person would desire it, and no honourable official would allow it. No honourable club or Friendly Society allows persons to become members unless they freely and honestly agree to its rules – ask the

Oddfellows, the Foresters, the Freemasons, the Good Templars, or members of the Phœnix. If these worldly institutions insist upon upholding their purity, how dare we, you, the Deacons, Pastor or Church members, allow the great doctrines, rules, orders, rights, privileges and responsibilities of the Church of God to be disregarded. The responsibility, before God, rests on you who are appointed Deacons. You are appointed as guardians of our constitution, and it is your duty to see that its demands are met and the Church kept pure. But it is slighted, despised, and trampled under foot.

The men of God who drew up the constitution of the Church of God meeting at the Metropolitan Tabernacle were not fanatics, nor heretics, nor knaves, but holy men moved of God. Amongst them were such men as James Low, Thomas Olney, G. Moore, Wm Potter Olney, Thomas Cook, T. H. Olney, H. Tatnell, Wm Higgs, E. J. Inskip, B. W. Carr, F. Passmore, Henry Greenfield, John Ward, and, greatest of all, Charles Haddon Spurgeon, of whom the Church of to-day is not worthy. These holy men, moved of God, not only provided a house for us to meet in – of which we are glad to avail ourselves – but they left us a sound organization, resting on a sound foundation, from which we have broken away. The constitution of the Church was expressive of their will and of their solemn convictions and faith, and by it every member and officer and pastor is in duty bound to stand.

Why then is it that so little regard is shown for it? Why do you Deacons pay so little regard for it? You have allowed many of its provisions to be ignored as to doctrine and order. The very first of these provisions is that the Pastor shall be a man holding and maintaining the doctrines commonly called Calvinistic, and he is only to hold office so long as he does so. The pulpit itself is denied him if he fails in this. But you allow these truths to be forgotten, and Arminianism to take their place. Another provision is, that "no person is to be admitted into the Church who does not hold and maintain the doctrines commonly called Calvinistic;" but all sorts of people are admitted; no effort is made to secure unity of the faith; nor is there any unity amongst us. Neither Elders, Deacons, Treasurer, nor Pastor hold office in harmony with the constitution of the Church. Everything is down-grade. Failure is everywhere, and yet you do not seem to care. All our rights and liberties and powers have been stealthily snatched away from us, and a tyrany set up by which we are degraded and enslaved. God's people are treated as if they were your people. You and the Pastor 'lord it over' them, and you are responsible for all the confusion and strife and division and bitterness and hatred that prevails in the Church – and there is very much of it. The works of the flesh are in the ascendant; it has been going on for a long time, and you are largely to blame.

If we follow the Pastor's example and go back a few years, as he did in stating his case against Pastor Edwards, we shall be able to see how this is. Let us take the election of Dr. Dixon to the Pastorate. A matter so serious should have been conducted very prayerfully and openly, and with full confidence in each other, and every effort should have been made to ascertain the fitness of the man and the feeling and convictions of the Church. You ought to have known his beliefs and received from him a promise 'to preach and maintain the doctrines commonly called Calvinistic,' and generally to act in harmony with our constitution. We supposed you had done so. But if we judge by his works we can find no evidence that you did anything of the kind. You seem to have thought yourselves free to get any man you liked, and to have conspired to give him a free hand to completely revolutionise everything dear to us.

In order to get what might look like an unanimous vote in favour of the invitation to Dr Dixon to come over to us, you pressed the Church to make a show of unity and unanimously to consent to his coming by none voting against him. He ought to know this. Very soon after he was settled you agreed to a change being made in the mode of letting the seats. A nonsensical scheme was put forth about free seats, subscribers were not to have seats of their own, but to pay all the same. They were to be miserably disturbed to make room for phantom congregations of strangers who were to crowd the Tabernacle, but they never came, and a large number of the old seatholders refused to come too. Many other offensive changes were allowed – amongst them Tithes. Tithes were demanded and money grabbed in every way. You smiled on all this and were responsible for it. In like manner you allowed the Thursday evening service to be converted into a sort of blackboard class for children. Funny anecdotes were told to make us laugh, and curious criticisms were indulged in about the ancients with modern applications. Of course for all this we had collections. We were admitted free, but paid to come out. All spirituality was lost. There was no worship of God in it. But you allowed it. It was the same with the holding up of hands after every service, which was an effort to hustle people into making some sort of profession of faith and desire to come into the Church, so as to look like doing wonders in the way of conversions and additions. Moses wrought great wonders before the King of Egypt and the magicians tried to do likewise, and they did 'so' with their enchantments. What they did we know not. We were used to real conversions through the Gospel of the grace of God, and it has been thought necessary to do something if only 'so'.

Well, great offence was given to our minds, and many left our fellowship. You ought to have stopped it. You could have done so, but you did not, and the responsibility rests with you. You also allowed Arminian lectures to be given to the workers on soul-winning. Much nonsense was talked about the ease with which people could be converted to God; and when told our views on one occasion, he professed to believe in Calvinism, but said the question was 'as to whether we could not hurry things up a bit!' Just fancy, a Calvinist talking about hurrying God up a bit – to be hurried up by Dr Dixon and the Church at the Metropolitan Tabernacle! Think of a professed believer in eternal election, in predestined times and means for effectual calling, talking about hurrying God up a bit! Yes, and he has been driving along these lines ever since, and you have been letting him try his hand at this all the time. To hurry God up a bit all the old workers were superseded by a lot of in-experienced boys or youths and girls, and such as were Arminians, and we were going to have hundreds of new members by the next Annual Church Meeting; but it did not come off. He did not come up with his contingent of so many per day, week and month; nor did any one else. If you had done your duty, these absurd dreams had never been heard of, nor would the tried and faithful Church workers have been pushed aside. You gloried as you saw these men and women ousted and a parcel of boys called to take their places, as it gave you mastery.

Then later Tithes were introduced, and the Law was hooked on to the Gospel. 'But we are not under the law, but under grace,' which you so soon forgot. It was Paul speaking by the Holy Ghost, who said that 'Christ had abolished in His flesh the enmity, even the law of commandments;' and James, speaking to the Church at Jerusalem, of the Gentiles, said, 'we will lay on them no other burden than that they abstain from fornication and from things offered to idols and from blood.' Tithes were not named, nor called for in the early Church for hundreds of years. Only when she became corrupt were they called for, and then by a greedy, extravagant, pocket-picking priesthood. Tithes caused trouble enough in this country, and yet you allowed Dr Dixon to preach sermon after sermon on our duty to pay tithes. In order to deprive the Church of its right to elect the Elders you suffered a monstrous request to be made at a small Church meeting that the Elders should be elected by a committee, and that the committee should be chosen by the Pastor. Our constitution says "they are to be chosen by the common suffrages of the Church.' It designs that they should be the servants of the Church, having their call and appointment from the Church the same as the Pastors and Deacons; but Dr Dixon asked a few simple members, taken unawares, to give him power to choose a committee to elect the Elders. They gave that power, but had no right to do so, and the result is that a committee of his own sort is chosen and Elders of his own sort are chosen, and as they are all his choice and take their office from him they are his servants. So the Church has no servants. You chose the Pastor, he chooses the Deacons and Elders; we only assent to it afterwards, but we have no servants taking their office from us as a Church. This is disorderly and illegal. Those who you call Elders have no constitutional standing and have no claim to be recognised. Yet you allowed the suffrage of the Church to be snatched away, and still allow the Church to be defrauded of its constitutional rights. This is a great shame. It insults us.

Nor is this all. Not only are the men you call Elders set to do the work of Elders, but you sit with them, and work with them, in a so-called Court of Conciliation. A fine name truly, but from what I know of this Court it is more deserving of the name of a Court of Inquisition. Persons summoned to appear before it are accused, called upon to confess sins, to be absolved or to be condemned, and virtually excommunicated. It only remains for the names of such persons to be placed before the Church, with a request that they shall be removed from the books and the work is complete.

The Church is the proper and constitutional Court, and no other exists either for members, or officers, or pastors. I shall never acknowledge any other, and advise all Church members to do the same. You are responsible for the existence of this Court, and so you are for the strife and division at the Lord's Table. Here a large part of the Church have been taught and encouraged to refuse to eat and drink with the other part. They sit apart, fearing defilement if they drink with others of the same cup. Probably this is the sign of the division amongst us. It is one of the consequences of smuggling unsuitable persons into the Church, and you are to blame for this also.

You defy the Church, you defy the constitution of the Church, but you ought to stand by the Church and serve the Church – not yourselves nor the Pastor. It is monstrous to sing 'Crown Him Lord of all' in public, and then in private to slip the crown on your own heads. As I and many others see it, you are responsible for much of the wrong that is going on in the Church – for the oppression, the strife, the back-biting, the anger, the hatred, the distrust, the abstentions, the withdrawals, and for all the grief and tears and mourning of God's people because of the calamities that have come upon the city of God. There is no effort to win the souls of God's people, but rather to offend and drive away. 'But woe unto him by whom the offence cometh.'

The great charge made by the Lord Jesus against Jerusalem was that "she stoned the prophets and slew those who were sent to her.' Even this is now our case. The more true and faithful men are to God the more sure they are to be cast out; men who have stood fast by the faith once delivered to the saints have been stoned and slain (I speak figuratively); Elders who were and are sound in the faith, and right in the manner of their lives, have been ill-used, goaded and bitten (I again speak figuratively), until resignation has been the only course before them; and men employed to do the work of the Church in the office, with solemn promises of support and co-operation, have been sacrificed to Moloch (I still speak figuratively). I have in my mind our beloved Elder, Class Leader and Clerk in the Office, Thos. Cox, who was abused unjustly, denied the right of a criminal to defend himself, and then cast out of the Bible-class Room, together with the class, for no other reason than that they wanted justice, and after this driven from the office and deprived of his daily bread. I am thinking also of Pastor Reeve and of Pastor Edwards. These were all of them shamefully treated, wrongfully accused and abused before the Church by your consent. They were stoned and figuratively slain; they were real martyrs for right and truth.

When you came to the Church to ask its support in order to compel Pastor Edwards to tender his resignation, you said in your written address, drawn up by you as a body, that you were grateful to God for all the good work that had been done by Pastor Edwards during all the nine years that he had been serving the Church. Then you said there was one thing, however, that made you think that his resignation was desirable. You did not tell us what that one thing was, nor whether it was a fault of his or someone else's; you made no charge against him, yet you asked us to give our vote against him. We were asked to exercise implicit faith in you and cast out a faithful servant of the Church. This was an outrageous request to make; had there been any wrong in Pastor Edwards no doubt you would have told us, but there was nothing, and the Church voted against you.

It was a vote of censure and want of confidence in you, so you disputed the validity of the vote, and, ignoring the Church Deeds, you consulted outside authority. You went to lawyers, who they were you did not tell us; I expect they were of no authority; and then you called another meeting and put a partial man in the chair, and a disgraceful leadership it was. Every effort was made to induce us to vote Pastor Edwards out of office without discussion and blindfolded, although you found no fault with him. The Church, however, would not agree, and you were compelled to adjourn the meeting. A week or so later we met again, and Pastor Edwards' case was to be discussed. Dr Dixon said that we were there to discuss Pastor Edwards' resignation, but he would allow no discussion. He angrily refused and suppressed all discussion. He made a long excited speech, covering the whole of the seven years that Pastor Edwards had been assisting him, and charged him many faults and made many inconsistent complaints in a manner that few could follow. Then Pastor Edwards was allowed to speak in his own defence, and afterwards Mr Passmore said a little and revealed to us the 'one thing' that made the Deacons think it necessary for Pastor Edwards to resign. But there was no discussion. There was a charge made, a defence offered and one witness. There was no discussion, and a hasty vote was taken, and a biased and prejudiced crowd gave you your vote. Sad have been the consequences, and you are responsible for them.

As a constitutionalist, I call upon you to stand by our constitution, to insist upon the preaching and maintaining of the doctrines commonly called Calvinistic – they are as true and important now as of old – to purge the Church of all those who do not hold and maintain the doctrines commonly called Calvinistic, to conduct all Church affairs according to our constitution, and to walk in the spirit of Christ in all your dealings with Church members, or else resign your office and membership. It is dishonourable and immoral to insist upon holding the position you do unless you intend to be faithful to your obligations. Should you fail to do these things you must be prepared for disaster. Your pride and unfaithfulness will fail; they cannot prevent right-minded and freedom-loving persons from thinking. Remember the Church is not your Church, nor is it Dr Dixon's Church. He has no right in our pulpit, and you have no right to support him, as he is not true to our faith and constitution.

At the last Church meeting in reference to Pastor Edwards, when referring to those who thought he (Dr Dixon) ought to go, he said, 'I won't go!' and you go on to support him. Later, he said, 'If you vote for Pastor Edwards to remain I won't employ him or give him anything to do, and so he will have to sit down there in one of the pews.' Is not this defiant? Is not this the very spirit of rebellion against the Church? He was glad to come at the call of the Deacons, but now he defies us, and says, 'I won't go.' No, he won't obey, he means to stick like a leech. Wanted, or not wanted, he won't go. I wish *he* would remember that 'no gentleman comes or stays where he is not wanted.'' He should not make any mistake; he can be removed if the Church really wishes it. But if the Church cannot be prevailed upon to remove him as yet owing to the unfit persons who have been brought into it through your carelessness, then corruption and rottenness will go on apace, lower and lower standards of godliness will prevail. False reports of prosperity will be often made. The spirit of evil will increase, gross darkness will be upon your hearts. The grace of God in Christ will be forgotten, and your house will be left unto you desolate. Nothing is so desolate as where God is not. The house built for the use of a holy and peculiar people, elect and zealous of good works, holding and maintaining the doctrines commonly called Calvinistic, will fall into the hands of a worldly people, dependent on worldly instruments, concerts, soloists, and the purse of the rich but worldly men, regardless of the truth as it is in Christ Jesus, or it may have to be sold for other purposes altogether; so it will become a monument of failure and unfaithfulness.

What a prospect for the Church to contemplate! May God forbid, and send forth the beams of the light of His truth and glory to illuminate your understandings in the knowledge of Him and His righteousness, and may He make bare His holy arm and remove every stumbling-block out of the way, and again revive His work in the hearts of His people, and give them peace, unity and love. How long! O Lord, how long! And, O arm of the Lord, awake, put on strength. May the Church put on the armour of righteousness and go forth, 'fair as the moon, clear as the sun, and terrible as an army with banners.' Own Christ as King, let His truth be law, and His Spirit our Guide, and we shall be saved.

This letter is a brotherly word to all my fellow-members and the Church officers. I trust it will be received and considered as from one who sincerely desires the welfare of the Church, and that it may lead to the making of some effort with a view to arresting the downward trend of things. We must gather up our forces, and do our best to get better known one to the other. I should be glad if as many as are in sympathy with the foregoing will kindly drop me a line and let me have their address. The Church roll cannot be got at, so we are obliged to use other means. The rights and powers given by our constitution cannot be taken advantage of unless we know each other and where to find each other and can unite and combine;

or I should be glad to see any who desire more light on the provisions of our constitution and the great Truths for which we stand. You will find me at almost any time at 28, Grove Lane, Camberwell, S.E.

Now, with brotherly love, I am yours sincerely in Christ,

CHAS. NOBLE.

Index

**Some other
Banner of Truth Trust
titles**

C. H. Spurgeon Autobiography

VOLUME 1 *The Early Years* [1834–1859]
566 *pp, illus.*
VOLUME 2 *The Full Harvest* [1860–1892]
600 *pp, illus,* June 1973

In the whole history of the Church there can be
no autobiography which for informative spiritual
usefulness and all-round fascination, ranks with
Spurgeon's.
Notwithstanding all that has been written about
him, the Autobiography (completed by others
after his death) remains the most authoritative and
authentic record of his life. The original four
volumes have been carefully revised, with some
additions and some abridgement. The result is
two beautiful volumes, lavishly illustrated.

The Metropolitan Tabernacle Pulpit
C. H. Spurgeon

Spurgeon's sermons provide the most valuable source of material upon the Bible ever gathered into one set. To maintain his ministry for more than thirty years, Spurgeon went deep into the finest expository and devotional works of the whole Christian era – having some 12,000 volumes in his own library. Today the man who does not himself have the resources to possess or the opportunity to read such a wealth of literature, will find its riches ready to hand in the *Metropolitan Tabernacle Pulpit*.

While each volume is complete in itself the purchaser who builds up the whole series will come to have what amounts to a commentary on the whole Bible. By use of the *Textual Index to Spurgeon's Sermons* the possessor of the series has immediate access to the finest pulpit exposition on a very large amount of Scripture. This *Textual Index* is given freely on request with an order for two or more volumes.

Volumes 26 to 37 [1880–1891] approx 700 pp per volume, £1·50 each
Volumes 32 to 37 are also available in leather binding

An All-Round Ministry
C. H. Spurgeon

In his day Spurgeon was an inspiration to many
of his colleagues in the ministry and through his
writings he continues to challenge and stimulate.
This work contains twelve addresses delivered to
his annual ministers' conference. In lucid language
enlivened by delightful illustrations and
irrepressible humour he supplies exposition,
exhortation, advice and prophetic warning for
the greater efficiency of the Gospel ministry.

'This is a deeply moving book. Spurgeon loved
nothing more than the fraternity of ministers of
the Pastors' College he himself had founded.
For more than a quarter of a century he opened
his heart to these men on deep and burning issues.
And Spurgeon had a largeness of heart, a
greatness of mind and a balance of truth as none
other had in his day.'

STANLEY J. VOKE *Crusade*

402 *pp, pbk,* 55*p*

Commentaries

*NEW TESTAMENT COMMENTARY
William Hendriksen

The Gospel of Matthew [*in preparation*]
The Gospel of John, 768*pp*, £1·50
Galatians, 264 *pp*, £1·25
Ephesians, 304 *pp*, £1·50
Philippians, 224 *pp* [*reprinting*]
Colossians and Philemon, 256 *pp*, £1·20
1 & 2 Thessalonians, 224 *pp*, £1·25
1 & 2 Timothy and Titus, 408 *pp*, £1·50

GENEVA SERIES COMMENTARIES

Genesis, *John Calvin*, £1·75
Leviticus, *Andrew Bonar*, £1·50
Proverbs, *Charles Bridges* £1·50
Daniel, *E. J. Young*, £1·50
Zechariah, *T. V. Moore*, 75*p*
Haggai and Malachi, *T. V. Moore*, 52*p*
John, *George Hutcheson*, £1·80
Romans, *Charles Hodge*, £1·50
James, *Thomas Manton*, £1·50
1 John, *Robert Candlish*, £1·50

*Not for sale to the USA or Canada

Paperback titles

The Best Books, *W. J. Grier*	176 *pp*, 22*p*
The Bible Tells Us So, *R. B. Kuiper*	144 *pp*, 25*p*
The Christian's Great Interest, *William Guthrie*	208 *pp*, 25*p*
The Christian View of Man, *J. Gresham Machen*	254 *pp*, 25*p*
Five English Reformers, *J. C. Ryle*	160 *pp*, 17*p*
For a Testimony, *Bruce F. Hunt*	160 *pp*, 25*p*
Genesis 3, *Edward J. Young*	176 *pp*, 25*p*
God-Centred Evangelism, *R. B. Kuiper*	240 *pp*, 30*p*
Hebrews, *Geoffrey Wilson*	192 *pp*, 30*p*
Jeanette Li, *Rose A. Huston*	384 *pp*, 60*p*
Letters of John Newton	192 *pp*, 22*p*
The Momentous Event, *W. J. Grier*	128 *pp*, 25*p*
Precious Remedies Against Satan's Devices, *Thomas Brooks*	272 *pp*, 37*p*
Profiting from the Word, *A. W. Pink*	128 *pp*, 25*p*
The Rare Jewel of Christian Contentment, *Jeremiah Burroughs*	240 *pp*, 22*p*
Reformation Today, *K. Runia*	160 *pp*, 25*p*
Romans, *Geoffrey Wilson*	256 *pp*, 30*p*
*A Summary of Christian Doctrine, *Louis Berkhof*	192 *pp*, 25*p*
Today's Gospel, *Walter Chantry*	96 *pp*, 25*p*
Warnings to the Churches, *J. C. Ryle*	176 *pp*, 25*p*

Other titles

The Beatitudes, *Thomas Watson*   320 *pp*, £1·20
A Body of Divinity, *Thomas Watson*   328 *pp*, £1·25
Charity and its Fruits,
   Jonathan Edwards   372 *pp*, £1·25
*The Child's Story Bible,
   Catherine Vos   732 *pp*, £2·10
George Whitefield, *Arnold Dallimore*   624 *pp*, £2·10
The History of Christian Doctrines,
   Louis Berkhof   296 *pp*, £1·25
John G. Paton: Missionary to the
   New Hebrides   528 *pp*, £1·25
The Log College,
   Archibald Alexander   256 *pp*, £1·25
The Lord's Prayer, *Thomas Watson*   320 *pp*, £1·25
The Office and Work of the Holy
   Spirit, *James Buchanan*   296 *pp*, £1·25
The Puritan Hope, *Iain Murray*   328 *pp*, £1·20
Robert Murray M'Cheyne: Memoir
   and Remains, *Andrew A. Bonar*   664 *pp*, £1·50
*Romans: Atonement and
   Justification, *D. M. Lloyd-Jones*   272 *pp*, £1·25
*Romans: Assurance,
   D. M. Lloyd-Jones   384 *pp*, £1·50
*Systematic Theology, *Louis Berkhof*   784 *pp*, £2·10
Thoughts on Religious Experience,
   Archibald Alexander   368 *pp*, £1·25

For free illustrated catalogue write to

THE BANNER OF TRUTH TRUST
78b Chiltern Street, London WIM IPS
Box 652, Carlisle, Pa 17013, USA